Praise for *Here We*

The struggle for the freedom of Soviet Jewry depended upon the unified efforts of Soviet, American, and Israeli Jewry. Once the global Jewish community joined forces and operated as a collective, only then did the exodus from the Soviet Union materialize. Rabbi Jonathan Porath's valuable contribution to the struggle, to the absorption of Soviet Jews in Israel, and to the reclaiming of post-Soviet Jewish identities in the FSU is unique in the multiple fronts he encountered and the vantage points he experienced. In *Here We Are All Jews*, he delivers a moving message of Jewish connection and an important perspective on a chapter in Jewish history worthy of being told.

– **Natan Sharansky**, former Prisoner of Zion

We all remember how the Communist regime oppressed the Jews in the Soviet Union and its hostile relations with Israel.

However, the Jewish flame did not disappear.

We all remember the Prisoners of Zion, the Jewish heroes who founded the Zionist underground, who were imprisoned, who suffered torture in hard to live areas in exile.

And we all remember how the entire Jewish world and not just the State of Israel combined forces and efforts to maintain contacts with the Jews of the Soviet Union in order to help them restore their Jewishness and make aliyah to Israel.

Redemption came as a result of Jewish solidarity and as a result of Jewish fire which secretly continued to burn.

But mostly the rescue of the Jews was a result of the activities of dedicated people who worked tirelessly to achieve the goal.

One of the most prominent activists was Jonathan Porath. The Jews who lived in Russia, struggling to revive their Judaism, as well as Israeli Jews, must express their appreciation and gratitude to Jonathan Porath. He has written an important and significant chapter in Jewish history.

– **Aliza Shenhar**, Israeli Ambassador to Russia, 1994–1996

Jonathan Porath's moving and inspiring memoir recounts his fifty-year engagement with the Jews of the Soviet Union and the post-Soviet Jewish community that he personally helped to shape. Filled with unforgettable vignettes, the volume serves both as a primary historical source on the Soviet Jewry movement and as a monument to a proud Brandeis alumnus who helped transform the Jewish world.

    – **Jonathan D. Sarna**, University Professor and Joseph H. & Belle R. Braun Professor of American Jewish History, Brandeis University

How did the Jewish people defeat the Soviet Union's attempt to spiritually erase three million Jews? No one is better positioned to answer that question than Jonathan Porath. Though Porath notes that he "is not a Soviet Jew," he came as close to joining the Soviet Jewish experience as any outsider possibly could. The remarkable stories he tells of his decades of intimate encounters with Soviet Jews, across the Soviet Union and in Israel, offer one of the most vivid accounts I know of the modern exodus. This book belongs on the very short list of essential books on Soviet Jewry.

    – **Yossi Klein Halevi**, senior fellow, Shalom Hartman Institute; author, *Letters to My Palestinian Neighbor*

Most people are spectators to history; Rabbi Jonathan Porath created Jewish history. Many people speculated how they would act on a visit to Jews in the Soviet Union; Rabbi Porath led students on daring multiple missions to Jews in the USSR. Most people would say that the job was done when the Kremlin was forced to open its iron doors to emigration; Rabbi Porath led the hard work in his Jerusalem community to warmly welcome Russian immigrants. Most people have almost forgotten the many hundreds of thousands of Jews still left in the vast former Soviet Union; Rabbi Porath spearheaded fifteen years of efforts to organize post-Soviet Jewry into caring, cohesive Jewish communities.

    The pages of *Here We Are All Jews* are bursting with story after story of the transition of Soviet Jewry from mostly fearful – some defiant – under the Kremlin's oppressive heel to an awakening from a seven-decade enforced slumber to energetically joining the worldwide Jewish community. His riveting, inspiring narrative ends with questions about and hope for post-Soviet Jewry's future. *Here We Are All Jews* is one heck of a read.

    – **Glenn Richter**, National Coordinator, Student Struggle for Soviet Jewry 1964–1991

For several generations, most of the Jewish world considered Soviet Jewry "lost" to the Jewish people. Subject to unrelenting persecution, lacking the institutions generally charged with educating and inspiring potential community leaders and activists, and living within closed borders that did not allow a natural connection with Jews and Jewish life elsewhere, there was little hope and even less expectation that someday things would change. With the passage of time, a reversal of this fate seemed increasingly unlikely. Soviet Jewry would disappear.

And yet, Soviet Jewry did return to the Jewish people, and the concept of a "post-assimilationist Jewish community" became a reality. To understand how that could happen, one needs to turn to a firsthand witness, an artist who uses words to paint a picture of the trends, the people and the forces that came together to make this a reality. Rabbi Jonathan Porath is that artist, and this book gives profound insight into the rebirth of a community long considered lost.

Rabbi Porath's descriptions and insights from more than fifty years of visits to the Soviet Union and its successor states are meaningful first-person testimony that sheds light on a reality few believed possible. It takes a special skill to communicate this story with passion, empathy, and understanding. That is what Rabbi Jonathan Porath has done in his book.

– **Asher Ostrin**, Senior Executive for International Affairs, American Jewish Joint Distribution Committee; former Director, JDC Former Soviet Union Department

Rabbi Jonathan Porath has written an inspiring and compelling memoir, which can be seen as a most moving and almost miraculous response to Elie Wiesel's agonizing *Jews of Silence*. Porath himself was a disciple and admirer of Wiesel, who had painted a tragic picture of a deafeningly silent Jewish world in the face of the Soviet Union's suppression not only of Jewish religious activity (circumcisions were banned, yeshivot were closed down, Hebrew books were confiscated...), but also of personal autonomy, as Jews were held captive and not allowed to emigrate. They could neither live as Jews in the Soviet Union nor leave as Jews to the State of Israel. And so Porath took up the gauntlet from his mentor.

Yes, the silenced Jews could hardly be expected to rebel against the mighty Communist regime, but he believed there had to be a meaningful Jewish reaction, especially since the Soviet onslaught was being perpetrated less than two decades after the Holocaust. And Porath understood that our tradition has maintained for thousands of years that all Jews comprise one family, that we are all siblings and therefore responsible for each other – no matter where in the world we may be living. And so, Rabbi Porath began in 1969 under the auspices of United Synagogue Youth to bring American Jewish teenagers to the Soviet

Union with the aim of giving hope to Soviet Jews and faith that they were not forgotten.

As you read the accounts of these trips, it becomes clear that heroic educational leadership and inspired and inspiring youth could provide a significant voice and push-back on behalf of Jewish rights – at least their right to leave the Soviet Union. At the same time, organizations such as Student Struggle for Soviet Jewry and adult political groups sprang up all around America, replete with marches, rallies, and political lobbying. Mirabile dictu, in 1990 the gates of emancipation to Israel were opened, and by the next decade's end, over a million Russian Jewish immigrants came to Israel. Jonathan Porath proved that when Jews worldwide work together on behalf of persecuted brethren, not only do we survive, we prevail.

– **Rabbi Shlomo Riskin**,
President and Rosh Hayeshiva of Ohr Torah Institutions

PRAISE FOR PREVIOUS WORK BY RABBI JONATHAN PORATH

For some time now, I have been meaning to write about Rabbi Jonathan Porath and his book, so let me tell you about a young, dynamic rabbi and his splendid work on behalf of Jewish young people in America and Soviet Russia. Many Jewish parents have him to thank that their children remained, or suddenly became, proud Jews, fiery Jews. Every year he would lead a group of Jewish students and travel out over Russian cities, where he would warm the hearts of local Jews, who were glad to know that they hadn't been forgotten. Most important was the very fact that they had come. Rabbi Porath's book *Jews in Russia: The Last Four Centuries* is one of the best books dealing with the condition of Soviet Jewry. It contains information, anecdotes, facts, figures, excerpts, and a great, great deal of Jewish fervor. If you would like a Jewish student to know more about the history and struggle of the heroic Jews in Russia, how the Jewish revolution has won out over the Communist one, give him Rabbi Porath's book.

– **Elie Wiesel** (*Der Algemeiner Journal*, December 6, 1974, p. 4)

Rabbi Jonathan Porath

Here

ЗДЕСЬ МЫ ВСЕ ЕВРЕИ

We Are All

ZDES ME FSE YEVREI

Jews

175 Russian-Jewish Journeys

Foreword by Professor Gil Troy

gefen גפן
publishing house בית הוצאה לאור
JERUSALEM ◆ NEW YORK   Est. 1981

Cover Design: Leah Ben Avraham/Noonim Graphics
Map Design: Leah Ben Avraham/ Noonim Graphics
Typesetting: www.optumetech.com
Index: Fern Seckbach

ISBN: 978-965-7023-92-1

1 3 5 7 9 8 6 4 2

Gefen Publishing House Ltd.
6 Hatzvi Street
Jerusalem 9438614,
Israel
972-2-538-0247
orders@gefenpublishing.com

Gefen Books
c/o Baker & Taylor Publisher Services
30 Amberwood Parkway
Ashland, Ohio 44805
516-593-1234
orders@gefenpublishing.com

www.gefenpublishing.com

Printed in Israel
Library of Congress Control Number: 2022904279

In honor of our parents
David and Judy Birenbaum Wachs, ז״ל
Dr. Milton, ז״ל, and Evelyn Birenbaum Graub, ז״ל
for having the wisdom and courage to send us on Eastern European USY
Pilgrimage during the height of the Cold War in 1971, 1972, and 1974.
Rabbi Jonathan Porath was our fearless leader, whose passion and commitment to the Jewish people inspired us to strengthen our own commitment to the plight of Soviet Jewry, Israel, and world Jewry.

Rachel Wachs
Philip Wachs and Juliet Spitzer
David and Pearl Graub Goldstein

***

In honor of Rabbi Jonathan Porath, dedicated teacher, inspired leader,
committed activist, and beloved cousin.

Rabbi Yocheved Mintz
***

In honor of our Rebbe and friend, Rabbi Jonathan Porath, who has been
a teacher, mentor, and source of inspiration to our family for over half a
century.

With respect and gratitude,
Larry Jefferson and Nancy Beren
***

Dedicated with deepest gratitude and respect to Morton and Malvina
Charlestein, *z"l*, whose kindness, warmth, generosity, and wisdom propelled their advocacy for all peoples, thus elevating and sanctifying our
world.

למען ידעו דור אחרון בנים יוולדו יקמו ויספרו לבניהם
"So that future generations of children and grandchildren might know
and in turn tell their children." (Psalms 78:6)

To Deena, without whose love and support, sacrifice, and patience, none
of the stories of the past forty-seven plus years would have happened
To our children Yehuda Aryeh, Batsheva Miriam, Akiva Yisrael and
Miriam, Yael Bat-Tzion and Haim, and Shlomo Reuven
and grandchildren Renana Osher, Yair Tzvi, Roee Lev, Tzruya Noa, Yoav
Meir, Avigayil Esther, Lavie Shalev, and Eitan Aryeh
for enabling me to fulfill my life's mission and journey.

I love you all,
Jonathan/Abba/Zadie

Contents

Foreword

An existential problem haunts us all. We remember history from back to front, but we live it front to back. As a result, our understanding of history is often over-simplified by knowing the happy – or unhappy – ending. But life itself – in the moment – often feels overly complex, because who knows how things will end?

That thought hovers over Rabbi Jonathan Porath's extraordinary book. To appreciate the courage, the confidence, the sheer love of the Jewish people required at the beginning of this journey in the 1960s and 1970s, we need to forget what we know – that the Soviet Union collapsed by 1991, and three million Soviet Jews were finally free to emigrate (or remain by their choice). This book helps return us to that terrifying time when we did not know what the outcome would be – and many of us simply got involved in the movement because we thought it was the right thing to do, even though we *knew* it would never succeed.

Porath's crisp, compelling prose shows both a master educator and a master activist at work. The educator accompanies wave after wave of students on this extraordinary journey into unfreedom; the activist helps lead the fight. Again and again, we as readers get a firsthand look at Jonathan Porath's passion and creativity, his courage, and his sense of history. From the start, he understood that he was not just fighting for Soviet Jews' souls but for his American students' souls as well. This movement to help others thousands of miles away gave many a sense of purpose right in their backyards. And the gift of feeling a part of the Jewish people and on the side of freedom fighters everywhere that Porath gave to so many can now be widely shared in this book.

Like Porath's students, I was a spoiled brat of Jewish history. Born in New York, I could not fully appreciate what it meant to be free, until 1985 when I visited the Refuseniks in the Soviet Union during Passover. That experience with unfreedom taught me just how free we were as American Jews – and just how obligated we were to do whatever we could to fight for Soviet Jewry, even if the cause seemed hopeless.

It is all too easy in today's world to feel our weakness, our insignificance, our irrelevance. Pessimism and passivity come naturally; optimism and activism require leaps of faith before leaping into action. This important memoir challenges us not to despair! It helps remind us that each one of us can make a difference.

The book is an important firsthand testimony to a great story not told often enough – how Jews around the world from the 1960s through the 1990s mobilized to make sure the Soviet Jews of Silence not just found a voice but found their way to freedom. Its vivid, you-are-there tone will help historians in the future understand just what we all did to help our brothers and sisters at that particular time and place, even as it reflects the timeless love and sense of responsibility one Jew has for another.

Hopefully, this book will spur our generation of parents and grandparents to follow in Jonathan Porath's footsteps. Even if we lacked the energy to replicate his itinerary or today lack the skill to mimic his literary achievement, those of us who were lucky enough to participate in this long struggle should testify. We need to retell the story about what we did to help those Jews in need. At the same time, all of us need to cultivate that sense of Klal Yisrael (Jewish peoplehood) and of *ahavat Yisrael* (love of the Jewish people and Israel) that leaps off every page in this extraordinary, enlightening salute to the magical power of Jewish memory, identity, solidarity, chutzpah, and hope.

Professor Gil Troy
Jerusalem, October 2021

Preface

THE GIFT BEHIND THE TITLE

The words of a group of wonderful Jewish children in Ukraine still resonate in my ears, thirty years later.

It was May 1992, just a few months after the collapse of the Soviet Union, and I was visiting the Jewish school in Kiev, going from class to class to meet the lovely, exuberant youngsters.

I posed the following question to a fifth-grade class: "Last year, you were all studying in a state Ukrainian school, and today you are in a Jewish school. Which do you like better?"

They immediately called out with great enthusiasm, "Here! Here!"

"Why?" I asked, and they responded, "*Zdes me fse yevrei!*" (Here we are all Jews!).

I had never imagined in my wildest dreams, during all of my many previous visits to the Jews of the Soviet Union, that I would ever hear Jewish children say those proud Jewish words.

Under the Soviets, such expressions were barely a fantasy and a hope. Afterwards, though, they became a dream come true and resonated over and over again during the course of my many visits to the Jews of Russia. That is the story that will be recounted in these pages.

This story is their gift to us.

BOTH A WITNESS AND A PARTICIPANT

I was a personal witness to the unfolding of one of the great sagas of modern Jewish history, the near loss and ultimate revival of Soviet Jewry after more than seventy years of Communist rule. An oppressed Jewish community returned to life and rejoined the Jewish people after decades of government-imposed suppression and state-backed antisemitism.

I not only followed these events from afar but was a part of them as well.

Others have written eloquently about the history and politics of the struggle. My story is different, as I was privileged to experience and interact with Soviet

Jews on the ground for more than half a century: in the Soviet Union and the former Soviet Union, in Europe, America, and Israel.

My 175 trips, from 1965 through 2019, spanned the entire modern-day experience of Soviet and post-Soviet Jewry. I first visited at the peak of the Brezhnev period and was present at the initial sparks of Jewish national rebirth in the wake of the Six-Day War. I followed the lives and struggles of Soviet Jews as a leader of American Jewish youth tours to Soviet cities, wrote articles, and published a textbook about Russian Jews. I met them departing the Soviet Union via Vienna on their way to Israel, welcomed them when they arrived on aliyah en masse following the dissolution of the Soviet Union, and participated actively in the reconstruction of post-Soviet Jewish life. And I have continued to follow their progress in person until the present day.

Over the course of the years, I visited more than fifty cities across the former Soviet Union, many on numerous occasions, from the current and former capitals (Moscow, St. Petersburg/Leningrad, Riga, Vilna, Minsk, Kyiv/Kiev, Kishinev, Tbilisi, Tashkent) to the periphery (Murmansk and Archangelsk in the far north, Lake Baikal and Irkutsk in Siberia, Magnitogorsk in the Urals, Orsk and Orenburg in the south, Samarkand and Bukhara in the southeast, Brest in the west, Odessa on the Black Sea), and dozens of other locations in between.

I came into contact with tens of thousands of Jews. In Soviet times, we met in public, at mass celebrations and large gatherings, such as Simchat Torah in Moscow and the Georgian synagogue in Tbilisi. We encountered each other near synagogues or by happenstance on buses, in restaurants, beaches, Young Pioneer Camps and concerts, or sometimes, just walking down the street.

They came from all across the political and Jewish spectrum, ranging from aliyah activists and refuseniks to pro-Soviet Jewish officials and spokesmen. They were Zionists and Communists; believers, agnostics, and atheists; school-age children, university students, adults, and pensioners; chief rabbis and Jewish Intourist guides.

When they made aliyah to Israel, I greeted them at transit centers in Vienna and Israel's Ben Gurion International Airport. I welcomed them as they moved into their new apartments in Jerusalem and accompanied them as they went through the process of (re)discovering what it meant to be a part of the Jewish people in the Jewish homeland – not as a response to the outside pressures of official antisemitism, but as a matter of personal choice.

Following the disintegration of the Soviet Union in December 1991, as a member of the senior staff of the American Jewish Joint Distribution Committee's Russian Department (known as the JDC or the Joint), I met and worked with many who were instrumental in rebuilding post-Soviet Jewish life.

These included community leaders, rabbis, Hillel pioneers, emerging Jewish professionals, Jewish and non-Jewish academics, Hesed Community Welfare Center and JCC staff and volunteers. I was also privileged to work closely with many of the local and international Jewish organizations that fostered and supported post-Soviet Jewish renewal.

And, perhaps most significantly, I was able to meet those fifth-grade Jewish schoolchildren from Kiev, whose words inspired the title and theme of the book.

TRAVEL OVERVIEW AND TECHNICAL NOTES

To place my various trips in order and context, the following is a travel overview (with chapter references):

1965 – First trip while a student at Hebrew University (chapter 1)

1968 – Simchat Torah in Moscow (chapters 2, 14); visit to Georgian Jews (chapters 3, 9)

1969 – Met with Soviet Jews traveling through Vienna on their way to Israel (chapter 4)

1969–1974 – Led United Synagogue Youth (USY) Eastern European/Russian Pilgrimages (chapters 4–12)

1969 (and following) – Shared the stories and developed educational materials (chapters 13–14)

1984 – Our family made aliyah to Israel and settled in Jerusalem (chapter 15)

1989 – Established the Jerusalem-based Keren Klitat Aliyah-Neve Orot organization to assist in the absorption of incoming Soviet Jews (chapters 15–16)

1992 – Visited the then former Soviet Union (FSU) under the aegis of the Wexner Foundation (chapter 17)

1993–2008 – Member of the senior staff of the JDC's Russian Department, responsible for overseeing field operations in the Urals, Central Russia, St. Petersburg and the Northwest and Belarus, with special focus on academic Judaica, Hillel, and creating YESOD/St. Petersburg Jewish Community Home; commuted back and forth from Jerusalem to the former Soviet Union every month for fifteen years (chapters 18–24)

2014 – Returned to Moscow as guest speaker at academic conference (chapter 19)

2018 – Scholar-in-Residence for Keshet Educational Tour's "Russian Jewish Journey" to St. Petersburg and Moscow (chapters 23, 25)

2019 – Traveled to Moscow for twenty-fifth anniversary of founding of Hillel in Russia (chapter 20)

PLEASE NOTE: Individual stories have sometimes been relocated for clarity. Each incident in the book is dated, either in the chapter introduction or in the text. The phrase "Jews of Russia" is used in the popular sense and often applies to the entire former Soviet Union and not only the Russian Federation. A number of the events described in the book have been illustrated by photographs in the picture section. The reader is encouraged to refer to the pictures while reading the text.

ACKNOWLEDGMENTS

This volume is a follow-up to my first book about Russian Jewry, which was published nearly half a century ago, *Jews in Russia: The Last Four Centuries; A Documentary History* (United Synagogue Commission on Jewish Education, 1973), the first textbook on Russian and Soviet Jewry for Hebrew high schools and adult education.

I opened that volume with the following dedication:

> To Some Very Close Friends –
>
> Chacham Yitzchak from Tbilisi; Reb Yonah from Moscow; Reb Nechemyah and Reb Meir from Leningrad; Shimon and Yitzchak Emmanuelovitch from Odessa; Reb Eliezer from Sighet; Reb Aharon from Turetz; Ya'akov Yitzchakovitch from America.
>
> This story belongs to them.

We will be meeting each of them and following their stories over the years. Save for Ya'akov Yitzchakovitch from America (the author and teacher Danny Siegel), they have all passed away. They are the real narrators of this story: Jews – mostly Soviet but also from America and other parts of the Jewish world – whose voices are deeply embedded in this telling.

Over the years, many urged me to undertake this project. The words of my longtime friend Dr. Larry Jefferson from Oklahoma City and Houston were especially evocative: "You have a unique perspective over time about the Jews in the USSR and Russia that few know about. Maybe the reason Hashem [God] sent you there on so many occasions was to be the scribe of His tales. It would be a big sin to let your unique stories fly away and be forgotten."

Larry's words spoke to me deeply. The stories and experiences were not mine alone but belonged to the Jewish people and the Jewish future.

They echoed my final conversation with my friend and mentor Elie Wiesel, may his memory be for a blessing, whose description of Simchat Torah in Moscow in *The Jews of Silence* inspired one of my earliest journeys and propelled me to return time and again. When I told him that I was contemplating writing up the stories of my visits, he responded with great passion: "Do it! Do it!" Reb Eliezer and Larry's encouragement, among others, were critical in motivating my writing, and I am very thankful to them for their words.

In addition, several of my closest family and friends helped in the preparation of this text.

To my beloved wife and partner Deena, thank you for your solid wisdom, insights, patience, spirituality, and for being my first editor, helping to elevate both the content and the style of the book; to my dear *chaver* and colleague Rabbi Yossie Goldman, whose mutual friendship and partnership has been so crucial for us both as we move into this stage of our lives, the publication of your book *Let My People Grow* (Gefen Publishing House, 2020) inspired me to begin the rigorous ritual of daily writing, the results of which you are holding in your hands today; to Danny Siegel for our sixty plus years together going back to our high school days in USY, for his words of Torah and valuable editorial comments; thanks to my sister and brother-in-law, Sara Porath and Jonathan Katz, for their continued words of cheer and reassurance, and for their invaluable proofreading skills; special eternal gratitude to my parents, Rabbi Tzvi and Esther Porath, may their memories be for a blessing. I know how much they would be delighted with the publication of this book. I am equally proud to be their son.

Todah to my "Friendly Readers," Gil Troy, Yossi Klein Halevi, and David Geffen, veteran authors with heartfelt feelings for Soviet Jews, with whom I shared the initial draft. Their early encouraging comments were very important.

Spaceba to our neighbor and friend of thirty years Sveta Goldes, for her inestimable help with the Russian and her invaluable first-person observations; to Masha Aryeva, Victoria Mochalova, and Steve Zerobnick for permission to use their pictures; to David Curwin for his timely translation help; to Glenn Richter for his May 2015 video interview for the Yeshiva University Soviet Jewry Movement History Project, where I recounted my entire story for the very first time; to Larissa Konshina, my favorite St. Petersburg guide, for her insights over the years; to Lila Korn for her illuminating help with the photographs.

I would like to extend my special thanks to Ruchel Wachs, Phil and Juliet Wachs, David and Puah Goldstein, Rabbi Gary and Laya Charlestein, Rabbi Yossie and Judy Goldman, Rabbi Yocheved Mintz, and Dr. Larry Jefferson and Nancy Beren, for their support. We go back many years together; I don't have the words to express how much your help has meant to me.

The team at Gefen Publishing House has brought encouragement, enthusiasm, professional knowledge, and insights to this project. I would like to thank Publisher Ilan Greenfield and his staff, especially Project Managers Shiran Halimi and Daphne Abrahams; Senior Editor Kezia Raffel Pride; graphic artist Leah Ben Avraham for her map skills and for the cover; and, in particular, my editor, Sam Sokol. Sam's sagacity, skills, and outstanding journalistic style, as reflected so wonderfully in his pioneering work *Putin's Hybrid War and the Jews* (ISGAP, 2019), which I highly recommend, are deeply embedded in this volume.

Since my first trip to the USSR back in 1965, I have been keeping diaries and notes of my visits, and I relied on them to recreate the stories. Any errors in the book are my own.

I would like to conclude this preface by stating the obvious: even though I have visited the Soviet Union on many, many occasions, *I am not a Soviet Jew.* I am an American Jew, who made aliyah and was blessed with many opportunities to visit the Jews of Russia as well as to welcome them as they came home to Israel.

These stories represent my observations, perceptions, and understandings, which I am certain vary greatly from those raised there. Nonetheless, I was not a "tourist" who came, saw, took pictures, and then departed for the next stop on an itinerary. The Jews whom I met there stayed with me not only as memories but impacted me tremendously, in far more ways than I would have ever imagined. Our meetings certainly changed the course of my life, and I hope had a positive impact on them as well. I was extraordinarily blessed to be able to serve God, our people, and the Jews of Russia, in the field and from afar, over the course of my lifetime.

Ultimately, this is not a travelogue of my trips over the past half century. It is a story about us and them, about the essentials of Jewish life and Jewish tradition, Jewish pride and Jewish courage, qualities that we need so much these days. It is a story of Am Yisrael – the entire Jewish people.

This journey of a lifetime began nearly sixty years ago, in a movie theater in Waltham, Massachusetts.

NOTE: In early 2022, as *Here We Are All Jews* was about to go to press, Russia invaded Ukraine. At the time of this writing, we do not know how this will end, and at what cost. This does not detract from the theme of this book: against seemingly insurmountable odds, the Jews of the Former Soviet Union ultimately survived and even flourished. Their struggles, courage, and resilience serve as a beacon of inspiration. Their story and ours are still being written.

PART I

Under the Soviets

CHAPTER 1

In the Footsteps of James Bond

EXPANDING HORIZONS

It was May 1964 and I was a nineteen-year-old student at Brandeis University. I had just completed my final exam sophomore year, in elementary Russian, and was about to pack my bags for a life-changing junior year abroad at Hebrew University, when a new hit motion picture came to Waltham, Mass. It was *From Russia with Love*, starring Sean Connery. I was mesmerized and captivated by the film: the excitement, the girls, the gadgets, the scenery, the travel, and especially by the title. I thought if 007 could have a Russian adventure – so could I! I would be a "James Bond with a kippah!" That movie planted in my mind the idea of traveling to Russia for the first time.

It was not connected to anything academic, Soviet-American politics, or the Cold War. I was not thinking about finding Jews or visiting shuls (synagogues). I would just be a Jewish kid having a great college experience.

That sense of adventure never left me.

As I disembarked from the SS Israel in Haifa harbor that July, after the thirteen-day boat trip from America, entirely new experiences awaited me. I had never been to Israel before, but I already had a personal connection. My father was the fourth generation of our family to be born in Jerusalem. We had arrived from Kovno, Lithuania, in 1837, with the students of the Vilna Gaon. Even though my father was brought to America in 1923, when he was a child of six, Israel was where we came from, and I would be meeting our extended family for the first time. I was coming home.

My Jewish perspectives were about to expand as well. As I was growing up in suburban America in the 1950s and early 1960s, the Shoah had barely been mentioned. I don't recall meeting any survivors or their families, though I am certain now as I look back, that they were there. I was familiar with *The Diary of Anne Frank*, the documentary *Night and Fog*, and Elie Wiesel's *Night*, but they were in no way as significant as they would become.

On Tishah b'Av, the solemn fast day in the heart of the summer, just a few days after my arrival, I found myself at Yad Vashem, Israel's national Holocaust memorial and museum. I can't even recall why I decided to go, but something drew me there on that day. The exhibition area was almost totally desolate, save for myself and a couple of other visitors. Room after room of black and white Holocaust scenes captured my mind and heart. I was intensifying and deepening my place as a part of the Jewish people.

I also decided to immerse myself in one of my long-time academic interests, Russian studies. Since taking an eleventh-grade class in Russian History at Bethesda-Chevy Chase High School, I was fascinated by the world of the Tsars. I registered in the Hebrew University Department of Russian Studies. I was the only American among the sixty or so students, most of whom were born in Romania and had already learned Russian before arriving in Israel.

I studied with some of the greats in the field: Russian literature with Israeli author-laureate Leah Goldberg, Jewish history with Professor Shmuel Ettinger, and Russian History with Professor Michael Confino. I also took an intensive Russian Language course eight hours a week. Reviewing the university catalog years later, I noted that I had not selected any of the few courses then being offered in Soviet Jewish history. That topic was not yet on my personal radar, but the idea of visiting Russia remained very enticing.

PREPARING FOR AN ADVENTURE

Upon examining a map of the Middle East and the Mediterranean, and noting how close Israel was to the Soviet Union, I began to take the idea of traveling there seriously. I went to Peltours, the long-established Israeli travel company in downtown Jerusalem, and learned that the Turkish Maritime Lines had regularly scheduled passenger sailings between Haifa and Istanbul. Even more appealing, I would qualify for round trip, off-season, and student discounts, kosher meals included, for a total of $45! From there I would have to make my way on a Soviet ship to Odessa, fly via Aeroflot to Moscow and Leningrad, exit via Kishinev, and, most enticingly, take James Bond's fabled Orient Express from Bucharest to Istanbul on the way home.

It sounded magical – and within reach. Hebrew University had a month-long spring break before Pesach, and I could be back in Israel well before the holiday.

My parents, however, were less enthusiastic. After all, who was traveling to the Soviet Union during the Cold War? They ultimately consented, and to this day I am not quite certain why. They sent me a $500 Israel bond to cash, which would more than pay for the trip. My Zadie (grandfather) in Minneapolis, who had been born in Tsarist Russia and escaped to America before World War I to avoid the draft, was against my going and especially fearful for my safety, a concern others voiced as well, but I was not deterred.

By December 1964, I was well on my way to planning the itinerary, going to Peltours on a weekly basis to check cables from Intourist, the official Soviet travel agency.

That month I attended the Twenty-Sixth Zionist Congress in Jerusalem as a youth observer from the United Synagogue of America. During the Congress, we younger participants were invited to a reception with Israeli president Zalman Shazar. As I shook his hand in an official "receiving line," I greeted him with some words in Russian (he had come originally from Belarussia) and mentioned that I was planning on traveling to the Soviet Union in a few months. He responded with a surprised smile and said with great interest that we would be in contact. (See photos.) A member of his staff spoke to me about possibly carrying a private letter from the president to his family in Moscow. I was reluctant and the matter was not followed up.

I was subsequently contacted by a member of the Israeli Security Service to meet privately in a Jerusalem cafe. I had recently visited the Soviet embassy in Ramat Gan to apply for a Russian tourist visa (it would be on my American passport). The Israeli security officer was very interested whom I had met at the Ramat Gan embassy. He showed me candid photographs of various Soviet diplomats and asked me to identify any that I recognized. When I pointed out one or two, he said that my prospective trip sounded OK and reassured me that I had nothing to worry about. Obviously, the word had gotten out that I would be traveling to the Soviet Union.

Not quite James Bond – but it certainly raised the level of seriousness and potential anxiety for the trip.

My departure date arrived, the day before the holiday of Purim, March 16, 1965, and I traveled to Haifa to begin my journey. I didn't realize it then, but it was to prove to be a pivotal experience in my life.

ENTERING AN UNKNOWN UNIVERSE

When I arrived in the Soviet Union in March 1965, I knew that I was traveling behind the Iron Curtain and was aware of the anxieties of my parents and family, but felt, perhaps like any other self-confident twenty-year-old, that I was embarking on a great adventure and could take care of myself. Certainly, I had no awareness of what it meant to be a Jew in the Soviet Union.

In those days, the plight of three million Soviet Jews was scarcely discussed; not in Israel, which wished to keep relations with the USSR as "correct" as possible; nor in America, which was still reeling from the assassination of President John F. Kennedy just over a year earlier and was absorbed in the struggles over

Civil Rights and Vietnam. Elie Wiesel's epic book about the Jews of Russia, *The Jews of Silence*, would not be published for another year.

I barely recall hearing anything about what it was like to be a Soviet Jew. Even though I had grown up as an active member of the Jewish community, a rabbi's son and grandson and a Jewish day school graduate, had served on the regional and national boards of Jewish youth organizations and as a counselor at Camp Ramah, Soviet Jewry was simply not on our radar.

However, one incident does linger with me. Rabbi Mordechai Leifman, from the Jewish Theological Seminary, had traveled to the USSR a few years previously. While visiting Camp Ramah in 1962, he shared stories from his trip. He recounted, in his compelling dramatic style, walking down the street in a Russian city with the copy of a Yiddish or Hebrew newspaper deliberately sticking out of his pocket, on a "fishing expedition" for Jews – and it worked! Maybe that was buried deep in my subconscious.

To my mind, on this trip, which was to prove to be the first of many over the years, I was going as an ordinary tourist…or so I thought.

MEETING JEWISH FRIENDS IN ODESSA

On my first evening in Odessa, I took a walk from my hotel to the most famous landmark in the city, the 192-step Potemkin Staircase. It was constructed in a unique architectural style. Seen from the top, the steps seemed to disappear, with only the plazas below visible, an optical illusion that created a mesmerizing effect. The stairs were the "star" of Sergei Eisenstein's epic 1925 silent film *Battleship Potemkin*. The scene of Tsarist troops marching down the stairs, shooting into the crowd, with a baby carriage careening out of control, lurching step by step to disaster in slow motion, was unforgettable. No visitor to Odessa could resist its allure.

While finding my way in the enveloping darkness, I came across two students, about my age, and introduced myself. I was an American, studying in Jerusalem.

"And you?" I asked one of the young men.

They laughed at me and responded: "*Me iz Tel Aviva!*" (We come from Tel Aviv!).

Now these young Soviet Jews had never left Odessa, and certainly in their wildest dreams had never been, nor would ever be, in Israel, but they chose to introduce themselves with a touch of Odessan chutzpah and class, identifying as proud Israelis and Jews. Israel was where they were really from!

I knew they were joking, and maybe they thought I was as well; after all, how could an American from Jerusalem end up in Odessa? That was their spontaneous response, perhaps a kibbitz, but also from the heart.

Would I meet any more Soviet Jews, I wondered. And what would they have to say?

A Surprise in the Leningrad Shul

With that first contact still resonating within me, I proceeded to Leningrad, the former capital of the Tsarist Empire and now the second-largest city in the Soviet Union.

I made my way to the only synagogue in town, on Lermontovskiy Prospekt, passing through the very impressive iron gate featuring, in Hebrew, the biblical verse "For my house shall be called a house of prayer for all peoples," which was topped with a Magen David (Star of David). I would visit there often in the decades to come, but I had not the faintest inkling of that back then. I ascended the front staircase into the once very imposing, but now rather dilapidated, Moorish structure.

Inside, I noticed several older folks carrying large shopping bags and spotted workers in long smocks and what seemed to be tall white baker's hats. Behind them were what looked like large ovens and a conveyor belt carrying a strange, twisted cardboard-like substance.

Suddenly it dawned on me: I was witnessing the baking of Soviet matzah! Jews were coming from all over the city and beyond, to purchase the precious symbol of Passover. I was to learn that almost none of them had a Seder, knew about the four cups of wine, nor had any access to a Haggadah, save perhaps for those who still had them from before the Revolution nearly fifty years earlier. Moreover, as I was to discover on my future visits to Russia, even the stories of Jewish slavery and the Exodus from Egypt were almost certainly lost, yet the matzah itself still held a deeply symbolic place in the lives and identities of Soviet Jews.

As I departed the Leningrad synagogue with two pieces of matzah in hand, I noted that the local Jews had wrapped up and hidden their matzah in copies of *Pravda*, the Communist daily newspaper whose name meant, ironically, "truth." I was struck by the contrast between what the Soviets claimed to be the truth and what *we* knew to be true, symbolized by the matzot.[1]

The following morning, I returned for services and was directed to the weekday prayer room to the left of the main sanctuary, at the end of the courtyard. About forty or fifty men were davening (praying). There were not enough tefillin

---

1. A version of the preceding text was published as "Pieces of Matza Wrapped in Copies of Pravda," *Jerusalem Post*, April 16, 2017, https://www.jpost.com/diaspora/pieces-of -matza-wrapped-in-copies-of-pravda-488088. Used by permission of the *Jerusalem Post*.

(phylacteries) to go around, and they switched off towards the end of the services. When I went to take mine off, I lent them to another man standing with his arm bared. We spoke in Hebrew and Russian. *Shalom aleichem* (welcome) greetings resounded.

When I said to the prayer leader that I had just come from Israel, he asked in Hebrew, "Is it very good there?" I nodded yes, and he sighed and said: "How fortunate, how lucky." For whom? Certainly not for him. I received requests for Hebrew calendars but had brought none. The only one I spotted hanging at the back of the shul was large-sized and hand-printed in Hebrew and Russian by a scribe. I overheard three of the older women looking in my direction and saying, "How nice that such a young person should come to shul."

Apparently, only pensioners frequented the services.

THE CHIEF RABBI

A few days later, I visited Moscow's Choral Synagogue on Arkhipova Street, the most prominent shul in the USSR. They were accustomed to receiving inquisitive and skeptical foreign Jewish tourists and knew exactly what to do. I asked to see matzot and was taken to the office of the chief rabbi of the USSR, Rabbi Yehuda Levin.

We spoke Hebrew and I addressed him as "Your Honor, the Rabbi." He gave me all of the "official" facts: matzot were available for 10 kopeks a kilo (although you have to bring your own flour); there were five additional sites for matza distribution in Moscow, for a city of perhaps half-a-million Jews; all of the private parcels of matzot sent to him from foreign Jewish organizations and communities, more than fifty tons worth, were received; he stays out of politics and deals exclusively with the religious needs of his people. He showed me a *get* (religious divorce) he had received from Tel Aviv, and he was planning on publishing a siddur (prayerbook) and a Jewish calendar next year. He said that he does not know what is going on outside of Russia on behalf of Soviet Jews. He was totally "apolitical."

The position and role of Rabbi Levin, and all of the other remaining Soviet rabbis, was a matter of great discussion and controversy in the West. Were they government "agents" and "collaborators" who actively presided over the steady disappearance of Jewish life in Russia, or, rather, were they attempting to keep aflame the dying embers of Judaism in an untenable and uncompromising situation, the very last of a vanishing breed?

Rabbi Levin and I were to meet several times over the next few years and would share some private moments.

On Shabbat morning, I arrived at the packed synagogue by 9:15 a.m., was greeted by numerous *shalom aleichem*s, and was seated in the special "box seats" in the front of the shul, reserved for foreigner visitors and separate from the local Jews. Israeli embassy personnel arrived around 10:30 a.m., with new siddurim (prayerbooks) in hand, for private distribution to eagerly awaiting congregants. They were newly printed and the diplomats had to separate the pages. I counted over six hundred people both downstairs and in the upstairs women's section, nearly all of them elderly pensioners.

In the middle of the services, a tumult broke out in the main sanctuary. A Soviet film crew had entered the shul, powered up floodlights, and began filming Rabbi Levin leading the prayers from the bimah (pulpit). Some voices of protest were raised since this was an obvious public desecration of the Shabbat. Nonetheless, the rabbi stood erect at his place and proceeded with the prayers. He took a Torah and recited the official Soviet Prayer for Peace as was done in every Soviet shul on Shabbat mornings. "Master of the universe, bless the government of the USSR, the defender of peace in the entire world, and let us say Amen!" The film would be used to show how "normal" and unhindered Jewish life was in the Soviet Union.

If I had any questions previously about the power of the Soviet state and the relative place of religion, they were graphically answered that Shabbat morning. Everything in the Soviet Union was under the tightest of controls.

IN THE CITY OF SLAUGHTER

The following day I flew to Kishinev, the capital of Soviet Moldavia. From there I was slated to depart the USSR for Romania, where I would board the legendary Orient Express to Istanbul on my way home to Israel. An overly solicitous local guide from Intourist met me at the airport and kept me under very close supervision.

I inquired about visiting the local Jewish cemetery, where victims of the 1903 Kishinev Pogrom were buried. Haim Nachman Bialik, the great Hebrew author, had immortalized the event in his epic poem "In the City of Slaughter" (B'ir Hahareigah). The guide said that it was very far from the city center and was closed, and there was no operating synagogue. "Phooey," I wrote in my diary, and, after he dropped me off for the afternoon, I went looking by myself and, of course, found both.

The cemetery, located not far from downtown, was certainly dilapidated, if not desecrated, with broken tombstones laying at crooked angles, overgrown weeds and plants surrounding the graves. Standing at the holy site, I felt a close kinship with the Jews of Kishinev, both past and present. A local cabbie was very helpful in locating the shul. One of the gabbais (synagogue officials) greeted me and showed me his congregation's matzah, and I stayed for the afternoon service.

As my first trip to the Soviet Union was coming to a close, I sensed that something about the experience of meeting Soviet Jews, which I barely understood or could articulate, had affected me to my core. The feelings of Soviet Jewish pride and courage, intensely felt but often hidden and suppressed, would capture my heart and actions in ways I could never have anticipated or imagined. Whether teenagers in a park in Odessa, adults picking up matzah in Leningrad, or older Jews still clinging to their synagogues, the dedication of Soviet Jews touched me deeply. Without question, and quite unexpectedly, this visit became the first step in an ongoing journey that would continue for the next fifty years.

CHAPTER 2

The Spirit of Simchat Torah

SOVIET JEWRY FINDS A VOICE

First quietly, and then with increasing urgency, the plight of Soviet Jewry began to make its way into public consciousness. More than a decade afterward, I wrote an article that appeared in *The Third Jewish Catalog*, the last in a trilogy of very popular Jewish how-to books.[1] My piece entitled "Saving Soviet Jewry" opened with the following:

> Any connection between the Soviet Jewry protest movement of today, and the small, loosely organized student group that first demonstrated in 1964, is purely coincidental. Then the few scholars and professors who took part always seemed to be out of place at a "student" rally. I remember the late Abraham Joshua Heschel invoking the prophets to protest Soviet injustice, seemingly the solitary member of the Jewish establishment who would join in the early "Children's Crusade." Mass rallies and protests, involvement on the highest political levels, the existence of an infrastructure of local and national organizations were then beyond the realm of possibility.

Two critical events marked the change. *The second* was the 1967 Six-Day War, which ignited and spurred Soviet Jews to take their future into their own hands. Their courage and acts of protest captured the attention of world Jewry. *The first* was the 1966 publication of a first-person report by a Jewish journalist about his visit to the Soviet Union.

Elie Wiesel's book *The Jews of Silence: A Personal Report on Soviet Jewry* electrified an entire generation, especially younger Jews. His report on his 1965 visit to five cities in the Soviet Union during the Jewish holidays was nothing less than earth-shaking. As Glenn Richter, the founding National Coordinator of the Student Struggle for Soviet Jewry (SSSJ) wrote:

---

1. Material from my essay "Saving Soviet Jewry" is reprinted from *The Third Jewish Catalog: Creating Community*, compiled and edited by Sharon Strassfeld and Michael Strassfeld (Philadelphia: Jewish Publication Society, 1980), 51–61.

For my contemporaries in high schools and universities in the 1960s, Wiesel's passionate outcry was the first of three shocks that would galvanize our nascent public student Soviet Jewry movement into a tidal wave of action. Wiesel ended *The Jews of Silence* thus: "What torments me most is not the Jews of silence I met in Russia, but the silence of the Jews I live among today." Not yet the icon he later became, Wiesel reinforced his written, searing recollection of his visit with Jews in the USSR in talks to our Student Struggle for Soviet Jewry members. We immediately connected with him and his message.

A year after *The Jews of Silence* was published, the Six-Day War propelled us into a deep-rooted connection with Israel and our own Jewish identities. And when, a year after that, Arthur Morse's *While Six Million Died* exposed the relative silence of our parents' generation during the Shoah, we vowed that our generation would not be guilty of the same sin.

Elie Wiesel was our moral compass. In between our numerous demonstrations at the Soviet mission to the United Nations, SSSJ produced a stark white-on-black lapel button challenging the Jewish community: Are We 'The Jews of Silence'? (JTA, July 3, 2016)

Wiesel's description of Simchat Torah in Moscow was breathtaking and overwhelming, particularly the scene of thousands and thousands of Soviet Jewish young people filling Arkhipova Street in front of Moscow's Choral Synagogue in a demonstration of Jewish identity, feeling, and joy. I was incredulous. I had visited Moscow not-so-long-ago and did not see a hint of such numbers, especially among younger Jews. I had met older folks but almost never any of my contemporaries. Who were they? Where did they come from? What propelled them to come to a synagogue for a Jewish holiday?

Did you ever read a book that changed your life? I had. Directly as a result of reading *The Jews of Silence*, I resolved to return to Moscow for Simchat Torah and to see for myself. This decision led to my meeting Elie Wiesel and forming a decades-long personal friendship with one of the greatest Jews of our time (see chapter 14).

SUKKOT WITH THE REMAINING JEWS OF WARSAW

Originally, spending the first days of the Jewish holiday of Sukkot in Poland in 1968 was only an afterthought. I was on my way to Moscow to celebrate Simchat Torah with young Soviet Jews and thought that Warsaw would be a good "stopover" on the way to my real mission. Little did I realize what such a visit, only twenty-three years after the end of World War II, would mean to me. The near-destruction of Polish Jewry only highlighted the fact that Soviet Jewry, however repressed, was still very much alive.

Landing in the Warsaw airport and armed with a local map I had picked up on the plane, I went searching for Jews. On that Sunday afternoon, everything felt desolate and deathly quiet. I passed a house that was still a pile of rubble a quarter of a century after the war. I finally found my way to the Nozyk Synagogue on Twarda Street, the only remaining shul in Warsaw, but it was locked. I was spotted by a grizzly looking fellow who took me to an adjacent apartment block to meet the wife of the late chazzan (cantor) of Warsaw and her two sons. Soon their uncle entered. He was the current shochet (ritual slaughterer) and prayer leader of the Holy Congregation of Warsaw. They told me that Jewish life was almost nonexistent. Most Jews were leaving or had been forced out by a government purge. There was no future for Jews in Poland.

As evening approached, a dozen of us gathered at the shul for the start of the holiday. The biblical description of Sukkot as "The time of our joy" did not seem to apply to Warsaw that day. The men were very open: virtually no Jews remained and the situation was hopeless. One had been employed as a teacher in the Jewish community but could imagine no work in the future. The once glorious life of Polish Jewry was no more.

I returned the following morning for services. As I opened the door, the large prayer hall was dark inside. There had been an electrical blackout. The flickering candles called to mind a haunting deathbed scene. I received the honor of reading from the prophets following the Torah reading. That day, the selection was from Zechariah chapter 14, which describes the future battle for Jerusalem when "The Lord will be king over the all the world, and on that day, He will be One and His name One." Earthly Warsaw seemed to merge into a heavenly apocalyptic nightmare.

After services and lunch at the community soup kitchen, I wandered through the remnants of Jewish life in Warsaw: the Jewish Museum, the site of the former Warsaw Ghetto and Mila Street, where Mordechai Anielewicz and his band of valiant fighters fought and fell in the 1943 revolt. As I stood at the imposing memorial, with the inscription: "To the Jewish People – Its Fighters and Martyrs," I took out my siddur, and it fell open to Psalm 20:2: "The Lord will answer you on the day of trouble." Smokestacks loomed on the horizon.

Even though it was time for the evening services, I was overwhelmed by a feeling of sadness. I felt useless and tired, and I was ready to return to the hotel for a needed rest, but at the last moment decided to stop by the shul. It was good that I had. *I was the tenth man for the minyan* [prayer quorum]. Warsaw, which before the War had been home to nearly 400,000 Jews, could barely scrape together ten for holiday services.

We adjourned into the sukkah. When I mentioned to them that I was studying to be a rabbi, one of them asked if I had brought a *Shulchan Aruch* (Code of Jewish Law) with me. I laughed at his joke, but afterward understood that he was serious. He wanted me to conduct a Jewish wedding! It was for a Jewish couple that was leaving Poland imminently, and the mother, who was remaining behind, wanted to be present at their chuppah (Jewish wedding ceremony). At first, I refused the great honor, for even though I had witnessed my father perform many Jewish weddings, I was still a student and had not been ordained.

"Why me?" I asked.

"You are worthy" was their response, and when someone says you are worthy of something, it is hard to refuse.

One of the women called me "an angel," and I replied: "Maybe a mensch, but definitely not an angel!"

Maybe that was the reason I was supposed to come to Warsaw in the first place.

A few days later, we gathered at the shul for the wedding ceremony. The mother arrived with the couple. He was an international pianist who came dressed in his best concert tuxedo. His bride came in a party dress, accompanied by a few friends. Save for the mother, none had ever been to a Jewish wedding before. We filled out the ketubah (marriage contract), I put on a tallit (prayer shawl), and I stood with them under the chuppah.

Conducting a wedding in the nearly empty synagogue produced a striking combination of isolation and intimacy. I explained to them, a bit in Russian, a bit in Hebrew, with a Polish translation, that the chuppah symbolized God's watchfulness and protection, and that their future life together should be as sweet as the wine we were blessing.

As we were about to conclude the ceremony, I noted that at every *simchah*, each joyous occasion, we recall sadness and invoke our hopes for a better future for us and our people. I thought how fitting this was, especially in the presence of the surviving remnants of Jewish Warsaw a generation after the Shoah. We broke the glass and there were many tears and mazal tov wishes.

The mother would not give me their names, for fear I might be stopped and searched at the border, but allowed me to take their "wedding picture."

PILGRIMAGE TO AUSCHWITZ

My final stop in Poland was Auschwitz. This was long before the days of the organized tours and memorial marches. It was a lonely and desolate journey. The by-now-familiar images of "*Arbeit macht frei*" (work makes you free), the gas chambers and crematoria and the railroad tracks to Auschwitz II Birkenau all of a sudden came alive.

In one corner of the camp, a French film crew was shooting a scene, with actors dressed as SS guards and armed prisoners in camp uniforms, with a burning German car in the background.

"Was all of this a movie set?" I asked myself. "Is all of this a dream?"

As I stood in the crematorium, I recited the same Psalm as I had in Warsaw, only this time with a different emphasis: "They bent and fell – but we arose and were encouraged" (Psalms 20:9). I thought of the State of Israel, which was where I was headed after visiting Poland and Russia. In our time, I resolved, that was the only possible Jewish response to such tragedy and powerlessness.[2]

With a heavy heart, I boarded my Aeroflot flight from Warsaw to Moscow. Even after leaving the vestiges of once-magnificent Jewish Poland, the echoes of my visit lingered. I wondered what I would find at my next stop.

ANTICIPATING SIMCHAT TORAH

I had enough time in my schedule to fly up to Leningrad on Friday morning and spend Shabbat visiting the Choral Synagogue. Some eighty older men had come for Friday evening services; a number of whom greeted me with questions in Hebrew.

"Where are you from?" they asked.

One older gentleman leaned in and cautioned me to watch what I said.

"We can't speak openly here," he whispered urgently, warning me that there were "informers" in the congregation who reported to the officials everything I said. It was a strange feeling to be engaged in an animated conversation, which suddenly halted in mid-sentence as a suspected informer came near. You could suddenly hear the silence. For a Soviet Jew, even speaking to a foreigner in a synagogue could be perilous.

But even if some of them were too scared to approach me, their eyes were always focused on my davening; warm, friendly, and soundless handshakes were our means of communication. I told some of them that I had come to meet, touch, and encourage Soviet Jews, and that they were not forgotten.

After services, we adjourned to the cramped and rather dilapidated sukkah in the shul courtyard. There were no decorations, nothing festive inside, save for

---

2. A version of the preceding text was published as "The Fallen Sukkot of Jewish Poland," *Jerusalem Post*, October 15, 2019, https://www.jpost.com/diaspora/dateline -warsaw-1968-604450. Used by permission of the *Jerusalem Post*.

a bottle of wine. I was surprised to find a young person there, perhaps sixteen years old.

"Why are you here?" I asked him.

He said that he was the only one. The others did not want to come.

As I made the Kiddush blessing over the wine, I felt them all staring at me. When was the last time they saw a younger person who could recite the prayers?

The following morning at services, a crowd of 250 arrived at the shul. Apparently, tourists were a rarity and I was not forced into any "honored" reserved seating, as was the rule in Moscow.

Even though I was free to converse with those around me, we always spoke "indirectly" to each other. To my "how are you doing?" they responded laconically: "It is hard to be a Jew and there are places where it is more difficult and places where it is less difficult."

They had greater faith in the coming of the Mashiach (messiah) than in their ability to leave Russia.

Following Shabbat, and with great expectation and trepidation, not knowing what would be taking place on the upcoming holiday, I traveled to Moscow for Shmini Atzeret and Simchat Torah, the two concluding days of Sukkot.

The evening of Shmini Atzeret was rather disappointing. Only a few younger people had gathered at the back of the main Choral Shul and in the street. I greeted them and said, "*Gut yontif*" (happy holiday) and got only lukewarm responses.

"When will they let us go to Israel?" they asked.

I could only shrug my shoulders in response.

I met two young women in their early twenties who were coming to shul for the first time.

Naively, I asked if they were satisfied and if they wanted to leave.

"Of course, I'm happy here," one responded, adding that the Soviet Union was her home. I felt rather foolish for having posed the question. Obviously, she could not have given any other answer to a foreigner. I could have been a provocateur or government agent.

The following morning, the synagogue was packed with over eight hundred men and women. Many of them had come for the recitation of Yizkor, the memorial prayer, which is central to the holiday liturgy. After all, it had been barely two dozen years since the war, and who had not lost someone to the Nazis, either in the Holocaust or while serving in the Red Army?

I was amazed by the size of the crowd. If the Jews in Poland were disappearing, millions still lived in the Soviet Union.

One man motioned to me to approach him. He wanted to show me something he had hidden in the pages of his siddur. It was a picture of the Western

Wall in Jerusalem. My heart skipped a beat as he showed me his secret treasure. I felt deeply privileged that he trusted me despite the risks involved.

I wanted to engage the older men in conversation as I had in Leningrad, but they would not let me. They were afraid to talk. I felt myself in a vise, with informants all around.

After services, I found a few people who recalled some Hebrew from their youth.

"Why have you come?" they asked.

"Jewish solidarity," I responded.

One of the Hebrew speakers invited me to come home with him, but he would be traveling by subway on the holiday, which I would not do, and I reluctantly had to decline his most gracious offer. I saw his disappointment.

I returned to the sukkah for a festive meal with Chief Rabbi Levin. He told me rather bitterly, of a delegation of some fifteen American rabbis who had visited him that summer and had spread *lashon hara* (derogatory and negative reports) about what they saw. He was deeply upset and hurt because they had not been discerning enough to understand that their actions could have real-life consequences for Moscow's Jews. Rabbi Levin and I would continue to meet in the ensuing years but had no hint of that at the time.

It was hard to predict what the turnout would be on that long-anticipated Simchat Torah evening. Would it be a modest group of young people as on the previous night, or more like that morning's crowd of only old people? Would I be disappointed, having come thousands of miles in anticipation of a mass display of Jewish pride and celebration, only to find that no one had bothered (or had not been permitted) to show up? Had my trip to Moscow in Elie Wiesel's footsteps been in vain?

MOSCOW SIMCHAT TORAH DIARY

"He who has not witnessed Simchat Torah in Moscow has never in his life witnessed joy!"[3] When I read these words by Elie Wiesel in *The Jews of Silence* echoing the Talmudic description of Sukkot celebrations in the Temple in Jerusalem thousands of years ago, I knew I had to see the celebration with my own eyes. I had traveled nearly five thousand miles from the US for this one evening.

Would I experience that joy as well, or had I come in vain? Perhaps what Elie Wiesel had seen a few years ago was the exception, and no one would show up

---

3.   Elie Wiesel, *The Jews of Silence: A Personal Report on Soviet Jewry* (New York: Schocken, 2011), 37. Copyright © 1966, 2011 by Elie Wiesel. Reprinted by permission of Georges Borchardt, Inc., on behalf of the author's Estate.

this year? There was no way to know but to be there with them. As I recorded in my diary for Sunday evening, October 14, 1968:

> I arrive at Arkhipova Street in front of Moscow's Choral Synagogue at 5:00 p.m. The crowds have already begun to gather. They are of all ages; the older folks go inside the shul, while the younger people remain outside. The interior of the synagogue is foreign territory to them, unfamiliar and unwelcoming, while the dimly lit street has become a giant Jewish pedestrian mall. Standing amidst the masses who are streaming there that night makes it seem somehow "safe," almost tolerated by the authorities. Surrounded by throngs of people, I still feel a sense of intimacy, like being at a giant outdoor family wedding.
>
> The previous year, the authorities had set up giant klieg lights in front of the shul to illuminate and expose the crowds, to discourage and frighten them off, but not this time. Activists reported that government agents were there as well, monitoring the crowd, but we do not care.
>
> I am standing in the crush with only a modest knowledge of Russian, looking in vain for an English- or Hebrew-speaker, when a guitar suddenly appears, and we start to sing. It begins to get joyous. We grasp hands on shoulders and circle around and around to the music. Familiar words flow from my mouth: "David Melech Yisrael," "Heveinu Shalom Aleichem," "Havah Nagilah," "Am Yisrael Chai." They ask me to lead them. I sing and so do they.
>
> In the fervor of the moment, a crowd gathers around me, and I switch to Israeli songs from the Six-Day War: "Machar," "Sharm El Sheikh," and even "Exodus." I sing "Yerushalayim shel Zahav" (Jerusalem of Gold) in Hebrew – and they sing it in Russian: "Zalatoy Yerusalim."
>
> "How do you know that?" I ask.
>
> "We listen to the illegal Israeli radio station Kol Yisrael [Voice of Israel] every night," they reply.
>
> The swell of the crowd is too great, and we break off into a smaller group. I teach them a Chabad song I had learned: "*Nyet-ne bayus ya nikavo; tolka boga adnavo*" (I am afraid of no one, only of the one God)! I deliberately whisper the phrase about God, fearing that such songs are off-limits and even seditious in the Soviet Union, but the

Soviet Jews in the street that evening are not afraid. They are delighted, and exuberantly shout out, over and over again: "*Tolko boga adnavo! Only one God! Only one God!*" I am startled, even a bit fearful, but they are not. I suddenly recall that the synagogue is located only a few blocks away from Red Square, and I could imagine Lenin turning over in his mausoleum grave at the sound of Jews praising God not far from the Kremlin.

My newfound Russian Jewish friends invite me to lead them in singing the same songs over and over again. I meet a twenty-six-year-old girl from the town of Ufa near the Ural Mountains, and greet her with *shalom*! She says that this is her first time at synagogue in her life and asks me what that unfamiliar word means. She had never heard *shalom* before, and so I teach her: "*zdrastvuyte, da-svidaniya, mir*" (hello, goodbye, peace).

The entire street is packed from top to bottom, with perhaps fifteen thousand people or more, including staff from the US embassy who have come to monitor the event. As there are very few foreigners present, we end up meeting each other. One of them says that from all of the festivals and celebrations he has witnessed during his time in the USSR, including May Day and the anniversary of the Bolshevik Revolution, none compares with the heartfelt joy and spontaneity of Simchat Torah. His Jewish wife adds that she has been to shul more in their year in Russia than in the previous ten years of their marriage. They were sent to observe but ended up as active participants. He invites me to stop by the US embassy before I leave, which I eagerly accept.

As I stand amid the throng, a young man approaches me and begins to whisper a familiar phrase in my ear: *Modeh ani lefanecha* (I thank you), the words of the morning prayer. I ask him how he knows it and he says that his grandmother from Riga taught him. I ask him if he believes in God, and he answers "yes."

"But aren't you also a Young Communist," a member of the state-run Komsomol youth movement? "How can you still say you believe in God?" I ask. He responds with a smile: "We all believe in God. We just say that we don't!"

He asks me to sing "Avinu Malkeinu" (Our Father, Our King, from the High Holiday service) together with him. Perhaps I have a spare Magen David neck chain, he asks. Regretfully, I had none left to give him.

It begins to rain, and we gather under an umbrella. The main synagogue building had closed its doors at the conclusion of services hours ago, but the festivities continue unabated in the street. This is the one night of the year when younger Jews, in particular, have the chance to be Jewish and to be proud of their Jewishness, and they want to keep it going as long as possible.

I am buffeted with questions: "Why did you come to Russia? Is there antisemitism in the US? How old are you? Where are you traveling next?"

One topic particularly excites them: "What is it like living in Israel?"

I ask them, almost disbelievingly: "Is it really true that I am in Moscow? Can this all be happening to us this evening?"

When I tell them that in the entire Jewish world, no one is celebrating Simchat Torah with as much heartfelt abandon as we are here tonight, they rejoice even more.

A tall, imposing young man stands at the edge of our circle of celebrants. Turning to him, I ask, first in Hebrew: "*Ma shlomchah?*" (How are you?)

He does not reply so I repeat the same question in Russian: "*Kak dela?*" (How's it going?)

Again, no answer, so I say: "Why won't you speak to me?" which finally elicits a response. He looks down at me almost disdainfully and says proudly: "*Ich bin a Yid*" (I am a Jew!) He wanted to speak only in Yiddish; this is his expression of his special Russian Jewish pride. I admire his steadfastness.

The end is drawing near, but the singing and joy continue unabated. At 11:15 p.m., unmarked police cars begin driving slowly up the street in front of the synagogue, to signal to the crowd that it was time to disperse, and finally, at a quarter to midnight, one of my new-found friends says to me: "Yonatan, it is time for you to go."

And so, with great reluctance, I make my way back to my hotel, over-flowing with tremendous feelings of joy and exuberance which I have never experienced in my entire life. I can barely fall asleep from so much excitement and emotion.

JEWISH POWER VERSUS SOVIET POWER

Elie Wiesel was right. If I hadn't come to Moscow for Simchat Torah I would have never known what true joy and *simchah* are. My entire trip was worth it just for this evening and I must return again. Only, I feared that I was witnessing the demise of Soviet Jewry, the last gasp of a dying community. In this unprecedented public Simchat Torah gathering, allowed only once a year for a few hours, they are permitted to be Jews; however, on all of the other days of the year, it is totally forbidden. It was inconceivable to me that Simchat Torah could ever compete with, much less triumph over, Soviet power.

As events were to unfold, it turns out that I was wrong, but that, only time and future events would tell. The exultation and national renewal in the wake of the Six-Day War would catalyze and embolden the demands of thousands upon thousands of Soviet Jews to leave and would culminate, within the lifetime of many of those with whom I danced on that Moscow street more than fifty years ago, in their exodus to Israel or the West.[4]

Even for those Jews who decided to remain in the former Soviet Union after the fall of Communism in December 1991, these Simchat Torah moments were precious and life-shaping. In the course of conversations in Moscow years later with Jewish academics and professors, many described their first contact with the Jewish people at these Simchat Torah gatherings back in the late 1960s. Perhaps we were even together in the crowd that evening. Only God knows.

I arrive at the synagogue the following morning at 10:00 a.m. The mood is festive and joyous. Today it is the turn of the older shul crowd. Unlike the previous day, they all speak with me. There is no fear or unease. This is the only day like it the entire year.

I am flooded with questions: "Where are you from? What do you want to be?"

They are very impressed when I tell them I am studying to be a rabbi.

---

4.   A version of the preceding text appeared as "A Moscow Simhat Torah Diary," *Jerusalem Post*, September 30, 2018, https://www.jpost.com/israel-news/a-moscow-simhat-torah-diary-568028. Used by permission of the *Jerusalem Post*.

"Why don't you speak Yiddish?" they ask me. "Are you married? If you are single, why are you wearing a large tallit?" which is usually worn only by married men.

I open my shirt to show them my tallit katan (mini-tallit) which I always wear. One of the men breaks into tears at the sight.

Rabbi Levin notices me and refers to me as "The guest." They honor me, together with others, as one of those chosen to begin anew the reading of the Torah, which is completed on a yearly cycle. I am not certain how much Torah will be studied that year in the Soviet Union, but we did, at least, mark a symbolic renewal.

"How do you like our Simchat Torah in Moscow?" I am asked repeatedly. On this day they want to feel like every other Jewish community around the world. I assure them over and over again that it is truly wonderful. They are so happy to greet me, a visiting Jew from the West. I tell them that we have not forgotten them, and they love hearing that. Many are gathering outside as well, where they request a spare siddur or tallit. Unfortunately, I have none left to give.

No one realized it then but following the dissolution of the Soviet Union in 1991, the Jews of Russia and the former Soviet Union would indeed resume their place among the world's Jewish communities. Their Simchat Torah yearnings would ultimately be fulfilled.

Some college-age students have assembled in the street. Three of them speak to me in Hebrew. They are desperate to make aliyah. As we walk, they are constantly on the lookout for the KGB. They stop and check every few steps. One of them stuffs his local address into my glove and returns it to me. The words of the Torah echo in my ears: "Don't stand idly by the blood of your brothers" (Leviticus 19:16) and "Whoever saves one life is as if he has saved the entire world" (Mishnah, *Sanhedrin* 4:5). I must do something to help them when I return home.

I speak with Nina, who also came last evening. She is a member of Komsomol, the youth division of the Communist Party and sees herself as a loyal Soviet citizen. She trusts what is reported in *Pravda*, the daily paper. She can't explain why so many Jews were in front of the synagogue last evening, including herself. Ninety percent don't believe in God, but after last night, it is hard *not* to believe. As we walk the Moscow streets, she is very wary about approaching my hotel. It is dangerous for her to be seen there.

Later on that day I meet with David from Poltava, Ukraine. We speak entirely in Hebrew, which he had learned from his father. They have been studying the Bible in the original for the past dozen years, ever since he was thirteen. He contends that life for a young Jew in Russia is satisfactory. The big problem is not the government, rather assimilation and the lack of desire of Jews to affirm their own identity. Here is an undeniably Jewish young man who is not sure if he believes in God or not, a member of the Communist Party and a loyal Soviet citizen who recognizes "the advantages," in his words, of the Communist system. I wonder how many more like him there are in the Soviet Union.

MY FINAL DAY IN MOSCOW

On my final day in Moscow, I went to the US embassy to visit the diplomat whom I had met on Simchat Torah evening. He told me that it was even a more enthusiastic celebration than the previous year. In his words, he was struck by the "abandon of it all," particularly in the regimented and closely watched Soviet society. KGB agents were taking photographs throughout the evening but were ignored by the crowd.

He told me that the listing of the word "Jew" on the "fifth line" of the internal Soviet passport, denoting nationality, emphasized the incongruity of the situation: a local minority, part of an international people.

I departed Moscow feeling both humbled and privileged to have witnessed and participated in this extraordinary Simchat Torah celebration. I was on the way to my final stop, Tbilisi, the capital of Soviet Georgia.

I had no expectation of returning to Moscow ever again. This was a once in a lifetime visit.

Or so I thought.

CHAPTER 3

The Steadfast Jews of Soviet Georgia

THE TBILISI SYNAGOGUE SCENE

In 1980 I wrote an article for *The Jewish Almanac* entitled "25 'Must' Places to Visit for the Jewish Tourist (outside the US and Israel)" especially so I could describe what I had experienced during my visit to the Georgian Synagogue in Tbilisi:

> The Georgian Synagogue, located on 71 Leselidze Street, is full on weekdays as well as on Shabbat, when hundreds of people, young and old, are in attendance. The synagogue's courtyard is the center for the most active Jewish community in the Soviet Union. At almost any hour, Jews can be found discussing the events of the day, plans for aliyah, or the latest government ordinances.
>
> The Jews of Tbilisi are extremely traditional, within the limits permitted by the exigencies of Soviet life. Holidays are celebrated, Shabbat is observed and kosher meat (mostly fowl) is available. They are extremely hospitable to travelers from abroad and are eager to hear about Jewish life in Israel and America.
>
> It is important to visit people whose fierce loyalty to their past and insistence on living a Jewish present has made them a model for Jews throughout the USSR.[1]

All of this was unknown to me before setting foot in Tbilisi in 1968.

I had first felt the mystique of the Caucasus in Professor Leah Goldberg's Hebrew University class Masterpieces of Russian Literature. I was captivated reading Lermontov's *Hero of Our Time*, an evocative nineteenth-century novel set

---

1. From Jonathan Porath, "25 'Must' Places to Visit for the Jewish Tourist," in *The Jewish Almanac*, comp. and ed. Richard Siegel, and Carl Rheins, comps. and eds., 151–52 (New York: Bantam Books, 1980). Used by permission of Penguin Random House.

in the region. The Caucusus Mountains were the border between East and West, Christians and Muslims, the tsar and the local kingdoms. Its inhabitants lived by their own rules and did not take central authority too seriously. I also knew of one of their "favorite sons," an erstwhile seminarian who became a revolutionary and bank robber and ultimately went into politics. Named Ioseb Dzhugashvili by his parents, he was better known by his chosen appellation: Josef Stalin.

Jewishly, however, the Caucusus were a total blank. Almost all the reports I had heard about Soviet Jewish life focused on Moscow, Leningrad, and Kiev.

I had chosen to visit Georgia almost on a lark. Rabbi Yechiel Orenstein, a friend and colleague, had visited Tbilisi a few years previously and told me that he had met Jews there who spoke modern Hebrew. To me, the prospect of meeting Hebrew speakers in the USSR was a compelling enough reason to add it to my itinerary. I didn't know, at the time, just how much the Jews there would become a part of my life.

As I approached the Georgian Synagogue in Tbilisi's Old Town, it was obvious to me that I had entered a completely different Jewish universe from Moscow and Leningrad. Jewish pride and community life were evident for all to see.

The large, well-appointed, two-storied building displayed a Magen David prominently on the gate. A sign posted in Georgian and Russian announcing "*Sinagoga Otkrita*" [the synagogue is open] 6:00–9:00 a.m. and 6:00–9:00 p.m." Crowds of seniors were relaxing in the courtyard as well as some younger men. One of the locals took me and my Intourist guide around and showed off the prayer rooms, the stack of Moscow-printed siddurim, the sukkah in the courtyard, the Torah scrolls in the ark (I counted sixteen upstairs and was told of more than thirty downstairs). We were also introduced to the local shochet, who ritually slaughtered between one thousand and fifteen hundred chickens a week.

The next morning, I counted dozens of tefillin-wearing congregants in shul, including younger men on their way to work. I was told that many local Jews kept kosher and that intermarriage was rare. In the courtyard crowd, I met a member of the Communist Party who told me that his home was kosher. When I asked him how that matched the Party's ideology, which was militantly anti-religious, he explained that this is what local Jews eat, not for ideological or religious reasons, rather due to time-honored, Jewish custom.

I told a man in the crowd gathering around me that I was on my way to Israel, which immediately evoked blessings and elicited quotes from the Bible. Many expressed a deep desire to make aliyah and some had already applied for exit visas. I noted that in the Russian Federation, including Moscow and Leningrad, the local Jews were largely without religion or hope, while in Georgia it was the opposite: they had both.

Friday evening Shabbat services were filled to overflowing, with people upstairs, downstairs, and in adjacent rooms. It looked to me like there were five to six hundred participants, including boys, young men, and women. Save for Simchat Torah, this was by far the largest group of Jewish youth I had ever seen in the Soviet Union. I was particularly overwhelmed by the numbers of elementary school–age Jewish children and teenagers gathered in the courtyard in front of the shul, something unheard of in a Soviet context and, frankly, unimaginable anywhere else in the country.

As I began to explore, one of the officials, Avraham, kept a very close watch over me, not dissimilar to Moscow, only with more local finesse and outward "respect." Though I was not particularly conscious of it, I was under observation all the time, but that did not dissuade the local Jews from approaching me in the street or in private. I was invited to several homes for meals, and even accepted one invitation, but was reluctant to do so again for fear of endangering them and, perhaps, myself.

An Unexpected Job Offer

There was also an Ashkenazi shul in town, reminiscent of those in Moscow and Leningrad, with the same frightened old people and none of the sense of hope or optimism that one felt while visiting the Georgian community. When I told them that I was a rabbinical student, they inquired if I was interested in the position of "Chief Ashkenazi Rabbi of Soviet Georgia!" The gabbai said that he could locate a three-to-four room apartment for me, and even offered to find me a local Jewish girl! I could come to shul in the morning and evening and get a regular job during the day.

I thanked him effusively but declined his proposal, though, come to think of it, twenty-five years later, when I returned to the post-Soviet Union working for the JDC, at times I functioned in a "quasi-rabbinic" role, and that is how I was perceived by the local communities. Maybe that is what the gabbai intended without knowing it.

My Friend of a Lifetime, Chacham Yitzchak

Undoubtedly, the Georgian Jewish experience that left the deepest and longest-lasting impression on me was befriending one of the shochtim, Chacham (the Sephardic title for rabbi) Yitzchak ben Siman Tov Adziashvilli. He was about ten years or so older than me. We met in the synagogue courtyard during my first trip in 1968, then again in Tbilisi in 1972, and, after his aliyah the following year, in their new apartment in Kiryat Ata, near Haifa. My wife Deena and I visited his home and shared family simchas. Even after his passing away, our friendship continued with his widow Miriam and their children.

Decades later, it was very emotional for me to present to Chacham Yitzchak's youngest grandson, on the occasion of his bar mitzvah at the Western Wall in Jerusalem, a picture of his late grandfather that I had taken in Tbilisi nearly fifty years previously, wearing the tallit I had given him. The young man had no memories of his grandfather, but I did.

Our spiritual connections were very deep, and he is sorely missed, even today. (See photos.)

I only realized later that *he* was the Hebrew speaker I was supposed to meet in Tbilisi, and that gave us a "shared language" of Jewish expression and a lifetime connection. When I published my book *Jews in Russia: The Last Four Centuries* a few years later, I dedicated it to him: "To Some Very Close Friends – Chacham Yitzchak from Tbilisi…"

We initially met only in passing, when I visited the shul courtyard for the first time in 1968, and Yitzchak was slaughtering chickens. I was amazed to see kosher slaughtering in the Soviet Union, and we exchanged greetings in spoken Hebrew. He had studied at the Kol Ya'akov Yeshiva, which was opened in 1957 at the Choral Synagogue in Moscow. Only a small number of students attended, many of whom came from Georgia, including Yitzchak.

He wanted very much to invite me to his home for Shabbat meals but was under pressure from the synagogue officials not to do so, so I met him and his lovely daughters, Simcha and Rachel, together with the rest of the neighborhood children, in the shul courtyard.

We managed to find a few minutes to speak in private. He desperately wanted to make aliyah, to raise his daughters and family in Israel, but until now it had not been possible for him to leave. He gave me some of his food and apologized profusely for not bringing even more. I assured him, that, God willing, when we meet in the World to Come, we will share in the proverbial messianic "Banquet of the Leviathan" together. His face lit up at the mention of our future eschatological repast.

I asked him if I could give him a "souvenir," a gift from Israel, and looking at his rather worn tallit, handed him my own. It was a very emotional moment. He asked me what he could give me in return and I responded with words from *Pirkei Avot*: "Don't give up hope in the face of adversity" (Ethics of Our Fathers 1:7), to which he responded with a broad smile.

"*Betach!*" (Absolutely!), he rejoined in Hebrew.

This brief exchange encapsulated for me the extraordinary strength and glory of Georgian Jewry. They were the Jews of Steadfastness. They were going to survive as Jews and would never give in, not to the Soviets or anyone else.

Two Modern Tales from the Jews of Georgia

One could not help but be inspired by the heroic Jews of Georgia.

In the early 1950s, the Soviet authorities had embarked on a campaign to close synagogues across the USSR, including forty in Georgia alone. In 1952, KGB trucks appeared in the town of Kutaisi in western Georgia and prepared to expropriate the synagogue and empty the building.

Professor Zvi Gitelman described the scene as follows:

> The [Jewish] community, some 20,000 strong, organized a mass sit-in, placing their bodies in the way of the trucks that had come to take the synagogue's furnishings. Although this was just before the "Doctors' Plot" was "uncovered" [and Stalin was still alive and very much in power] and all citizens, not just Jews, were taking their lives into their own hands with such actions, the authorities retreated and the Jews of Kutaisi retained their synagogue and their honor.[2]

That story was known far and wide and was forever a source of great Georgian Jewish pride. Undoubtedly when I visited Tbilisi only some sixteen years later, the memories were still very strong.

A second event, unbeknownst to me, was also in the works. In August 1969, Israeli prime minister Golda Meir publicized an "open letter" written by eighteen religious Georgian Jewish families to the United Nations Commission on Human Rights, demanding that they be allowed to move to Israel.

While careful not to attack the Soviet Union – in fact, they even praised the "nationalities policy as formulated by the founder of the state, V.I. Lenin" – they noted that after receiving oral assurances that they would be permitted to depart for Israel, they were left in limbo, kept waiting for official word. They opened their letter with the famous words of Hillel: "If I am not for myself, then who will be for me, and if not now, when?"

My visit to the Jews of Georgia was almost magical, something out of a Soviet-Jewish fairy tale. Would I ever be privileged to visit them again? (See chapter 9.)

---

2. Zvi Gitelman, *A Century of Ambivalence: The Jews of Russia and the Soviet Union, 1881 to the Present*, 2nd, expanded ed. (Bloomington, IN: Indiana University Press, 2001), 200.

CHAPTER 4
The Mission of My Life

THE AEROGRAM

Arriving in Israel in October 1968, after my two-and-a-half-week European journey, from the depths of Warsaw and Auschwitz to the heights of Simchat Torah in Moscow and Shabbat in Tbilisi, I was overwhelmed with emotion. I could not imagine anything could match the lows and highs I had experienced in Jewish Europe, both past and present. I fully expected to continue with the rest of my studies and professional life.

I had traveled to the Soviet Union en route to Israel for my junior year of rabbinical studies at the Jewish Theological Seminary of America's Jerusalem branch, Neve Schechter. I assumed that I would spend the year studying, return to the US, receive my rabbinic ordination, and spend the next fifty years in the pulpit rabbinate, just like my father and grandfathers. The direction in which I was headed seemed clear.

An aerogram, a one-page airmail letter, awaited my arrival in Jerusalem, dated October 6, 1968. It was from Paul Freedman, then acting director of United Synagogue Youth, the youth arm of the Conservative movement. I had been a very active USYer during my high school years and was a proud alumnus of the program. Although he was a decade older than I, I knew Paul and we were personal friends.

The brief note inside was staggering in its impact, though its far-reaching implications were not obvious at the time: "Jonny – are you interested in a USY Pilgrimage to Russia?" To a twenty-four-year-old during those often-perilous times, an offer to lead trips to meet Soviet Jews was mind-boggling.

That unexpected ten-word invitation was to launch my life and career into an entirely new direction, which ultimately was to culminate, a quarter of a century later, in my working for the Joint Distribution Committee's Russian Department, rebuilding Jewish life in the post-Soviet Union.

I must have somehow sensed its significance since I kept the original aerogram for the next fifty years. I still have it today.

LEADING VISITS TO SOVIET JEWS

In my mind, my two trips, in 1965 and 1968, were to have been my only visits to the Soviet Union. I had come and seen and had no other reason to return. However, with Paul Freedman's out-of-the-blue message, my role and focus had totally changed. In accepting the invitation, I would be leading a group of American Jewish teenagers behind the Iron Curtain, with the express purpose of making contact with Soviet Jews. I knew full well of the seriousness with which USY took such summer programs. The organization was already sponsoring two trips, USY Israel Pilgrimage and USY on Wheels (a Jewish bus trip around the United States), both of which were profound experiences in Jewish living and were phenomenally successful.

Upon further reflection, a series of questions crossed my mind:

- Would parents agree to send their high school youngsters to the USSR in the current Brezhnev period, when US and Soviet relations were very strained?
- Would we be threatened, or worse, by the Soviet security services, which were notoriously wary of contacts between locals and foreigners?
- What responsibilities would I be accepting upon myself, together with other staff members yet to be selected, for the health and safety of the group?
- What about the Jewish components, including kashrut, Shabbat, daily prayer, and study?
- Would I be successful in orchestrating and programming contacts with Soviet Jews? After all, we would be traveling totally "under the radar."

To the best of my knowledge, no other Jewish-sponsored groups were traveling to the USSR during that period. A few individual Orthodox rabbis were going, notably Rabbi Pinchas Teitz from Elizabeth, NJ, and Rabbi David Hollander and Rabbi Arthur Schneier from New York, but they were focused largely on the religious needs of Soviet Jews. Some rabbinical delegations also visited but they were few and far between.

The Lishkat Hakesher, the Liaison Bureau of the Office of the Prime Minister of Israel, in charge of maintaining contact with the Jews in the Soviet Union, had briefed and sent selected emissaries, under the guise of tourists, to various Soviet cities over the years, with the express purposes of contacting refuseniks and encouraging aliyah. My future wife, Deena, was to visit Moscow, Leningrad, Riga, Tallin, and Crimea on one of those missions in 1971.

The political environment was changing as well. Since the June 1967 Six-Day War, Soviet Jews themselves had been taking their fate more and more into their own hands. Yuli Kosharovsky's *"We Are Jews Again": Jewish Activism in the Soviet Union* (Syracuse University Press, 2017) and Gal Beckerman's *When They Come for Us, We'll Be Gone: The Epic Struggle to Save Soviet Jewry* (Houghton Mifflin Harcourt, 2010) tell the story in great detail from both the Soviet and American perspectives.

As Kosharovsky described those early days: "Those labeled the 'Jews of Silence' by Elie Wiesel thus began to acquire a voice, gradually gaining confidence and strength. This voice of protest evoked a broad response in the West among those who were fighting for Soviet Jews' emigration."[1]

The plight and fate of Soviet Jewry were becoming a part of the public agenda of the Jewish people, which undoubtedly sparked interest in USY initiating such a program.

At this critical time, I had been invited to take the experience of my heretofore private visits and expand their reach, both among American and Soviet Jews.

TAKING JEWISH HIGH SCHOOL KIDS TO THE USSR

By any standards, it was an audacious proposal: *to send a group of American Jewish teenagers to the USSR to visit Soviet Jews*. Such a trip, certainly in the late 1960s and early 1970s, was without precedent. USY had run a European Pilgrimage, including Russia, back in 1960, but it was discontinued after one year due to the freeze in US-Soviet relations as a result of the Berlin Wall and the Cuban Missile Crisis. No other American Jewish organization, and certainly no youth movement, had attempted such an endeavor, because the logistics were so complex and the stakes so high.

In addition, following the Six-Day War, there was a consensus within the organized American Jewish community, that no Jewish organization should officially sponsor tours to the Soviet Union, and this policy remained in effect.

In November 1971, Rabbi Paul Freedman and I were invited to a meeting of the National Jewish Community Relations Advisory Council in NY, to report on the USY trips to the Soviet Union. I explained the rigorous selection and orientation process, the Jewish content and regimen of the trips, and our expectations for the participants to serve as community speakers and resources for local Soviet Jewry programs. The Chairman stated, that, as compared to general tourism, the USY trip "was thought to be a different program with a specially structured

---

1.   Yuli Kosharovsky, *"We Are Jews Again": Jewish Activism in the Soviet Union* (Syracuse: Syracuse University Press, 2017), 71. Quoted with permission.

intensive Jewish content experience for young people," and we were authorized to continue.

The challenges facing such a trip were beyond daunting, including:

- There was absolutely no local Jewish community to partner with. The few functioning synagogues discouraged such visits and their local officials closely supervised all occasional tourists who happened to stop by, usually with well-prepared and rehearsed pro-Soviet propaganda. Who would receive the group and make local Jewish contacts? How would we meet Soviet Jews?
- Intourist, the official Soviet state-run travel agency that was the exclusive address for travel within the Soviet Union, carefully monitored the movements of foreign tourists. An openly identified "Jewish" group would never have received visas, and if it managed to get in and was uncovered, would be subject to constant supervision and harassment, as ultimately happened to us on more than one occasion.
- We were traveling in the days before email and cell phones. In cases of emergency, international telephone connections were often unavailable. We were on our own and totally responsible in the field.

The strategies we developed to deal with each of them will be described in the pages to follow.

Undoubtedly, the staff was key to the success of the project. From 1969 through 1974, USY European Pilgrimage trips were led by: Rabbi Arthur and Kinneret Chiel, Rabbi Arnold and Nomi Turetsky, Rabbi Jack Reimer, Rabbi Yaacov Rone, Mira Katz, Libby Jochnowitz, Danny Siegel, and Aaron Shor as well as yours truly. Some two hundred young people took part.

The itinerary was critical and was fine-tuned over the years. The core of the six-week trip was always the same: Moscow, Leningrad, and Israel. Additional cities on the itinerary included London, Paris, Amsterdam, Helsinki, Vienna, Budapest, Prague, Krakow/Auschwitz, Warsaw; Riga, Kiev, Vilna, Tbilisi, Odessa; Bucharest, Istanbul, and Athens.

Rabbi Freedman, with the backing of the lay leadership of the United Synagogue, believed that such a trip would have an extraordinary impact on the lives of the USYers, their home synagogues, and communities, and hopefully, on the Soviet Jews themselves, and time was to prove him correct.

It was impossible to project or even imagine the life-changing Jewish educational potential of such a trip. Traveling as a self-contained Jewish religious community, we were going to the Soviet Union with the goal of reaching out and touching fellow Jews who had been forcibly separated from our people and bringing them messages of solidarity and hope.

In at least one respect, though, we were mistaken. We thought we were going to inspire them. We had no inkling then of how much they would inspire us.

PRE-TRIP PREPARATIONS AND ORIENTATION

I was deeply involved in reviewing the applications, and in interviewing, in person or by phone, as many of the prospective participants as possible. I wanted to ensure that they understood the goals and expectations of the trip. This was not designed to be just a "fun summer vacation" or "a tour of Russia." We were setting out on a mission and every participant was expected to take an active part.

After all of the preparations, memos, and packing, we met for an intensive two-day orientation before the trip, which also included learning how to read the Russian alphabet.

The following are from my orientation notes, as we prepared for our imminent departure:

- **PACKING CONTRABAND** – It is forbidden to take into the USSR "anti-Soviet" materials, including *The Jews of Silence* by Elie Wiesel, items from the Student Struggle for Soviet Jewry, USY baggage tags and membership cards, Israeli currency and Israel Bonds, obvious Israeli items such as an El Al bag.

- **SOVIET CUSTOMS** – Customs agents will open up 80% of the bags, especially flight bags and carry-ons. We are not smuggling anything illegal into Russia. For maximum security, do not pack all of your Jewish "gifts" in one place or one package.

- **SECURITY** – Your rooms may be searched. Carry personal items with you at all times (a diary, for example). The rooms may be bugged. No speaking about any Jewish activities indoors at all. If you write or talk, especially about Jewish subjects, do so circumspectly. It is nobody's business but our own what we think of the USSR or its nationalities policy. Don't mention USY in the USSR. We are officially the Youth Study Tour and have come to learn about life in the Soviet Union. [See photos.]

- **ABSOLUTELY FORBIDDEN!** – No taking of souvenirs (including hotel towels); no guests in rooms, locals, or other foreigners; no selling of clothes for rubles; no black-market exchange transactions. No baiting or challenging Intourist guides. Do not be critical of the Soviet Union. The Russians are especially touchy about this.

- **SPECIFICALLY JEWISH TOURING INSTRUCTIONS:**
  a. We will be maintaining a "double tour program" in the USSR: From nine-to-five we will be general tourists and will visit shuls in the early mornings and evenings.
  b. When you meet Jews, whether in shuls or in public, be circumspect. The local Soviet Jewish activists aren't even certain who their "friends" are. In the Soviet Union, nothing is as it seems. Different techniques of identifying fellow Jews include: whistling "David Melech Yisrael" in public, saying quickly "Hello/*Shalom*," fingering the Magen David charm you have with you around your neck, mentioning your next stop on your itinerary (Israel). No kippot in public. You may wear a hat if you wish. [See photos.]
  c. Especially be on the lookout for younger Jews or those coming to the synagogue for their first time, and welcome them. At 11:00 a.m. on Shabbat morning, refuseniks gather on Arkhipova Street in front of the Moscow Choral Synagogue to meet visitors like us.
- **GIVING GIFTS TO SOVIET JEWS** – It is not illegal but should be done selectively, as a token of regard and interest. Treat them as personal gifts. Don't give gifts to the shul officials if you can avoid it.
- **TRAVELING AS A USY GROUP** – It is vital to record your journey; keep a diary, document your Jewish experiences and meetings; take lots of pictures. You are expected to teach, speak, and retell your experiences. We will start by reporting to the other 650 members of the USY Israel Pilgrimage upon our arrival in Israel.
- **IN CONCLUSION** – During the coming few weeks, we will be living on a whole different plane than our normal high school lives. We will be meeting and encouraging fellow Jews around the world, and it will affect us deeply as well.

What would await us when we finally arrived at Soviet customs? We would soon find out.

But first, I had to make a stop in the heart of Europe.

DATELINE VIENNA: WELCOMING SOVIET JEWS

One of my dreams was to be the first person to wish a *shalom aleichem* to a Soviet Jew arriving in freedom and making aliyah to Israel, and suddenly and unexpectedly, it became a possibility.

In 1969, in response to pressure from refuseniks and others applying for exit visas in the wake of the Six-Day War, the Soviet government began to permit

Jews to move to Israel for "family reunions." Even though the numbers were still modest, they nonetheless marked a dramatic change: 230 exit visas were issued in 1968, rising to three thousand in 1969 – a more than twelvefold increase.[2] With the USSR's decision to sever diplomatic relations as well as direct travel connections with Israel, the only transit point for Soviet immigrants to Israel was Vienna.

Since I would be traveling from Israel to Paris in the summer of 1969 to meet the incoming USY group from America, I decided to add a stopover in Austria to my itinerary to take advantage of this not-to-be-missed opportunity. Through my father's contact with Rabbi Mordecai Kirshblum, the head of the Jewish Agency's Aliyah and Absorption Department in Jerusalem, I received a letter of introduction to the Jewish Agency in Vienna, where I was welcomed with open arms.

It was 1:30 p.m. as I stood at the entrance to platform 19 at the Westbahnhof, Vienna's central train station, awaiting the incoming train from Moscow. A call had come in from the Austrian border police saying that new *olim* (immigrants) were on board. It was an anxious as well as exciting moment.

I waited until all of the regular passengers had departed the train before going to see who remained. I spotted a couple in their mid-fifties, standing on the platform. They seemed somewhat bewildered. The husband was wearing an old-style blue double-breasted suit, with a small blue and white Israeli flag lapel pin. (See photos.)

I approached them, holding out my hand in greeting, and said in Hebrew and Yiddish: "*Shalom Aleichem. Vos machstu? Mah shlomchem*" (Hello. How are you)? He gave me a big smile and, flashing his gold teeth, said in rich European Ashkenazi-accented Hebrew, "*Ani loi dibarti Ivris zeh shloishim shonoh, v'ani noiseyah l'Eretz Yisroel*" (I haven't spoken Hebrew in thirty years, and I am going to the Land of Israel).

What a wonderful and emotional moment of a lifetime for us both. He, a Jew from Vilna, who had lived under the Soviets for the past thirty years, was finally going home. And I, an American Jew, with Lithuanian roots, was privileged to greet him on behalf of the entire Jewish People, something I had always yearned to do.

The Jewish Agency for Israel (JAFI) had set up a transit camp for the incoming Jews at the Schonau Castle, a secure location located some twenty miles outside of town, and all arriving *olim* were transported there before being sent on to Tel Aviv.

---

2. Based on figures from the Israeli Bureau of Statistics and Petrus Buwalda, *They Did Not Dwell Alone: Jewish Emigration from the Soviet Union, 1967–1990* (Johns Hopkins University Press, 1997), 221–24.

A small van took us to Schonau. As we arrived, a large sign in Hebrew and Russian greeted us: "Welcome! JAFI Transit Point." Some seventy newly arrived *olim* were eating in the communal dining room, a mix of families with young children, older couples, and working-age people. They were mainly from the "periphery" of the Soviet Union: the Baltics, Tashkent, Czernowitz. I spoke with an English teacher from Riga. She described the great ferment and anxiety among the Zionist activists in the city and of their keen desire to join those who were leaving for Israel. Those applying for exit visas were immediately fired from work and kept waiting in limbo for permission to leave.

In their desperation to leave, some were even contemplating an audacious plan to hijack a Soviet airplane and fly to freedom, which they would attempt to carry out in the following year.

Others were more hopeful. When I told an older couple, "It will be good in Israel," they replied, "*Im yirtzeh Hashem*" (God willing).

Four years later, in 1973, on our way to Russia with that year's USY group, I wanted to open our trip by greeting new *olim* in transit via Vienna. By then, over thirty-four thousand Soviet Jews were being permitted to emigrate annually, largely from the Soviet "heartland" (Moscow, Leningrad, and Odessa) but also from the periphery, including Soviet Georgia. The Georgians we met were the first ones to inform me that my dear friend, Chacham Yitzchak from Tbilisi, had just moved to Israel.

As we entered the large reception and dining hall at the Schonau transit center, our USYers immediately fanned out and greeted each of the *olim* with a *shalom* and a broad smile. They begin singing and dancing with the older folks as well as with the many sweet Georgian children. The JAFI staff was very moved. One of them, originally from Russia, who had been working at Schonau for the past four months, said that she had never seen a group of young people exude such Jewish spirit and feeling.

At the end of our Schonau visit, we parted. Both groups were anxious about what the future would bring. The *olim* were continuing their journey to Israel, and we were just beginning ours in the opposite direction, to the very place from which they were fleeing. I wrote in my dairy: "May God bless their paths as well as ours. Amen!"

Entering the Soviet Universe

Crossing into the Soviet Union was always accompanied by overwhelming feelings of anxiety and fear. Would the real purpose of our visit, to meet Soviet Jews, be discovered? Our 1972 trip was a particularly harrowing example. We boarded our two buses in Helsinki, Finland, and headed east. I was on the first bus and my friend and co-leader Rabbi Arnie Turetsky was on the second.

The previous evening, I had written in my diary: "We are going to leave for Russia in a few minutes. I didn't sleep well during the night. If God wills it, we will enter the Soviet Union in peace and leave in peace, only because we believe in God alone. Hope in the Lord, be strong, and let your heart take courage; whatever you do, hope in the Lord."

My prayers were not in vain.

We crossed the Finnish-Soviet frontier at about midnight, and the sun was still shining. During the long summer nights in the Far North, it barely gets dark, lending the nights an eerie, almost otherworldly, aura.

Aaron, one of the members of our group, described what happened: "We had been driving for almost five hours and the mood on our bus was very light, as though we had all forgotten that we would be in Russia in a few minutes. There was a lot of talking and laughing when, without a moment's notice, one of the people on my bus shouted, 'Oh, my God, we're here!' At that moment, I don't think there was a person on the bus whose heart did not skip a few beats."

The Soviet border and customs station were located behind rows of imposing and starkly lit fences, capped with barbed wire, complete with guard towers, and manned by armed KGB soldiers.

We all sat in stunned silence, each engrossed in his own thoughts about what might happen next.

As we pulled up to the customs point, I stepped out of the lead bus and addressed the very sleepy guards.

"*Zdrastvuyte*" (Hello), I said in the friendliest tone I could muster.

They seemed quite taken aback and even disarmed by my greeting – in Russian, yet – as I began my shpiel. We were two buses of American students and had come to visit the USSR. The USYers from my bus placed their bags on the tables, and the guards didn't even bother examining them! With a wave of his hand, the officer in charge passed us through, our luggage unopened and unchecked, with all our prayer books, Hebrew texts, and Jewish gifts undetected and unchallenged. We were overwhelmed with feelings of relief and unbelievable good fortune…only we were celebrating a bit prematurely. Our bus parked, awaiting the rest of our group, which was now approaching the checkpoint.

As Arnie stepped out of the second bus, his flight bag in hand, I greeted him, told him reassuringly that all was fine, and introduced him to my newfound KGB "friend." Still seemingly in a relaxed mood, the officer, in a rather off-the-cuff manner, asked him to open his bag.

As the KBG officer stuck in his hand, something caught his attention. He pulled out a small cellophane packet containing a costume jewelry neck chain, together with a Magen David; only it was not *one* chain, but a package of *ten* identical neck chains, each featuring the same Jewish emblem.

He was no longer smiling. As border guards led Arnie away into the customs station, the KGB commander demanded that everyone else on that bus come forward and present their handbags for inspection. From the backroom, I thought I heard what sounded like a slap, as if they were "working over" my friend Arnie. It turned out not to be the case, but I didn't know it then. I was now solely in charge.

The customs officers began scrutinizing the bags, removing dozens of books. When they discovered something, they unceremoniously tossed it in a growing pile on the table in front of them. Prayer books, Bibles, it didn't matter. The stack of books continued to grow. They threw them this way and that, upside down and right side up, back to front. I wanted to blurt out "Stop! You can't do that! You don't treat holy Jewish books that way, like pieces of trash!" But, of course, I didn't dare protest out loud.

After a two-hour search of the bags, dozens of books were heaped up on the table. At this point, the officer, no longer my "friend," turned to me and asked ominously: "Do you have books like this on your bus too?"

That was a particularly problematic question since there were three possible answers, all of which were wrong. I could state the facts and say yes, at which point he would demand that we hand all of them over to him, or I could say no, which was potentially even more dangerous since he could check for himself and uncover them. So, I finally said, "I don't know," which was not quite fully truthful, since I personally had given books and other Jewish items to the USYers, but it felt like the only answer I could give at the moment.

It was a question of situational ethics. Is it allowed to lie to the KGB? I think so. As long as you don't get caught.

"Let's ask them," the guard said menacingly, and with that, he led me to the first bus, where the USYers had been waiting in the parking lot for nearly three hours. They were extremely anxious. When the door open and I entered, they gave me a reassuring wave and were visibly relieved, until they saw the green-uniformed KGB border guard right behind me. The smiles melted off their faces.

"Show them the book," he barked at me.

As I demonstratively held up a siddur, the guard prodded me to ask the question: "Does anyone here have books like this one?"

There was total silence on the bus. I had told them repeatedly at orientation never to volunteer such information, and here I was, asking them in person. They froze and said nothing. I knew the guard would not accept that, so I began walking up and down the main aisle of the bus, opening up purses, examining jacket pockets, and selectively removing various books.

"I thought you had one of these," I said to one of the USYers, as I apprehensively passed them to the guard standing right behind me. "Perhaps you forgot."

"Is that all?" the guard asked me, after I had given him seven or eight books. I asked the kids once again, rather half-heartedly. They nodded their heads and the guard withdrew, apparently satisfied, his assignment completed.

After undergoing questioning, Rabbi Turetsky was returned to us, unharmed. Libby, our Russian-speaking USY staffer who had also been taken aside for further inspection, reported that when she was in the office, she had overheard a conversation between the officer and KGB headquarters in Leningrad. He reported what he had found and asked for instructions. He was told that since he had removed the illegal items, our group could be allowed to enter the Soviet Union.

I had visions of us either being turned back at the border or detained for a public confession. Fortunately, neither scenario came to pass.

At 4:00 a.m. we reboarded our buses and, with the sun brightly shining in the northern sky, began to make our way to Leningrad.

We sat silently on the bus, still very shaken by the experience. As we drove through the Russian tundra, those of us who were still awake began to daven the morning service. Words from the prayerbook I had never really noticed before leapt out at me: "Thank You, Lord, for freeing the prisoners."

Even though we were only now entering Soviet territory, I felt that we had come through an ordeal and had been saved. Our real trip was about to begin.

CHAPTER 5
Searching for Our People

HIDING IN PLAIN SIGHT

Our visits to the Soviet Union echoed an ancient conversation, more than thirty-six hundred years old. Our biblical ancestor Joseph is told by his father Jacob: "See how your brothers are faring." On his way, he gets lost and meets a stranger, who asks him, "What are you searching for?" to which Joseph responds: "I am searching for my brothers" (Genesis 37:14–16).

We came to Russia in Joseph's footsteps. The entire heart and soul of the USY Russian Pilgrimage, its raison d'être, was to meet our brothers and sisters, to connect with Soviet Jews.

It was an incredibly challenging task.

The most obvious places, the few synagogues that remained open, were tightly supervised and regulated. They had largely been abandoned by the local Jews, save for a handful of pensioners. Younger people, families with children, the working population, and anyone connected with the State or ruling Communist Party did not frequent them. There were no other public places where Jews could meet other Jews in the Soviet Union. The courtyard of the Georgian Synagogue in Tbilisi or Simchat Torah evening in Moscow were among the outstanding exceptions. How could foreigners make contact with local Jews? During the period of our visits, in the late 1960s and early 1970s, it was not possible for a group of foreign high school students to meet Jews in their homes.

Paradoxically and unexpectedly, the local Jews would often find *us*, especially in places where we would least expect it: *in public, in plain sight*.

ON TRAMS AND BUSES

It was a busy Moscow morning in the middle of rush hour during our 1969 trip, and we were returning by bus from an early visit to a small and remote prayer house. I was huddled together with four or five USYers, holding onto the straps and poles to keep our footing, swaying back and forth as we moved through the traffic, balancing a tallit bag that I had brought with me for davening.

Suddenly, the bus lurched, we grabbed on for dear life, and my tallit bag fell to the floor. I quickly picked it up, gave it a light kiss, and held on to it even more tightly. I had not paid attention, but the Magen David symbol on the bag, which previously had been facing down, out of sight, had flipped over in the fall and was now facing up.

Quite unexpectedly, I noticed a local young man, just beyond the circle of our group, who was staring at me and the Magen David, with a broad smile extending ear to ear, his eyes almost glistening with tears.

After a moment's hesitation, I pulled myself together and, being very careful to remain unobtrusive, said to him: "*Ve tozhe?*" (You too?).

"*Da*" (Yes), he nodded. "Me too."

The bus stopped. Our new Jewish friend got off, and we stood speechless until we reached our destination. We would never meet again, but the impact of that anonymous Jewish encounter remains with me until today. If we couldn't find them, they could find us.

In 1970, we were on a tram, a streetcar, in Leningrad. One of our girls, Divi from New Jersey, was standing next to me, absentmindedly fingering her Magen David necklace, when she was approached by a young woman with long blond hair, wearing a blue dress.

"*Yevreika?*" (Jewish?), the local asked. When Divi replied with a nod of her head, the local Jewish woman took the bouquet she was holding in her hand and gave it to her. And with a wave and a farewell *shalom*, she got off the bus.

We were astonished and stunned at the meeting. Where else did one receive flowers for being Jewish?

Our immediate excitement was mitigated by a profoundly unsettled feeling; perhaps others in the bus also witnessed the scene? I returned to our hotel feeling very uneasy and even a bit scared. Was my discomfort self-induced? Perhaps. Or perhaps not. In Soviet public spaces, one never felt secure.

IN RESTAURANTS

It was our first night eating at the hotel restaurant in Riga, during our 1970 visit. They set out a banquet for us. I had six tomato and cucumber salads. Delicious! We were celebrating the birthdays of two of our group members. Some of the other guests joined in, a table of Armenians from Yerevan, and even a tourist from Aleppo, Syria. We all drank toasts to "Brotherhood!" The ever-present restaurant band, invariably with a least one Jewish member, played a "*freilach*," a Jewish wedding dance, followed by "Yerushalayim shel Zahav" (Jerusalem of Gold)! Wow! That sure threw us for a loop!

By the following evening, the band had figured out who we were and welcomed us accordingly.

They played "Havah Nagilah" in our honor, and patrons and guests got up to dance, including Olga, a local woman who was in the restaurant by chance. When the song concluded, she approached our table and identified herself as one of us. We gave her a Magen David. Overcome, she stepped outside and began to cry. She bought a round of champagne and sat with us. We spoke for an hour. She told us that she would save the Magen David for her son. She was overwhelmed at having met us. We had given her some solace and even hope.

One Friday afternoon two years later, I was on the twenty-first-floor restaurant of Moscow's huge Hotel Rossiya – the largest in the world, according to the Guinness Book of Records – buying bottles of lemonade for our evening Oneg Shabbat. The man at the checkout counter spotted my Magen David neck chain, asked me where I was from and told me that he was a Jew as well. I was surprised at how open he was.

As I waited for an elevator to return to my floor, my new friend approached me and asked if I had a spare Magen David. Three more restaurant employees came out, including the Russian administrator. She told me that her husband was Jewish; might I have one for him? The other two knew a few words in Hebrew and said *shalom*. They asked for Jewish jewelry for their relatives and friends. They said that fully 80 percent of the restaurant workers were Jews.

And here I thought that I had come to buy some bottles of lemonade…

Our people were all over, in plain sight and eager for contacts. If we could but find the way to make ourselves known to them.

AT PIONEER CAMPS

The Young Pioneers (officially the Vladimir Lenin All-Union Pioneer Organization) was the mass youth organization of the Communist Party of the Soviet Union for children ages nine to fifteen. Every school child was enrolled. The summer camps were extremely popular and groups of foreign tourists were brought there as part of their standard Intourist itineraries. Over the years they provided our USY groups with some very powerful Jewish encounters, probably not what the Soviet authorities had in mind.

I noted the following in my diary during our 1970 visit to Riga in the Latvian Soviet Socialist Republic:

> We just returned from a visit to a Pioneer Camp. Our people were there. We met a newly married young Jewish couple. She was in her third year of the Institute; he was in his fifth. They wanted to leave. The

situation was very bad and getting worse. What will be their future? They are not allowed to be Jews. The camp's music teacher was one of us. He asked why we came to Russia. When Arnie responded that we came to meet him and to connect with Soviet Jews, he almost couldn't believe it. Our people are coming out of the walls. The English teacher is one of us as well.

After our 1971 visit to Vilna, I recorded the following entry:

The high point of our visit to a Pioneer Camp in Vilna, Soviet Lithuania, was the concluding outdoor concert. After the local children performed, they invited us, the members of the visiting American delegation, to sing for the entire group. I sensed that there were some Jewish mothers and children in the audience, but how could we identify ourselves only to them?

We ascended the stage and lined up choirlike. I said that we would open with "If I Had a Hammer," the folk song popularized by Pete Seeger, who was beloved in the Soviet Union for his left-leaning politics. This time the words: "It's a song about love between my brothers and my sisters all over this land" took on a double meaning. We were looking for our brothers and sisters all over this land. The audience applauded very enthusiastically, both the song and our "obvious" politics, when I suddenly realized what we should do.

I announced that we would now sing "a song of world peace," which evoked smiles and obvious approval from the crowd. I breathed very deeply, smiled as broadly as I could, and began: "*Oseh shalom bimromav, Hu ya'aseh shalom aleinu*" (May He Who makes peace in the world make peace for us). At that point, I modified the final words a bit. Rather than sing "*ve'al kol Yisrael*" (and for all of Israel), which was a step too far (singing about Israel in public in the USSR, just four years after the Six-Day War, was definitely not politically correct), I came out with "*ve'al kol ha'olam*" (and for the entire world).

The crowd applauded politely, though I noted the unhappy face of one of the camp administrators, and we hurriedly finished our performance.

As we were milling about in front of the stage, a local woman with dark hair approached me, flanked by her children, and inquired: "What is your nationality?" I told her that all of us were Americans, and some of us were Jews, to which she responded: "*Ve fse yevrei*" (You are all

Jews, aren't you)? I nodded and smiled. The woman introduced me to her sixteen-year-old daughter Bailah and her other Jewish friends. I told her how happy we were to be in the "Jerusalem of Lithuania," and she understood precisely what I was referring to. [See photos.]

Vilna had been the glory of the Jewish world, the prewar home to more than 100,000 Jews, nearly half of the city's population, with 110 shuls and ten yeshivot. Now barely a few thousand remained.

We gave out Magen David neck chains for the children. I hugged a seven-year-old Jewish child.

Jews were coming out of the woodwork to say hello and to contact us. We had a wonderful visit to Vilna.

Two years later we visited a Pioneer Camp in Kiev, the capital of Soviet Ukraine. I wrote the following afterwards in my diary:

As we entered the camp, we met Maria, the Jewish camp nurse. She was very eager to speak with us and asked us for a copy of the "Biblia" (Bible), which we, unfortunately, did not have. We took a walk together. "Ich ken a bissel Yiddish" (I speak a bit of Yiddish), she said. We told her about our visit to Auschwitz and the million Jewish victims there. Apparently, she had not heard of that previously. She approached her fellow workers to tell them the shocking news she had just learned: "Did you hear? A million Jews slaughtered?!"

It was very important for her to tell me that she believed in God. As we were about to depart, she gave me one of the most poignant and powerful blessings I ever received in all of my trips to the Soviet Union: "God knows that you and I are one."

I have quoted her heartfelt words on countless occasions. She summed up what brought us together. No matter what we gave them, they gave us even more in return.

When these visits originally appeared on our Intourist itineraries, I was initially very unenthusiastic. We had come looking for Jews, and spending time at a Communist Party youth camp did not seem like a worthwhile venue. It turned out that I was totally wrong. The relaxed outdoor setting allowed for many informal social interactions and contacts.

Every time we visited, discretely displaying some Magen Davids or singing Jewish songs, local Jews came forward and identified themselves to members of our group. If we were looking for them, they were looking for us as well, and we invariably found each other.

AT THE BEACH AND IN OTHER PUBLIC PLACES

Our 1972 group went for an afternoon swim in the Neva River, in the heart of Leningrad, on the banks of the Peter and Paul Fortress. As I stood on the pebble beach and took off my shirt, a local man in his mid-thirties approached me, pointed at my Magen David, and asked, "What is that?"

Even though it was clear what was about to take place, I still wanted to check further, so I told him that it was simply a piece of jewelry, nothing more. I inquired where he was from, and when he told me that he was born in Leningrad, I asked where his parents came from, to which he replied: 'My mother came from Zhitomir and my father from Berdichev.'

"Bingo!" I thought to myself.

"Wonderful towns," I responded. "Wonderful Jewish towns."

With a smile of recognition and familiarity, our newfound friend – who had been given the Hebrew name Yisrael by his Ukrainian Jewish parents – told us about himself. He was a local doctor, and like many Jewish young professionals, he wanted to leave for Israel but was concerned that he did not know the language.

He grasped Arnie by the arm and called him "*brat*" (brother). He asked what nationalities the members of our group were, and when we told him that all of us were Jews, he was very surprised and pleased. I offered to give him a Hebrew-Russian textbook, but he was afraid to accept it.

"They are looking at us," he said. "It is very difficult here."

I put on my shirt, surreptitiously placing the volume inside, and invited him to take a walk with me near the walls of the fortress. As I reached over to give him a farewell hug, I passed him the book. He opened the button of his shirt and slipped it in. He blessed me with *l'chayim* and quickly walked away.

I returned to Arnie at the beach and told him that if we had any doubts, we really had arrived in the Soviet Union.

In addition to the hidden Jews, who were all over the Soviet Union, a few urban Jewish neighborhoods still survived.

Walking in the Podol section of Kiev in 1973, it was almost as if we were on New York's Lower East Side or in Tel Aviv, there were so many Jews. We "collected" Jews left and right, including two grandmothers, one of whom had learned several words of biblical Hebrew as a child. We gave them some clothing for their grandchildren and she responded, "*Toydah rabbah*" (Many thanks), in a thick accent. We passed some older Jewish men sitting on a bench, whom we greeted with a *shalom*. Speaking in Yiddish, we wished them "*a gris*" (best wishes and regards). We crossed the street to greet two older women, dressed in classic babushka style, complete with shawls. At the metro station, we asked for instructions and thanked them in Yiddish.

We met dozens of Jews just walking the streets of old Kiev. We felt very much at home, as if we were coming back to our old Jewish neighborhood. I reveled in the familiarity and intimacy of being among my fellow Jews.

Strolling in public with a group of obviously friendly visiting American students provided an excellent cover for our real goal of identifying and greeting Jews in a "safe" manner, something I would not have done if I were alone.

At our group debriefing in Jerusalem a few days later, one of the USYers perceptively commented on what was really going on: "Rabbi Porath 'used' us – in the best sense of the word. Without us, he couldn't have done what he did. We served as his eyes and arms, and he served as our protector, as someone to run to in times of trouble."

Of course, the most natural and obvious place for meeting Jews was in and around local synagogues, where we spent much of our "Jewish time."

VISITING SOVIET SHULS

It is difficult to imagine what the old men thought when our USY group, quite unexpectedly and without warning, entered the doors of their small shul in Leningrad, late one summer's evening in 1969.

To be sure, occasional visitors – and even organized groups accompanied by Intourist guides – often came to visit, especially during the tourist season. They were greeted by the officials, all the lights in the main sanctuary were turned on, and they were taken around the building. They would be shown the "Wedding Hall" (rarely used in Soviet times), heard about how much the Soviet government provided for the religious needs of the "believers," and were given some time to take pictures. It was a great show!

But we were different. In those days, there were almost no other religiously observant Jewish high school groups visiting Russia. We came to Russian shuls not as tourists but as full participants. The boys put on tefillin and the girls knew how to daven. We led services, read the Torah and many of us spoke Hebrew as well as a few words of Yiddish. Clearly, our USYers felt at home in shul.

The reception we received was difficult to predict, depending upon the actions of the gabbai who was on duty at the time. These were not lay leaders, as in the West, but had an official or semi-official role sanctioned by the state. Their job was to keep the locals and foreigners apart and to report to the Soviet Ministry of Cults (aka Religious Affairs). The local Jews, of course, knew how the system worked, and, given no choice, went along. There were those, however, who couldn't resist the opportunity to symbolically "protest."

One of the Leningrad officials proudly showed off the kosher slaughtering rooms in the basement of the synagogue and described the rich Jewish life they had there. He was trailed by Reb Zalman, one of the shul's old-timers, who kept repeating to us in Hebrew, which the gabbai did not understand: "It's all lies and a cover-up. It's all a fake." We were all part of the "show," and each of us had our assigned role. That's how it was, traveling the Soviet Union in those days.

JEWISH OUTREACH IN LENINGRAD

We were always on the lookout for local Soviet Jews visiting the shuls. They were easy to identify. They stood close to the exits, sat by themselves in the women's section or waited around appearing a bit lost in the courtyard. They were either deliberately ignored by the officials or told to leave the shul premises. They were open and even eager to speak with us.

In 1969, we spotted a young man standing at the back of the Leningrad shul. His name was Misha. He was twenty-two-years old and hailed from Gorki, a town in Central Russia. It was his first time in shul in his life. I said hello and he began singing "Havah Nagilah" for me. I showed him a Magen David, which he recognized. When I placed it in his hand, he become very teary-eyed. He knew a smattering of Yiddish words like *gelt* (money) and *parnosah* (livelihood).

He asked about obtaining a visa to Israel, and I inquired if he would like to learn Hebrew. When he nodded his head, I gave him a Hebrew-Russian dictionary and a heartfelt embrace. Standing and speaking together, we were attracting too much unwanted attention. I told him that it was time to go and wished him *shalom*. There was no shul in his hometown, he said, but he hoped we would meet again someday.

Jews from the periphery, such as David and Lyuba from Tbilisi, would travel to Moscow and Leningrad for medical care and would visit the synagogue. Often, they were looking for needed religious items. It almost sounds ludicrous to state the obvious: there were no Jewish bookstores in Moscow, Leningrad, or anywhere else in the Soviet Union. Perhaps they thought that some tourist would stop by or a local Jew would come to sell or dispose of a family religious heirloom that was no longer of any value to him.

I met them in the shul courtyard and gave them a Hebrew textbook and a tallit. David asked me for a pair of tefillin and I promised we would bring a set in the morning.

The next day, both of them were eagerly waiting in the street near the shul and greeted us with joy and excitement. We went to the side of the building to pass him the tefillin. He wanted to pay for them but I adamantly refused. He then offered to give me his old pair of tefillin but I told him to pass them on to another young person. He tried to give me his watch, which I also declined. They were the parents of eight children and Lyuba said that I was just like a son to her, which was quite a compliment! We wished them well in their treatments. I wrote in my 1970 diary: "Dear, sweet, warm Jews. May God in His mercy protect them from all pain and suffering."

On the same trip, Rachel, one of our USYers, had brought a Magen David on a neck chain with her from the States, which she had received when she was born. As she unfastened the clasp to gift it to one of the younger women who came to shul, she gave it a loving parting kiss, saying goodbye to a part of herself.

I was thrilled to see that our USY girls, sitting upstairs in the women's section, were bonding with the local ladies. It was worth the entire 1969 visit just to see them at work, especially when, after services, two of them told me the following story.

They understood that most of the older women lived very meager and lonely lives. Many were World War II widows who had been living alone since their husbands were killed, more than twenty-five years before. As they sat next to each other upstairs, overlooking the congregation, our young ladies would hold their hands, and the older women would touch and caress our girls' arms with real affection and yearning for the families they did not have.

Our girls felt they had to do something. They left the synagogue, walked back to our hotel, gathered up their spare makeup and jewelry, and returned to shul to distribute their gifts to the astonished and thankful women. Our USYers message was heartfelt: We love you, you are beautiful, and Jews take care of fellow Jews.

I was full of admiration for what the young women had done. Sometimes, the rabbis tell us, if we are worthy, a single deed can redeem the entire world.

CHAPTER 6

Summer 1970:
A Time of Troubles

TENSION IN THE AIR

For those with an ear for Russian history, the phrase "Time of Troubles" will res-onate. It refers to the period of Russian civil unrest that began in 1598 with the death of the last tsar of the Rurik line, the son of Ivan the Terrible, and lasted until the establishment of the Romanov Dynasty in 1613. The final reigning Romanov, Tsar Nicholas II, was executed by the Bolsheviks in 1918.

The phrase also calls to mind my all-time favorite painting, by the Russian master Ilya Repin, "Ivan the Terrible and His Son Ivan on 16 November 1581," which depicts, in stark and graphic detail, Ivan killing his son in a fit of rage, setting off the Time of Troubles. You can almost feel the drops of blood on the canvas. The masterpiece is displayed in Moscow's State Tretyakov Gallery and should not be missed.

That phrase from Russia's past seemed to capture our mood as we arrived in Leningrad during the summer of 1970.

On June 15, 1970, the Soviet authorities announced that they had arrested a group of alleged hijackers who had planned on diverting a small passenger plane from the Soviet Union to the West and, ultimately, Israel. Sixteen people were charged with high treason, fourteen of them Jews and two non-Jews. They were put on trial in Leningrad in December 1970. Two of them were sentenced to death, and most of the rest received lengthy prison sentences.

The arrests and subsequent trial were accompanied by a crackdown on Jewish activists and other Soviet dissidents.

Following strong international condemnation of the verdicts, the Soviets commuted the death sentences and, hoping that the Zionist and dissident move-ments would be weakened if "troublemakers" were allowed to leave, the Soviet government sharply increased the number of exit visas it gave to Jews. In the entire decade of the 1960s, only about 11,000 Soviet Jews had been permitted to go to Israel, while in 1971 alone nearly 13,000 made aliyah. During the 1970s, over 225,000 Jews and their family members were allowed to depart, 150,000 of whom came to Israel.[1]

When our group arrived in Leningrad in July 1970, barely three weeks after the accused hijacking, we sensed that something had changed.

As we approached the shul on Lermontovskiy Prospekt, we felt the unwelcoming gaze of the locals staring at us, as if to say: "What are you doing here?" Inside the shul, it was no better. The chief gabbai told us not to speak: that would disturb the daveners. A group of twenty non-Jews entered the shul. We didn't know who they were. Afraid of provocations, we told our USYers not to approach them. Our group quickly departed and waited at the tram station with many others, including some soldiers and police.

I felt very uncomfortable and vulnerable, and I was certain that I communicated my anxiety to the group, even without thinking. We thankfully made our way back to our hotel. I was not even sure why I felt afraid: was it the fear of the tentacles of "Soviet Power," or was it perhaps an existential Jewish feeling of exile combined with our being strangers in such a foreign place? It was a deeply unsettling feeling, which I would later learn was not totally baseless.

Feeling uneasy and unsure of how to behave even in shul, we welcomed the opportunity to spend Friday evening at the hotel by ourselves. Since services did not begin at the synagogue in the summer until 11 p.m., we met earlier in Sid and Andy's room for our own Kabbalat Shabbat evening service. We lit candles, sang "Shalom Aleichem," made Kiddush over wine and Hamotzi over bread. Our fears and anxieties melted away, and we felt that we were standing in a protected and holy space. It was a precious feeling and gave us great strength and solace.

REB NOACH'S DESPERATE PLEA

I recorded the following in my diary during my 1970 trip:

> I just returned from a heart-rending meeting with Reb Noach, a member of the Jewish intelligentsia. We had met at shul yesterday morning after Shabbat services and he was desperate to speak to me but felt terribly vulnerable and afraid.
>
> "They are staring at us," he kept repeating.
>
> We arranged to meet today, on the Nevsky Prospekt, the main public thoroughfare of Leningrad, comparable to New York City's Fifth Avenue. I felt much more exposed in public, but he preferred the

---

1. Based on figures from the Israeli Bureau of Statistics and Petrus Buwalda, *They Did Not Dwell Alone*, 221–24.

anonymity of the crowded streets. As we walked, we spoke in biblical Hebrew, Russian, and some English.

In near-desperation, he reported that the local situation was getting worse and worse in the wake of the KGB crackdown, following the attempted Leningrad Hijacking on June 15, 1970, less than a month previously. (We were speaking on July 12.)

He poured out his anguish to me. The mayor of the city is an antisemite, hence the trumped-up airline case. Jews are living in the shadow of the Valley of Death under the yoke of the state. It is impossible to leave. He would come to Israel with his entire family if he could, but he sees no possibility now.

He spared neither words nor emotions in his criticism of the Jews of the Free World: "*Atem loi oisim maspik bishvileinu*" (You aren't doing enough for us), he kept pleading. "You in the West and Israel must be more insistent and more aggressive."

As I heard his heartfelt words, I knew that he was right. Certainly, he said, our coming to visit them in Russia gave them support, but they need so much more.

To grab the world's attention, Israel should establish a museum about Russian Jewry "Just like Yad Vashem!" he said. I cringed, knowing that Yad Vashem was for Jews who perished in the Holocaust, not for living ones. He quoted the famous words of Rabbi Tarfon from the Mishnah: "The day is short," and added: "Time is running out."

I returned to the hotel feeling hopeless, frustrated, and angry at the Soviets for what they were doing to our people as well as ashamed by what we in the Jewish community were not doing for them ourselves.

The Missing Gates

Reflecting Reb Noach's sense of dread and desperation, when we returned to the Leningrad synagogue a year later in 1971, we were shocked to find that the magnificently ornamented wrought iron shul gates, prominently displaying a Hebrew inscription and a Magen David, *were missing!*

They had been removed from their supporting posts and carted away. There was a gaping void where they had stood so firmly for so long – presumably since the building had been dedicated in 1888. We were told that they had been taken down "for repairs" though they had always seemed quite solid and sturdy to me.

Perhaps they had been removed as an "official response" to the Leningrad Trials, telling the Jews, in effect: don't get any "wrong ideas" from the failed hijacking. We control everything here, from who can leave the country to what you can display on the outside of your synagogue. The shul entry was now open and exposed, like a raw wound.

Although the gates were eventually restored, nothing better symbolized the vulnerability of Soviet Jews.

ARNIE'S STORY

We entered the small shul in Leningrad with great expectation as well as anxiety. How would we be received? For my friend and co-leader, Rabbi Arnie Turetsky, this 1970 excursion was his first day in the Soviet Union and his first time in a Russian shul. He approached one of the older men with a heartfelt greeting: "I am Turetsky from the town of Turetz. How are you?" There was no response. Figuring that perhaps the man hadn't heard or understood him, he went up to a second man and was met, once again, with silence.

In desperation, Arnie turned to yet one more person and poured out his heart, pleading: "I am Turetsky from Turetz; I have come thousands of miles to be with you, a fellow Jew. Why won't you speak to me?"

Finally, he received a response.

"We don't know you. Who are you?" the man asked. "Are you a provocateur? Why have you come?"

Chastened and humbled, Arnie spent the next few days attending services morning and evening, weekdays and Shabbat, meeting, gifting, becoming – as much as he could under the circumstances – a part of the congregation. Finally, as we left the shul for the final time, on our way to Moscow, he turned to me, told me the story, and wondered aloud, "What will happen if ever I come back again?"

A year later, in 1971, we returned to Leningrad and prepared to enter the same small shul. Arnie, hopefully yet hesitatingly, opened the door.

Aaron, one of the USYers, described what happened next: "When Reb Elya, one of the old men Rabbi Turetsky had become friendly with last year, saw the rabbi walk in, he ran to him and embraced him (as Rabbi Turetsky says) "as he had never been hugged in his life." Then, still not believing what he was seeing, Reb Elya exclaimed: "If you live long enough, you see everything, even miracles."

It was the kind of heartfelt greeting that one could only dream about.

We moved on to Riga, where the Jews were even more isolated than in Leningrad.

THE LONELY SHUL IN RIGA

After checking in to the hotel in Riga, the capital of Soviet Latvia, Arnie and I went searching for the shul. We found the building but the front door was locked, so we circled behind and in a small back alley found an open gate with an unlocked door. We went upstairs to the cavernous women's section, now vacant, and davened the afternoon service by ourselves. We wanted to identify with once-great Latvian Jewry, now only a shadow of its former glory.

Prewar Latvia had been home to over ninety thousand Jews, complete with Jewish schools, synagogues, theaters, and a rich cultural and communal life. The great Jewish historian Simon Dubnov had fled from Germany to Riga in 1938 to escape the Nazis, to no avail. Only fourteen thousand Latvian Jews survived. Notices from the end of World War II were still posted, requesting information about the remnants of destroyed communities.

We were overcome by an empty feeling: only us, the one shul, and a few old signs.

We went outside and came upon Gavriel, who was working on a woodpile by the side of the shul. He opened the building for us and turned on the lights so we could take some pictures. He said there was no Jewish life, no schools, no youth groups. There were minyanim every morning and evening, and on Simchat Torah the place was filled, with the crowd including young people, spilling onto the street. Some of the youths had attempted to return to the shul during the year, but the gabbai threw them out.

At about 9:30 p.m. we returned with the USYers. We were greeted by ten men waiting to begin davening. One told me that he wanted to leave for Israel but could not.

"We are afraid," he said.

Three of the Jews arrested in connection with attempted hijacking were from Riga: Yosef Mendelevitch, Sylva Zalmanson, and her brother Izrail. One of the men told me that he had recently attended one of their weddings. I understood from his descriptions that many local Soviet Jewish activists were clamoring to leave. Another said that many Riga Jews listened to Kol Yisrael, the clandestine Israeli radio station, every day and knew what was happening in the Holy Land.

Down in the basement another minyan was starting, affiliated with Chabad. One of the men from the main minyan claimed that this other group was full of informers. The person whom I thought was the chief informer himself was warning us about the others! It was impossible to know whom, if anyone, to trust.

I met a younger man who spoke to me during the davening. I told him that we had just come from Leningrad and that there was great fear there. He replied that he understood, but that he believes in God and is not afraid. We departed with a hearty *"Zei gezunt"* (Be well).

The most unsettling thing in Leningrad and Riga during that trip was that Jews were afraid of their fellow Jews.

We departed Riga for our final stop, Moscow.

SHABBAT MORNING IN MOSCOW

Arnie and I were seated in the "guest box" at the front of the Choral Synagogue when a tumult broke out in the congregation. Two men in military uniform entered the shul and begin searching the rows, one at a time, as if checking up on who was present. There was great unrest among the hundreds of old men. Nothing like this had ever happened before, we were told. The rabbi stood up and quieted the congregation.

During the Torah reading, I went outside. A large crowd had gathered in front of the shul, including at least half a dozen activists, many speaking Hebrew, who had come to meet tourists and to exchange the latest information about Israel. They told us they were about to take some "legal actions" to publicize their plight and to voice their demands to leave the USSR. They insisted that we tell people in the West that they existed and that they wanted to make aliyah.

They were fearless, something we had not seen in Leningrad or Riga. One person guessed that, if given the choice, half a million Soviet Jews would leave. It turns out that he had badly underestimated. Over the next forty years, over three times that number would depart for Israel, the US, and the rest of the world.

Congregating on Arkhipova Street that Shabbat morning, there was a sense of freedom and even optimism for the Jewish future. A small group, for now, but definitely growing, these young people in their twenties and thirties were aggressively fighting to leave. One accompanied us back to our hotel and wasn't afraid to be seen in our presence.

Another activist told us that when Rabbi Levin recently came out in support of the government's anti-Zionist and anti-Israel positions in a March 1970 letter to *Izvestia*, he had signed a letter of protest and was summarily fired from his work. Now he was free to do what he wanted and was no longer beholden to the Soviet system.

At our hotel, I met a visiting Jewish tourist. He said to me that the best gift we could give the local Jewish activists was for our group to come in person and give them encouragement, which was precisely the reason we were there.

FINAL DAY – TENSIONS AND EMOTION RUNNING HIGH

Arnie reported that his room had been searched and his notes in Hebrew and Yiddish were missing. Nomi, his wife and co-leader, was extremely anxious. We were scheduled to depart for Bucharest the following morning, and we still had a harrowing twenty-four hours ahead of us.

After a rather perfunctory tour of the Kremlin and Lenin's Tomb, we were just trying to get through the day and leave the USSR in peace. As a parting visit, a group of us prepared to travel to the most remote shul in Moscow, in the Chergizova neighborhood.

I had brought the USYers there the previous year. It was barely two rooms, an office, and a library with some aged and tattered books. There had been a rabbi, but he had recently passed away at the age of ninety-three. Save for our group, tourists never visited. A year earlier, we had left a treasure trove of gifts: a tallit and four pairs of tefillin, kippot, and Hebrew texts. We told them then that the entire group of twenty-five young people had brought these from America for them and wished them "Next year in Jerusalem." They echoed our words and added "Amen!"

I wanted to return this year as well. We were their only "lifeline" to the Jewish world.

As we descended the escalator on our way out of the hotel, Arnie and Alan, who were bringing up the rear, didn't get off. We waited, at first patiently, then increasingly anxiously, for them to appear. Ten minutes passed, and finally, blessedly, they came down. I told the group that they had lost their way, but I really feared that they had been detained by the authorities. With that less-than-auspicious departure, we were on our way.

I remembered the metro stops to the neighborhood, but once we left the station, I could not recall exactly where to go. I searched for a "safe" source to direct us and found a mother walking her school-age daughter. As we turned the corner, a detachment of four or five city police came walking down the street in our direction. Thankfully, we passed them without any problem, but I still could not find the shul.

Becoming increasingly anxious, I stopped another passing lady, who directed us to turn back in the direction from which we had just come. As we began to retrace our steps, the same police unit came towards us once again. It was a frightening moment. Two of the men took a step in our direction but, ultimately, left us alone.

We were carrying the still-undelivered tallitot, tefillin, and Jewish books we had brought to give away. I tried not to think about what would have happened if we had been stopped, questioned, and searched. Finally, we arrived at the synagogue, hidden away in a corner of Moscow. From the outside it looked like a garage. There was no sign, no Magen David, nothing to mark it as a Jewish place.

I am certain that the dozen old men gathered in shul thought they were dreaming as our group of USYers suddenly opened the door and walked in. I recognized a number of them from previous visits and they remembered me as well. We were overcome with feelings of gratitude and thanksgiving at having arrived safely. They were delighted to see us. Because of its remote location, there were no state-sponsored gabbais in the shul, so we could mix openly and without fear.

The scene hadn't changed since I had been there a year earlier. The elderly pensioners were still sitting around the table, studying the *Ein Yaakov*, a collection of Talmudic tales. The teacher greeted me with a heartfelt *shalom*. They were totally on their own. Our group the previous year had been the last foreign guests they hosted. They said that a hundred people came on Shabbat morning and twenty during the week. The only time that young people showed up was on Simchat Torah.

They loved seeing our girls and were amazed at how they knew how to daven. We left with them our remaining items including half-a-dozen Teitz Siddurim, published by Rabbi Pinchas Teitz of Elizabeth, NJ, specifically for smuggling in to Soviet Jews, which were very much in demand.

The experience was so emotional that Arnie began to cry. We felt a deep and real connection. Arnie told them that our boys and girls kept the Shabbat and davened every day, and repeated that to the USYers themselves. We were all overwhelmed by the moment and many of us were on the verge of tears.

Regretfully, it was time for us to depart. Reb Yonah, one of their most faithful stalwarts, a learned Jew and a person of great respect, said to us: "*Koshe olai preidaschem*" (Your leaving is so hard for me). As we departed, we wished each of them a loving "*Zei gezunt*" (Be well), followed by "Next year in Jerusalem."

I left feeling an almost overwhelming compulsion to return. I saw that it was possible to fulfill the mitzvah of *pidyon shevuyim* (freeing captives) not only *physically*, but *spiritually* as well, by coming in person, giving support, and extending words of encouragement. It applied to these old men in shul, to the young activists in the street, and to all of the Soviet Jews whom we were privileged to meet during our visits.

CHAPTER 7
With the Chief Rabbi of Russia

ON ASSIGNMENT FROM THE CHIEF RABBI OF ISRAEL

As the son and grandson of rabbis, I felt much sympathy towards Chief Rabbi Yehuda Levin. He was in an impossible position, stuck between the Soviet authorities who oversaw his every move; the Russian Jews, the overwhelming majority of whom had long ago abandoned their religious heritage; and the international Jewish community, which often criticized him for not speaking out against the policies of the government. To my mind, he was doing the best that he could under the circumstances. He and I had a number of contacts over the years, and he graciously met with our USY groups.

It was obvious that Moscow's Choral Synagogue, as well as the few dozen remaining Jewish houses of worship across the country, were permitted to remain open and functioning only at the discretion of the authorities, and if the government or the Soviet security services decided to limit the shuls' activities, or close them down, they would do so with little hesitation.

The rabbi was vulnerable and subject to attack wherever he turned, domestically or internationally, but he did have some ardent supporters around the Jewish world.

While studying in Jerusalem in 1969, I was contacted by the office of Rabbi Isser Yehuda Unterman, the Ashkenazi chief rabbi of Israel, to come and meet with him. He was a long-time friend of my grandfather, Rabbi Israel Porath from Jerusalem and Cleveland. I believe that my Zadie had mentioned to Rabbi Unterman that I was going to be in Russia that summer, and that was the reason for the invitation.

I was honored to be in the presence of the chief rabbi and soon understood why he had asked me to come. *He wanted me to be his private emissary to Rabbi Levin in Moscow.* As we sat together, he handwrote a letter that he asked me to deliver in person. He was afraid that I might be stopped, so he composed the note for Rabbi Levin in a classical Hebrew style, as if addressed to me.

Please, dear Jonathan, express warmest greetings to the distinguished
Rabbi Levin, who carries on his shoulders a most heavy and responsible burden. May God bless him in all his great work on behalf of the
people, and may he continue for many years to come.

And afterward, when you meet the local Jews, strengthen their
hearts and spirits in the Rock of Israel, and tell them that the entire
Jewish people is awaiting redemption. Even those who call themselves
freethinkers and secular still carry the spark of faith in their hearts, as
we say: "*Netzach Yisrael lo yeshaker*" (I Samuel 15:29), whose message
is "The Eternal One of Israel will never abandon His people."

I have refrained from writing letters directly to Rabbi Levin for
fear of censorship. When he recently celebrated his seventy-fifth
birthday, I sent a telegram and also blessed him in a radio broadcast,
but understood that even if I were granted a visa to attend the event, I
would not be allowed to address the congregation, so what would have
been gained by my visit?

I wish you all the best, and may the Lord bless you and protect you
in your mission.

Our USY group arrived in Moscow in mid-July, and we went to shul on our first
morning in town. After services, I met privately with Rabbi Levin and completed
my mission. He was very pleased and encouraged to receive Rabbi Unterman's
letter. Rabbi Levin extended his blessings in return, praying "God grant him good
health and strengthen him in his work."

I am not certain how many repeat visitors Rabbi Levin had from the West,
but I was becoming one of them.

OUR TEENAGERS MEET WITH RABBI LEVIN

I asked Rabbi Levin if he would be available to meet with our group, and he cor-
dially agreed. We met on two occasions, in 1969 and 1970, before he passed away
in 1971. (See photos.)

Here is how I described our visit in *Our Age*, a publication of the United
Synagogue of America's Department of Education:

A most memorable experience was our meeting with the Chief Rabbi
of Moscow. We were ushered into his reception room, which dou-
bles as a study hall. The Sefer Torah and Aron Kodesh, signifying
God's watchfulness, contrasted ironically with the careful eyes of the

synagogue officials who accompanied Rabbi Levin to the interview. He was taciturn but allowed us to ask questions of him in Hebrew or Yiddish.

He noted that we were the first group of Jewish young people that he had met since he assumed his position as Chief Rabbi. His quiet eyes, buried deep in his bearded face, left a haunting impression on many of us. One of our USYers even said that the two Russian faces most vivid to him were those of Rabbi Levin…and Lenin.[1]

In addition to one of the officials, there was a notetaker present, recording what was said. I sensed that, in response to our questions, the rabbi told us as much of the truth as he could: there is one yeshiva, but with very few students; kosher slaughtering and ritual items do exist, for those who want them; pocket calendars were published, but not large-format ones; there is no Jewish education, and in any event, there is no time for classes; the young people are not religious, and don't come to shul; the rabbis and other clergy would like to move to Israel, but nobody would remain to lead their communities; there are Russian Jews who want to leave, but first they are required to repay the state for their education.

He summed up his role as follows: "I am a rabbi and do not deal with politics, only with the religious needs of the community."

I can't say that he was forthright or candid, but certainly, for a group of visiting American high school students, he was very hospitable and welcoming. After our forty-five-minute visit, the USYers eagerly lined up for photographs with the rabbi. He agreed and posed patiently, shaking hands with each one as we departed, bidding us to "go in peace."

I was personally saddened that we were the only group of Jewish young people he had occasion to meet with, which summed up to me the unfortunate reality of the Jewish religion in the Soviet Union. The younger generation of Soviet Jewish youth was totally alienated from the synagogue. It would only be a matter of time until Judaism itself would completely disappear – or so we imagined.

WORLDWIDE RESONANCE OF THE VISITS

Our meetings with Rabbi Levin reverberated across the Jewish world. Articles appeared in the Israeli and American Jewish press, including the *Jerusalem Post*, the *United Synagogue Review*, the *Jewish Morning Journal*, and others. Most striking was a picture of our group with Rabbi Levin on the front page of the August 2, 1970, edition of the Israeli newspaper *Maariv*, with the caption: "A delegation

---

1. Jonathan Porath, "Visit to Russia," *Our Age*, October 5, 1969, 3. Reprinted with permission of the United Synagogue of Conservative Judaism.

of Jewish youth which just spent twelve days in the USSR, in conversation with Chief Rabbi Levin, in Moscow."

A group of American students holding such a meeting was big news fifty years ago.

An article by journalist S. L. Schneiderman entitled "Soviet Jews Are Silent No Longer," which appeared in the popular *World Over* magazine, was of particular interest.

> A highlight of my trip to the Soviet Union was a visit to the chief rabbi of Moscow, Yehuda Leib Levin, who had recently celebrated his 75th birthday. He had been much impressed by a group of American Jewish teenagers who had visited him, and he started his conversation about them. He was surprised that many of them were fluent in Hebrew. One astonished the old rabbi with his knowledge of the Bible and Talmud.
>
> I later came upon this group of young people in one of the long lines that move slowly through Lenin's tomb. Most of them were high school seniors from a number of American and Canadian cities, and one future rabbi from the Jewish Theological Seminary in New York, Jonathan Porath, who could speak Russian. It was Jonathan's scholarship that Rabbi Levin had praised.[2]

Rabbi Levin's very gracious comments, both regarding our group and me personally, were totally unexpected and much appreciated.

THE POSITION OF THE RABBI IN THE SOVIET UNION

As controversial as Rabbi Levin was around the Jewish world, some seeing him as a heroic individual who maintained a semblance of Jewish life under impossible conditions, while others viewing him as a state sponsored "stooge" and collaborator, to my mind he was a tragic figure who did the best he could in the face of overwhelming odds. I did not envy him. It was manifestly clear to me that his was a job I would never want to have.

Professor Mordechai Altshuler, in his illuminating and authoritative study *Religion and Jewish Identity in the Soviet Union, 1941–1964*, devoted a chapter to "Rabbis and the Congregational Establishment," writing as follows:

---

2.   S. L. Schneiderman, "Soviet Jews Are Silent No Longer," *World Over* (a publication of the Jewish Education Committee of New York), February 27, 1970, 6–7.

The official rabbis were charged with ensuring that the synagogue was used for ritual observance only, as defined by the Soviet authorities. The rabbis had to remain in constant contact with the regime's authorities and report to them on the goings-on in the synagogue; to certain circles of Jews in the USSR [and abroad – JP], this demand made the rabbis suspect....

These people lived and functioned under the terrible vise of Soviet religious persecution. To keep alive any permitted religious activity, they had to please the authorities and meet the regime's demands.[3]

Our experiences in the Soviet Union certainly supported Professor Altshuler's conclusions.

---

3.   Mordechai Altshuler, "Rabbis and the Congregational Establishment," in *Religion and Jewish Identity in the Soviet Union, 1941–1964*, trans. Saadya Sternberg (Waltham, MA: Brandeis University Press, 2012), 128–29. Excerpts reprinted with permission.

CHAPTER 8

Surprises in Vilna;
Jewish Joy in Moscow

THE DAY THE GABBAI DIDN'T COME TO SHUL

Our 1971 visit to Vilna was amazing and wonderful! We attended evening services in the Great Choral Synagogue, the only remaining shul in Vilna. To our delight, the gabbai wasn't there. It was like a Jewish Disneyland. We met many new friends: Reb Shlomo, a Red Army veteran; the shochet who reported that thirty families still keep kosher; a Hebrew-speaking friend of Rabbi Teitz from America. They held a Mishnah class between Minchah and Maariv, and I invited one of the USYers, Leibel Shmuel, to sit down next to me, so he could say that he once studied Torah in Vilna.

We spent almost two hours there.

They told us that they had never seen anything like our group of young people, who felt so comfortable davening in shul. For the first time in a long while, I felt relaxed, without the constant pressure from the ever-present gabbais. Additionally, for me personally, descended from Lithuanian roots on both sides of my family, it was very good to finally be "back home."

Our shul friends were overcome with emotion as we departed. We received many wishes for the New Year. We wished them "Next year in Jerusalem," and they responded: "We want to leave, we want to join you."

We felt enveloped by our people. Wherever we walked in public in Vilna, we met Jews: in the parks, at the cemetery, at the Pioneer Camp. We gave a teenager a Magen David neck chain, which he proudly wore in public. I was anxious but, apparently, he was not.

Even though Vilna was only a shadow of its former self, it was still Jewish Vilna at its heart.

A MESSAGE OF HOPE IN THE KILLING PITS OF PONAR

We journeyed to Ponar, on the outskirts of Vilna, a place of mass Nazi executions. Over seventy-five thousand people were murdered there, most of them Jews. As our bus made its way, we heard the shrieks of passing train whistles, the rustle of the wind and trees. We left the bus and felt the echoes of our footsteps and our barely audible whispers. We were afraid to shout or even to raise our voices.

Other sounds: the constant clicks of cameras, the silent gasps of those treading on a place where once corpses lay, the tearful wail of the El Maleh Rachamim memorial prayer, the murmur of orphans saying the Mourner's Kaddish, and, finally, the scratching of pens writing messages of hope.

We approached the pits where the Germans and their Lithuanian collaborators had murdered Jews in cold blood. As the USYers stood on the edge, peering down into the abyss, I climbed down inside, to the bottom, into the void. We were truly poised between heaven and earth, between this world and the next. We had become a part of Ponar, its living witnesses and storytellers.

We didn't know it then, but we were standing at the site of a singular act of Jewish heroism. On April 15, 1944, on the last night of Pesach, a group of Jewish prisoners who had been brought to Ponar by the Germans to exhume and burn the bodies of their victims, escaped from the pit in a makeshift 112-foot-long tunnel they had dug with teaspoons over the course of the preceding seventy-six nights. Eleven survived to tell their tale. The tunnel was only discovered in 2016, more than seventy years after their escape.

There were other surprises as well. The Ponar Historical Museum was the only memorial site I had ever visited in the Soviet Union with an explicit Jewish presence. There were guide books in Lithuanian, Russian, English…and Yiddish! Glass cases displayed Yiddish messages and notes. One recorded the murders of "*Mameh, Lubka, Feige, Chaya…mit noch toyzend Yidden*" (Mother, Lubka, Feige and Chaya…with thousands of other Jews) on April 12, 1944. At least here our holy martyrs were not ignored. By contrast, at Babi Yar in Kiev, the biggest single Jewish killing field in all of the USSR, the nationality of the victims was totally suppressed. At Ponar, one knew that Jews were killed because they were Jews.

On the way out, there was a memorial book for visitors to enter personal comments and reflections. Who knows who might follow us and leaf through the pages, after we departed? Wanting somehow to reach out to them, I wrote in Hebrew: "*Am Yisrael chai*" (the Jewish people lives). Arnie wrote: "*Netzach Yisrael lo yishaker.*" We hoped that our words of encouragement and prayer would give heart to some future Jewish visitors.

AN UNEXPECTED CONVERSATION IN THE SKIES

While flying on Aeroflot from Vilna to Moscow, I had a most unusual conversation. I noticed that the passengers seated next to me were reading *Sovietishe Heimland*, the only Yiddish-language publication in the Soviet Union. Despite my usually outspoken enthusiasm and Jewish outreach, I was wary of saying too much and resolved to mention nothing about who we were or why we had come.

I said hello and asked: "I heard that there are Jews who would like to leave the Soviet Union."

"Yes," they confirmed. "But we will never leave. Even if you offered us mountains of gold, we are not going anywhere." One of them was a professor of philosophy and other an instructor in comparative linguistics. They were loyal members of the Communist Party.

They asked me my opinion of the activities of Meir Kahana's Jewish Defense League, and I called them "hooligans."

I finally said to the senior of the two: "I am a Jew and you are a Jew. What does that mean to you?"

To him it meant nothing. To me, I said, it meant a shared common history, hopes, and homeland. I noted that without the valiant Soviet army in World War II and the decision of the Soviet government to support the creation of Israel in 1947, the Jewish people would not have survived Hitler, and we would not have a Jewish state. He agreed but said that is all in the past.

As we parted, I bid him "*Shalom, Reb Yid*" (Goodbye, my fellow Jew).

What was remarkable about this conversation was that *it was conducted totally in Hebrew!* He had attended a Hebrew-speaking school in interwar Vilna, then part of Poland. Even though the Soviet Union suppressed the Hebrew language as "Zionist," and officially supported Yiddish, my seat-mate had not forgotten the language of his youth.

The following day, I came across an English-language pamphlet in our Moscow hotel lobby entitled *Soviet Jews Reject Zionist "Protection,"* featuring a round-table discussion held in February 1971 under the auspices of *Sovietishe Heimland*. The final page was an interview with Professor Dr. Henrikas Zimanas, a former partisan in World War II as well as a member of the Supreme Soviet of the USSR and the Soviet Public Anti-Zionist Committee – whom I recognized from his picture. He sat next to me on the flight from Vilna! I had spent time with one of the most senior Soviet-Jewish officials and spokesmen in the country.

I was starkly reminded that, although we had come to the Soviet Union to encourage our Jewish brothers and sisters, most local Jews were loyal to the Soviet State and were content to stay put. However, as we were soon to find out, growing numbers were prepared to challenge the status quo.

ONEG SHABBAT

As the group leaders (myself, Arnie, Nomi, and Libby) gathered on Friday afternoon on the twenty-first-floor lounge of Moscow's vast Hotel Rossiya, two new friends from Tbilisi, Mordechai and Yitzchak, whom we had met that morning at shul, suddenly appeared, and threw a party! They ordered drinks and cognac, pastries and chocolates, setting an overflowing table full of treats, as only the Georgians know how to do.

We were sitting in a public area in a Russian hotel toasting "Next Year in Israel" and "If I forget thee, O Jerusalem." In exchange, we gave them a cigarette lighter that played "Hatikvah" and a copy of the Israeli newspaper *Yedioth Ahronoth*.

The joy and emotions were running high; what a feeling of Jewish unity. I learned only later that my future wife Deena had met the two of them in Moscow on her own trip to the Soviet Union only a few weeks previously. I was subsequently to meet them in Israel on a future visit.

We didn't know it then, but this was to be the opening to an unforgettable Shabbat.

We arrived at Arkhipova Street on Friday evening and unexpectedly found a whole new reality: young Soviet Jews who were no longer afraid. In addition to our Georgian friends Mordechai and Yitzchak, other local young Jews also came to shul. We all sang and danced together in the street, experiencing tremendous joy.

I had gotten a taste of the new spirit just a few minutes before, during services. A young man approached me in shul and introduced himself as one of the growing numbers of Hebrew teachers in Moscow. I asked him what Hebrew language text he was using for his classes, and he responded: "*Mori – Chelek Alef*" (*My Teacher – Part 1*).

With a big smile, I said to him, "*Yesh li Mori – Chelek Bet*" (I have brought with me *My Teacher – Part 2*)! In an instant, the curriculum of the underground ulpan was doubled!

At 11:00 p.m. we took a group stroll around Red Square, American Jews, and Soviet Jews together, singing "Am Yisrael Chai" and other Jewish songs. Some of the locals even put on kippot as we walked. Save for Simchat Torah gatherings, I had never experienced such public Jewish displays here before.

Undoubtedly, they were encouraged and energized by the conclusion of the Leningrad Trials, the worldwide condemnations, the eventual commutation of the death sentences, and the government's decision to allow unprecedented Jewish emigration to Israel. The word was out: the Jews have begun to leave, and these young people in Moscow were eager to be next in line.

No wonder they couldn't restrain themselves when our group of American Jewish teenagers came to town.

The following morning there were even larger crowds, both inside and outside the shul. People came from Moscow, Kishinev, Poltava; Jewish families with school-age children from Georgia and all over the Soviet Union. Arkhipova Street was crowded with people singing and conducting multiple conversations in Hebrew, English, Yiddish, and Russian.

One of our group, Riva from Long Island, recounted the following story from the just-completed morning services:

As she entered the upstairs women's section, she was escorted to her seat by one of the female gabbais and handed a siddur from a locked safe. This book was the property of the shul and must be returned, she was informed.

As Riva began to leaf through the holy book, she noticed a name written on the inside cover: "Chaya Rivka bat [daughter of] Devorah." Riva was stunned. Her Hebrew name was Chaya Rivka and her mother's name was Devorah. The siddur had her name in it! In effect, she was holding her own siddur.

She grasped and hugged the book. How could she part with it, to be locked up in a safe, for use only by visiting tourists, not even for local Jews?

When the official confronted her following services and demanded the book back, Riva had no choice but to return it, only with the greatest reluctance. She felt that she had left a part of herself behind.

CONTINUING CELEBRATION

After lunch and a rest at our nearby hotel, we returned to the shul for the afternoon service. A circle of Jews had gathered on Arkhipova Street, eagerly waiting for us to return. I read out loud from an Israeli newspaper we had brought with us, from the help wanted section: "Wanted: a teacher in Jerusalem! Job Offer: An engineer in Tel Aviv." Our Russian friends eagerly called out: "That's my job! Save that one for me!" Their hearts and minds were already home.

As we stood in the street, suddenly a rainbow appeared in the Moscow sky. They recited the blessing after me, word for word, praising God "who remembers His covenant with the Jewish People and who will never forget us." We all joined in saying "Amen" together.

We entered the small shul for Minchah and the Seudah Shlishit, the traditional third meal of Shabbat. Our USYers started dancing in the outside hall with the local Jews, just like on Simchat Torah. One of our staff, Rabbi Jack Reimer, spoke in Yiddish to the older men. We all gathered together for Havdalah and the end of Shabbat.

It was 11:00 p.m. on Saturday night. The shul closed its doors, and we continued our conversations in the street. Our newfound friends shared their deepest concerns. Many had been fired from their jobs or dismissed from the universities. The government had recently raised the exit and passport fees to 900 rubles ($1,000), where the average wage was 125 rubles per month. The word was out that an additional education tax would be levied requiring the repayment of thousands of dollars more before any exit visas would be issued.

They gave us many requests for visa invitations to take to Israel. Fearing that we would be searched on the way out, we photographed the letters in our hotel room, flushed the originals down the toilet, and gave the films to the Israeli authorities upon arrival. Our Russian Jewish friends invited us to come to their homes, but we refused. It was too dangerous for them and us.

One of the underground ulpan teachers told me that some two hundred students were currently learning Hebrew.

Our USYers were blown away with excitement and Jewish passion. They came to meet Soviet Jews, but never imagined it would be so intense and such a "high." They would never forget our Shabbat in Moscow.

SHABBAT IN KIEV

It was an hour's walk from our hotel to Podol, the old Jewish section of Kiev. We noted and acknowledged many Jewish faces as we approached the shul.

A young man from Tbilisi was waiting for us in the street. We had met his older brother in Moscow the previous Shabbat, and he had excitedly called home to tell his younger brother about "an American student group that was coming to Kiev." When he heard the news, the younger brother traveled from Georgia to Kiev to meet us.

Word about us was spreading around the Soviet Union.

In the courtyard, we mixed freely with the local Jews and exchanged Hebrew greetings. We felt welcome and at home. However, inside the shul, it was like an all too familiar prison. The gabbais ran a very tight ship, allowing no contact between the visitors and the locals. Two Americans were in shul already, one wearing a tie with a Magen David design, obviously fishing for Jews. I found out subsequently that they both were expelled from the USSR for "anti-state activities." We tried to keep our distance, not wanting to endanger ourselves.

Rabbi Jack Reimer recounted to me that he had met an older man outside of shul, Reb Yaakov, and offered him a wonderful gift: a glossy Hebrew-Russian calendar album, complete with pictures of Ben-Gurion, Golda Meir, and all the rest, really a unique treasure that we ourselves would love to display on our home coffee tables.

The old man was very reluctant and refused the gift. "But it's *gornisht*" (nothing), Jack said in Yiddish. "Yes," said the man. "But I once sat twelve years in jail for *gornisht*."

We were more than happy to be departing for Israel very soon.

CHAPTER 9

Old Friends, a Mazal Tov, and a Return Visit

THE FRIENDLY AND THE NOT SO FRIENDLY

Our "home synagogue" during our visits was undoubtedly the daily minyan of the small shul in Leningrad. The spiritual leaders were Reb Nechemyah, Reb Meir, Reb Elya, and others who had studied in yeshivot before the Bolshevik Revolution, more than fifty years before.

Every summer, they welcomed us and made our USYers feel at home. I would like to believe that as much as we looked forward to seeing them, they anticipated our arrival as well. After all, how many religious teenage groups came to visit them year after year who could daven, read Torah, sing, and infuse the shul with a feeling of life?

Perhaps we somehow represented their children and grandchildren, as well as all the other young Jews in Leningrad, who never came to shul. I was often struck by their near-paternal regard for our young people.

Our coming showed that they were not alone. Somewhere "out there" in the greater Jewish universe, the values and practices so precious to them would continue and even flourish. Indeed, following the collapse of the USSR in 1991, synagogues, Jewish day schools, JCCs, Hillels, and all the rest burst onto the post-Soviet Jewish scene in ways that would have made these old Jews justly proud.

As we came through the door, we were warmly welcomed and embraced as old friends. There were fewer daveners on this 1972 trip than on our previous trips. Some had gone to Israel, others to the World to Come. Reb Nechemyah asked about the Lubavitcher Rebbe, and I told him that the Jews of Russia were uppermost on the Rebbe's mind.

Reb Nechemyah pleaded with us not to forget them.

He quoted the haftarah (reading from the prophets) from Rosh Hashanah (Jeremiah 31:7) that God will rescue the Jewish people "from the depths of the earth." That referred to Russia, he told us, "the nethermost place in the world." Perhaps Soviet Jews would have to wait until the coming of the messiah to be free.

We sat in on their Torah discussion. I asked a question and Reb Meir responded in Hebrew. I was flattered to be part of this very special study group.

Not everyone in shul was happy to see us. For the synagogue officials, foreign visitors like us just presented more trouble and bother for them. Over the years, the reception we received ranged from the friendly – especially if the gabbai was not in attendance that day – to the sharply antagonistic, and even, as we were once to encounter in Odessa, to a virtual lockout, when they turned off the lights and closed the shul doors on us. Undoubtedly, they were following the political instructions from above, from the Ministry of Cults, though I never had the opportunity to have a heart-to-heart talk with a gabbai, to get the real story. Even though their treatment was not personal, it could be upsetting and even threatening at times. However, as we were to find out, not all was politics. There was some "monkey business" going on, as well.

The head gabbai in Leningrad was already accustomed to our USY groups. Once he complained to me that everyone else was getting gifts, but not him! I took out a lovely white leathered-covered siddur, but he was not interested. He was looking for items to sell on the side, and this American bat-mitzvah gift had no added market value for local Jews.

A few days later I had a similar conversation in the main Moscow shul. When one of the gabbais saw us giving out things, he demanded angrily: "Give us, too!" One of the older men told us that the local officials resold these items for up to 100 rubles, a month's salary. Corruption in the Soviet Union was rampant, and this corner was no different from anywhere else.

A MAGICAL EVENING

From all of our shul experiences over the years, one – from 1973 – stands out in particular.

Our group of twenty USYers arrived at the Leningrad shul for the evening services. One of our young men, Moshe, led the prayers with American-style group singing. The old men loved it and joined in. I showed the assistant gabbai who was present that evening the Polaroid pictures from our previous stops in Budapest, Prague, Auschwitz, and Warsaw, and he was very impressed, especially by the photograph of the grave of the great Cantor Gershon Sirota in Warsaw. He opened the large synagogue hall for us, turned on the lights, and invited us to take pictures of "his shul" as well, which we did with great pleasure. The tensions of our trip were replaced by feelings of relaxation and ease.

We returned to the small shul and I began our daily Torah session, while the old Jewish men of Leningrad gathered around to listen. As we were studying the siddur, the words of the familiar prayers suddenly leaped out at us and took on new meaning. I quoted from the Amidah (silent devotion) and added my own commentary (in italics):

- "Blow the great shofar of our redemption…and gather us all together," and I exclaimed: "*In Israel – now!*"
- "You, God, alone, rule over us." And I blurted out: "*Not any man-made government or regime!*"
- "May there be no hope for Jews who inform on their fellow Jews," and I looked around, acutely aware that we were in the presence of government spies, and culminated with:
- "We yearn to return to Jerusalem, Your holy city," and we all thought: "*Let the Soviet Jews come to Jerusalem, O Lord, now – in our time!*"

Inspired by the words and the setting, we broke into songs of hope and Jewish yearning and began singing with heartfelt joy and enthusiasm. We were swept up in the moment.

Our girls got up and began to dance in the middle of the shul, and invited the old men to join in. They had never seen young people, especially young women, express such Jewish feelings and *simchah* before. If I had not captured it on film, I would not believe it really happened. (See photos.)

Our learned friend, Reb Nechemyah, smiled broadly, and asked in Hebrew: "*Eifo Miriam?*" (Where is Miriam?), referring to Moses' sister who led the dancing after crossing the Red Sea. He told me how fortunate we were that "The Commissar," the chief gabbai, had not come to shul that evening. He would have stopped such a demonstration of Jewish joy dead in its tracks.

He then said to me with great emotion: "*Atem Yoisef*" (You are just like Jacob's son Joseph), and I responded in kind, or so I thought, "*V'atem: Reuven, Shimon, Levi, Yehuda…*" (You are just like the rest of the brothers).

"No," he interjected, "you don't understand, '*Atem Yoisef – loi shachachtem oisonu*'" (You are just like our long-lost brother Josef…you have not forgotten us). His words pierced my heart, for that was precisely why we had come so far: to show the Jews of Russia that we had not forgotten them. It was a precious moment I would never forget.

As we readied to leave, I wished our Leningrad friends a farewell blessing and they responded in kind. No one knew if or when we would meet again.

I told our USYers, that if God forbid, we were expelled that night from Russia for "anti-Soviet behavior," the entire trip would still have been worthwhile.

A Mazal Tov Surprise

It was, without doubt, the greatest surprise I ever experienced in all my trips to Russia.

We were sitting in the dining room of Moscow's Hotel Ukraine on a late Friday afternoon in 1973, when a local young man suddenly appeared, pointed at our kippot, and said, very excitedly: "Hats! You are wearing hats!" He asked if we were Jews, like him. Our new friend was an engineer during the day and a bandleader in the evenings, and he played Jewish music. He asked me if I would like to come to a Jewish wedding party with him.

Stunned at the invitation, the first I had ever received in Russia, I excitedly rose from my seat and followed him into the adjoining hall. The room was packed with some 150 guests. The formal marriage registration ceremony had taken place earlier at the Moscow City Registrar's Office, and this was the wedding reception. I was told that both families were Jewish, and I wished the bride and groom a mazal tov. When I told them that I was a rabbi, the bride asked where my beard was! We spoke excitedly in Russian and Yiddish.

I asked them if could bring our group of USYers into the room, and they agreed.

As we entered the hall, all eyes turned in our direction. We felt a bit tense and unsure as to how to behave when, luckily for us, our friendly band leader struck up "Havah Nagilah." The USYers circled, the Russian Jewish women kicked off their shoes, and we begin to dance, to really dance, with more and more gusto and joy. The local guests asked if we were Jews, and when I showed them my tzitzit and kippah, they were tremendously excited. Some kept repeating again and again: "*Ve fse yevrei*" (Are you really all Jews)?

"*Da!* Here we are all Jews!" I responded, to their great joy.

But not everybody was happy with our presence. One of the guests approached me and told me that we needed to leave. I told her that we were "friends and acquaintances" but she said no. I was certain that she was afraid of being seen with a group of foreigners.

As we readied to depart, I asked for permission from the father of the bride to say a few words, and without waiting for a response, called for quiet, and began in Russian:

"Comrades, Jews. We are visiting American students. I would like to say how happy we are to be here with brothers and sisters."

I continued in Yiddish: "We send you a *shalom aleichem* and best wishes from the Jews of America and the entire world. We have not forgotten the Jews of Russia." I turned to the bride and groom and wished them Mazal Tov and a long life together for the proverbial "one hundred and twenty years."

I was physically shaking, blown away to be addressing such a Jewish gathering in Moscow – my first time. The guests were "*kvelling*" (bursting with pride) with us. I left the room feeling that we had done what we came for, what we had been sent to do.

We adjourned upstairs and gathered in one of our rooms. We felt elated at what we had just experienced and were on an emotional high. We sang the Shabbat prayers ever so softly, so as not to arouse the attention of the ever-present Soviet floor lady, who watched every hotel floor like a hawk.

I recounted Talmudic tales about the coming of the messiah, and who would merit the World to Come. The Americans and the Soviets each had their own path for creating a vision of the future; so did the Jewish people. This summer our group had been bringing the ultimate redemption closer through our pilgrimage to places of Jewish tragedy and loss (Mauthausen, Budapest, Prague, Theresienstadt, the Warsaw Ghetto, Auschwitz) as well as through *simchah* and joy (a celebration in Budapest, an evening in Leningrad, and tonight's Jewish wedding party).

We felt like we were doing our small part to help to bring the Mashiach in our own time.

RETURNING TO GEORGIA WITH USYERS

I had been tremendously impressed by my 1968 post–Simchat Torah visit to the Jews of Georgia, by their feelings of Jewish pride, loyalty to tradition, and stability of family and community. I wanted to expose our USYers to this unique facet of Soviet Jewry, so I included Tbilisi in the itinerary for the summer of 1972. We were not disappointed.

It was our first day in town, and we made our way to the synagogue complex. We came upon a group of perhaps eighty or so local Jews, sitting and relaxing in the courtyard, as if on their own front porches or backyards. We greeted them with *shalom* and suddenly, as if out of nowhere, crowds of Georgian Jews, women with little babies, boys and girls, teenagers and adults, began to pour out of the neighboring apartment buildings and flocked to greet us with "*Shalom! Shalom!*" (See photos.)

We entered the shul for the afternoon service, and when we exited, we were welcomed with food, fruits, cold water, and sweets, as if we had just arrived from the parched desert to an oasis. After coming from the oppressive atmospheres of Moscow and Leningrad, that captured precisely how we felt.

Our teenagers were overwhelmed by the warmth and love expressed towards us. We had traveled all the way from America to visit with them, and the Jews of Tbilisi understood and welcomed us with open arms. On especially happy occasions, Jews express their gratitude with a blessing of thanksgiving and this was most definitely one of those moments. We felt privileged to be in their presence.

From across the courtyard, I spotted Chacham Yitzchak, whom I had last seen four years earlier. I approached him, but he could not immediately place me.

"Where have we met?" he asked.

"I was here four years ago," I responded.

Suddenly, as if a light went on, he exclaimed in his high-pitched voice: "Ben Tzvi? Yonatan?" He remembered my father's name and my name. We embraced with hugs and kisses, just as men do when they want to express their deepest closeness and emotion.

He had received my letters, only it was hard for him to write, but he had enjoyed them very much. I recalled our parting words: "Don't give up hope" and his response of "*Betach!*" (Absolutely!). He was even more confident than he had been back then, especially since the Jews of Georgia were being allowed to leave for Israel.

The following morning, we returned to shul. There were perhaps two hundred men of all ages present, many of whom were wearing tefillin.

Yitzchak told me that he had been offered the position of chief rabbi of Moscow following the passing of Rabbi Levin in 1971, but had refused. It was "too big" for him, he said. He did not speak Yiddish, and also he knew that accepting the post would forever preclude him from making aliyah.

After services, we entered the slaughterhouse and he showed me the tallit I had given him four years ago, which he used only on Shabbat and holidays. I gave him some Israeli jewelry for his wife and daughters.

When it came time to part, he began to cry. There were tears in my eyes as well. We shared goodbye hugs and kisses.

Our USYers were tremendously excited and engaged by the visit. We came to shul at 8:00 a.m. and stayed for two hours, surrounded by crowds of local Jews.

We left the Georgian Shul in Tbilisi enormously encouraged and uplifted. The Jews told us that life here was good, but they still had one more stop to go on their journey, echoing the words of Rabbi Nachman of Bratzlav: "Wherever I go, I am headed only to the Land of Israel." We hoped to meet them there in person in the future.

We had come to give them support and encouragement, and they gave us even more in return.

Exchanging Gifts in the Ashkenazi Shul in Tbilisi

Meeting and interacting with local Jews could at times be very challenging for the USYers. They often found themselves dealing with situations they had never had to face before. So it was on our last night in Tbilisi, as a small group of us entered the lone Ashkenazi shul in town.

It was as if we had been instantly transported back to Moscow. It was a much darker and confined place. There were officials in charge, and everyone was under scrutiny all the time. They could barely gather ten men for a minyan and relied on their Georgian neighbors for help.

It was our final visit to a Soviet shul. Since we were about to depart the following morning for Israel, we wanted to hand out all of the remaining Jewish items and gifts we had brought with us. One of our USYers, Eliezer, spotted a man standing in a corner by himself. There was the hint of an odor about him, like from someone you might see sleeping on a bench in a bus station, whom you normally would not approach. However, it was our last night, and there were things to give away.

The man was dressed in a very worn jacket and stood with both of his sleeves thrust firmly into his pockets. Eliezer approached him, smiled, took out a Magen David on a neck chain, and offered it to him. The man was eager to accept, and signaled Eliezer with a motion of his head, to place it into his pocket, all the while keeping his sleeves firmly in place.

Eliezer saw that the neck chain had become twisted and knotted, and fumbled with it for a few moments, which only snarled it even more. He signaled the man to pull his hands out of his pockets, so he could place the gift inside, which the man could straighten out afterward on his own. Only, as the man pulled out his sleeves, Eliezer saw that at the end of them – there were no hands. *The man had no hands.*

Eliezer, now thoroughly flustered, felt under intense pressure to give the chain away as quickly as possible without attracting too much attention, since several people had begun to look in his direction. He realized, however, that he had to untangle the chain himself. Getting himself under control, Eliezer unsnarled it, placing it over the man's head. Giving him a kiss and a hug, he said a parting *shalom*. The man began to cry from emotion.

These were mutual gifts: Eliezer gave away a highly treasured Magen David neck chain, and the man-with-no-hands gave Eliezer the opportunity to overcome his fears and rise to the occasion of the moment. Both were blessed.

CHAPTER 10

Two Special People

LUBA, OUR JEWISH INTOURIST GUIDE

Cultivating a friendly relationship with our Intourist guides was always a key to the success of our summer trips. If they were suspicious of our motives or felt we had come to the Soviet Union for some "ulterior" purposes (for political protests or to meet with Jewish activists), they could have made our situation very difficult and severely hampered our movements, including interfering with our attending synagogue services and meeting with Jews. We were aware that, since they were dealing with foreigners, in the eyes of the authorities they were not merely tour chaperons. Intourist was responsible for our actions, and our guides reported to their superiors on our activities.

When we first met our Intourist guide Luba at our Leningrad hotel, I was impressed. She seemed very competent and professional. Libby, our Russian-speaking long-time USY staff member, told me that she remembered her from her first visit to the USSR, five years earlier. I told Luba that we were looking forward to all of the excursions and tours and that we liked to take early morning and late evening walks to see the city, which was more than fine with her. When we said that we were all "vegetarians," and handed her a meatless menu, she was a bit surprised but, ever a professional, said it could be arranged.

And so began a unique relationship that was to go beyond the few days we spent together in the summer of 1973. (See photos.)

I noticed that she was always curious about our strange eating habits, and the fact that we wore those "caps" when we were dining. My senses alerted, I asked her very nonchalantly if, perhaps, any members of her family happened to be Jewish.

"Well, yes," she replied. "Me, for example."

By chance or by fate, we had been assigned a Jewish Intourist guide. It was to prove to be a most complex and ultimately, life-changing, relationship. In previous years, when we had non-Jewish guides and might get questioned or reprimanded for giving out Jewish items, or for going to shul so often, I was not overly concerned, for the authorities could not associate or blame our guide for

75

our actions. Now, anything we did might cause problems or difficulties for one of our own.

Luba had almost no knowledge of Jewish life or culture. Her grandfather had been a religious Jew from Vitebsk in Belorussia, the home of the legendary Marc Chagall, but she knew almost nothing. She told me that she identified more with the Russian people than with the Jews.

But little things crept up. During our Moscow tours, she would disappear for hours on end. She reported that she had been attending the Moscow Foreign Film Festival, held once every five years, and had seen seven movies in five days! I called her "*meshuga*" (crazy) and she said that her father had also called her a "*meshugener*" when she was a child.

We showed her pictures of our visit to Auschwitz. She had been to Buchenwald and Ponar. Those interested her much more than Babi Yar in Kiev, which was, after all, in her words "only a stone marker." She said that when she was younger, she had visited the local shul on Simchat Torah, out of curiosity, but had never returned. She accompanied an American tourist there four years ago but found it run down and sad. It was not for her.

I invited her to join our Friday night Oneg Shabbat as our guest, and she accepted. We gathered in our hotel room, sang softly, and danced Israeli dances ever so quietly. She had never seen Jews do that before.

Near the end of our visit, we took a walk outside in the open. She would never speak to me about personal or Jewish things indoors, where we could be overheard. She showed me her internal Soviet passport with the word "*yevreika*" (Jew) listed as her nationality. I asked her if this had ever given her a problem. She responded with laughter and said that I was smart enough to figure that out for myself.

"Do you have to report on our group to anyone?" I asked, and she answered that I should be able to guess that as well.

"Is there antisemitism in Russia?" I further queried.

"As an Intourist guide, the answer is 'no,'" she replied, to which I said that "as a tourist," I was certain she was correct.

She confided in me that our group was under suspicion because I had been to Russia so many times, and they were curious to find out why.

Her next comment came from a totally different place. She asked if I had a spare Hebrew language textbook handy. I said that I would try to get one for her. The following morning, on our way on the bus to the airport, I passed to Luba a copy of the Soviet satirical magazine *Krokodil*, with an anti-Semitic caricature of Moshe Dayan on the back cover, drawn by one of their most popular cartoonists, M. Abramova, a Jew. Inside I had placed an Aleph-Bet primer for children, the last remaining Hebrew book we had. I said goodbye and *shalom*, and had no expectations of ever meeting again.

Our Paths Cross Again

The following summer I returned to Russia with USY. By chance, Luba and I ran into each other in the lobby of the largest Intourist hotel in Moscow. She was in a rush and we arranged to meet a few days later. She asked who our guide was, and I answered that it was Margarita Nikolayevna.

"Be careful, Jonathan, she is not one of us," Luba cautioned me.

Two days later, we walked and talked through the streets of Moscow. All of her masks and pretenses evaporated, and she spoke from the heart. Her aunt had just left for Israel, and she expected her cousins to follow soon. She was thinking of trying to get out as well but did not believe she would succeed.

When she was younger, she had tried to get a job with Intourist but was refused twice because she was Jewish, even though she was the most qualified and was one of the top finalists. She was told that there was "no need or place for you," and "don't call us, we'll call you." A few years later, she finally got the position, at first only temporarily and then on a full-time basis, but now she was in a terrible dilemma. If she applied for a visa, she would undoubtedly be fired, only she couldn't imagine being permitted to leave, especially since Intourist has a "quasi-security" status, dealing with foreigners. She had thought of changing jobs, but that would be too suspicious.

She grew up with the Russian people and felt herself a part of their culture. She did not want to go to Israel – it was too foreign to her – but she was desperate to get to freedom, wherever she could. She spoke very deliberately and calmly but was painfully aware that she was potentially in very grave danger.

All I could do was to listen to her with all my soul, and acknowledge that sometimes being a Jew was very, very difficult. I tried to encourage her and left her a copy of Leon Uris's epic novel *Exodus*, the inspiration and "Bible" of Soviet Jewish activists and refuseniks.

When we had met the previous year, Luba had given me a Russian record as a parting gift. I recalled what she had written on the cover: "In memory of our wonderful though brief journey together. Hope to meet you soon." Her wish had come to pass.

That was in the summer of 1974.

Nearly two years later, in April 1976, I received a long-distance phone call. It was from Luba. She had just left Russia and was in a transit camp run by HIAS (the Hebrew Immigrant Aid Society) in Rome, waiting to come to the United States. Among the first people she called was me.

I had thought that our relationship was passing and distant, but obviously, it meant much more to her. She had forwarded her books and papers from Russia to our home address in New Jersey.

She was alone in a strange place and clearly needed some help. I approached some members of my congregation to send her aid, and they met her in Rome on their vacations.

I received the following letter from her: "Dear Jonathan, I got the money order ten minutes ago and received your telegram last Friday. Thank you very much! There is an old saying that 'a friend in need is a friend indeed.' For me, the check is not only financial help but also great moral support. I feel very lonely here, and I cried today for the very first time."

Several months later, just a few days before Rosh Hashanah, we received the following card: "For a Special Friend. At this special time of the year, this brings warm thanks for your friendship and wishes for a year filled with health and happiness. Good *yuntif* [a happy holiday] and kisses to you and your wife. Luba"

The return address was her new home, in Albany, New York. Our Jewish Intourist guide and friend had made it to freedom.

SHIMON FROM ODESSA

We were sitting in the community dining room of the Jewish Federation of Romania in Bucharest in the summer of 1970. Our USY group had just arrived after ten days in the Soviet Union, and we were eagerly anticipating that evening's El Al flight to Tel Aviv. As we sang and danced with the older folks in the canteen, celebrating our imminent departure for Israel, we spotted a young man sitting alone at a corner table, and we assumed that he, too, was a local. It turned out that he was a twenty-four-year-old Jewish tourist named Shimon (Semyon in Russian), and he was visiting from Odessa, Soviet Ukraine. He had come to a neighboring Socialist country to be with other Jews.

Libby, Shimon, and I immediately bonded and we invited him to became part of our group for the day. He joined us on our touring bus, we gave him a kippah and a Magen David...and the USY European Pilgrimage added one more participant! He came from a very Jewish family. His mother was a pediatrician, his father an engineer. His nearly ninety-year-old grandfather, who lived with them, was raised in a religious home and used to sing in the Odessa synagogue children's choir.

Shimon was amazed when our group davened in public. As we sat in the back of the bus, we sang "David Melech Yisrael," "Havah Nagilah," and other Jewish songs in Yiddish and Russian. When, with great emotion and anticipation, we shouted out the words to "Hatikvah," he recognized it as the "sign off" melody from the Kol Yisrael radio broadcasts. He didn't know that it was the national anthem of Israel and the Jewish people. He told us that his Jewish friends in Odessa won't believe it when he tells them that Jewish teenagers filled the bus with songs of freedom and in praise of Eretz Yisrael. He was eager to come to Israel. We told him about the courageous Jews of Moscow and the Baltics who were writing open letters to the Soviet government demanding to leave. We had just spent a Shabbat with them on Arkhipova Street in front of the Moscow shul. I spoke about Elie Wiesel and the Simchat Torah celebrations in Moscow.

I came up with a daring (and perhaps foolhardy) thought. How about if he and I switched passports? He would go through Romanian border control as "Jonathan Porath," and I would report to the US embassy that my passport had been lost. Would that work? Could we dare to do it? Ultimately, we dismissed the idea (and undoubtedly were correct), but we felt so close that we did not want to part.

As we passed through the Bucharest Airport departure gate on our way to our Tel Aviv flight, we spotted him lingering in the main hall, looking in our direction. Neither of us wanted that magical day to end. We did not know it then, but this was to be the first of many meetings over the following years.

We corresponded. He wrote to me a few months later:

Shalom, my dear friend Jonathan,

Thank you for all the gifts you gave me in Bucharest. I show them to all my Jewish friends. I wore your small and modern knitted Israeli *yarmulka* [kippah] when I went to synagogue in Odessa on Rosh Hashanah. Some of them said that I did not have a *yarmulka* on my head, and when I bent my head, they were smiling. Thank you for it once more.

I remember the nice day we had in Bucharest. It is good that American Jews don't forget Russian Jews. I think that all Jews must be together. Perhaps we will have the chance to meet once again in the future. Shalom [in Hebrew letters]

Shimon

HAVDALAH ON THE MOSCOW-KIEV EXPRESS

A few years later, in 1973, I dropped Shimon a note from Leningrad, telling him that I had returned to Russia and that we would be spending the following Shabbat in Moscow. On Shabbat morning, as we entered the shul on Arkhipova St., who was there but Shimon! He had received my letter just a few days before and flew up to meet me. It was like someone living in New York flying to Miami to meet a friend coming from Israel!

We spent the entire afternoon walking and talking. He had received a letter of invitation to go to Israel, but was in the Soviet army at that time and could not leave. He was learning Hebrew in a clandestine ulpan in Odessa. He knew that he and his friends were under surveillance and that there were informers among his group; one of their number was seen departing the local KGB headquarters.

He arranged to take the train with us to Kiev that night after Shabbat. As we walked the streets, he told Libby and me that this was his first time in Moscow, and he kibbitzed: "Jonathan knows Moscow better than I do!"

As nighttime fell, we boarded the Moscow-Kiev Express, and Libby, Shimon, and I gathered in my compartment. I explained to him the Havdalah ceremony, teaching him the words to Eliyahu Hanavi, the closing song of Shabbat, and told him about our yearning for better times for the Jewish people and the entire world. I turned off the lights, Shimon held the candle, and we began to sing ever so quietly. I translated from Hebrew to Russian, and he eagerly joined in. He smelled the spices with great enthusiasm. We wished each other a "Shavua Tov" (good week) in Hebrew, Yiddish, and Russian. I was close to tears.

We spoke through most of the night. Libby gave Shimon her copy of *The Traveler's Guide to Jewish Landmarks of Europe* (Postal and Abramson, Fleet Press, 1971), which was of great interest. He immediately turned to the Soviet Union section and discovered Jewish places that he had never heard of before, including in his own city of Odessa. I gave him my own tallit, a gift from my parents. I told him that I had dedicated my book *Jews in Russia: The Last Four Centuries* to him ("To Some Very Close Friends – Shimon and Yitzchak Emmanuelovitch [Isaac Babel] from Odessa"), and he was eager to see it.

I wanted to teach him all the Torah I could during our few precious hours together, as our train rumbled through the Russian and Ukrainian countryside. We posed for a picture at the Kiev railroad station. (See photos.) Shimon continued on his way home, and our USY group went to tour the capital of Ukraine.

I resolved that the next time I returned to the Soviet Union with a group, I would include Odessa on our USY itinerary.

VISITING "ODESSA MAMA" WITH FRIENDS

The following summer, in 1974, we traveled to Odessa with USY. It was a wonderful reunion. My first steps in the Soviet Union and my initial meetings with Russian Jews had been there, nine years previously, when I had visited the USSR for the first time as a college student.

This time I was returning as a rabbi, a former Hillel director, author of a book about the Jews of Russia, and a USY group leader on my eighth trip to the Jews of the USSR.

Our non-Jewish guide, Alla, had been born in Birobidzhan in the Russian Far East, known as the Jewish Autonomous Region, and had a birth certificate in Yiddish. Raised in Ukraine, she spoke an Odessan patois of Russian, Ukrainian, Yiddish, and Hebrew, similar to the slang of a New York City cab driver. When she wanted us to hurry up, she would urge: "*B'kitzer, b'kitzer*" (Yiddishized Hebrew for "quickly"). Shimon met us at the Hotel Odessa. Knowing that the guides reported all contacts with locals to their superiors, I introduced him as a distant cousin. Whether they believed me or not, he was allowed to accompany us on our morning tour.

We walked the streets of the city, imbibing the atmosphere of "Odessa Mama," as "Mother Odessa" was famously known. It was founded on the shores of the Black Sea at the end of the eighteenth century as a free port and became a magnet for a diverse population, including many Jews wanting to leave the confines of their Ukrainian shtetlach. It developed into a hub for Jewish culture, politics, and Zionist activity. In the 1897 Tsarist census, nearly 140,000 Jews lived in Odessa, 37 percent of the city's population. It was famous as a warm and welcoming city (notwithstanding some pogroms and revolutions) with an illustrious Jewish past. Ahad Ha'am, Chaim Nachman Bialik, S. Y. Abramovich (Mendele Moicher Seforim), S. N. Rabinovich (Sholem Aleichem), Isaac Babel, Simon Dubnow, Zev Jabotinsky, and many more, had called Odessa "home."

My introduction to the city preceded my physical arrival. I was in love with Isaac Babel's short stories. Odessa-born and raised, Babel was the premier Soviet short story writer. His tales of the Jewish underworld, of proud Jews who were confident and afraid of no earthly power, spoke to my heart. I had been collecting books by and about Babel for the past fifty years, and they filled an entire shelf in my library in Jerusalem.

My favorite story was called "The Rabbi's Son." It spoke to me personally. It portrayed a young man torn between the Revolution and tradition. As Babel encapsulated it so brilliantly, "the portraits of Lenin and Maimonides lay side by side."[1] Most powerfully, at the conclusion of the tale, the narrator described the end of his Jewish compatriot: "He died among his poems, phylacteries, and foot-wrappings…I received my brother's last breath."[2]

Across from our hotel, we saw Jewish grandmothers sunning themselves in the park and exchanged a few Yiddish words of greeting. We approached an older

---

1. Thanks to Svetlana Goldes for the English translation.

2. Idem.

lady and asked her, first in Russian and then in Yiddish, how she was coming along, to which she responded: "*Nisht koshe*" ("Not so bad" in Hebraicized-Yiddish).

As we walked, I was aware that I was strolling through the legendary Odessa of my imagination. Part of my soul deeply identified with the spirit of Odessa.

Our Intourist itinerary included an official tour of "Jewish Odessa." We paused at Babel's home address with its memorial plaque, which left out the fact that he had been a victim of Stalin's terror and was executed in 1941. We passed by the Odessa City Archives, housed in the former Brodsky Shul nationalized by the Soviets, and the new Jewish cemetery.

As we drove down Shalom Aleichem Street, Shimon and I pressed the guide to stop at the old Jewish cemetery, but she refused, saying it was "closed." We entered the main Christian cemetery to see the grave of the great Yiddish author Mendele Moicher Seforim, with inscriptions in Hebrew and Russian. When I asked her why he was buried here, she responded that the old cemetery was no longer operating, and the family asked to move the body here.

As the group wandered about, Shimon and I quickly slipped away, crossed the street, and found a breach in the wall of the old Jewish cemetery. We hurriedly entered and were shaken and distressed to find tombs smashed, gravestones uprooted, Russian graffiti on monuments, and metal latticework lying broken on the ground. We quickly took some pictures and rushed back to the bus.

Our guide was very displeased with us, figuring out where we had gone. She told Shimon that he was no longer welcome on our tour bus. I told Shimon to "get lost." It was becoming too dangerous for us to be seen together. We resolved to meet that evening at his parents' home. We tried to placate Alla with gifts of flowers, nylons, and a transistor radio, to no avail. I have no doubt that we got taken apart at Soviet customs during our departure two days later, because of her critical reports.

AN EVENING AT HOME WITH SHIMON'S FAMILY

As I entered Shimon's family's apartment, his mother – Tzila – and I exchanged warm kisses and hugs. They introduced me to his ninety-two-year-old grand-father, born in 1882. I could only begin to imagine what he had experienced in his lifetime: Tsars, pogroms, the First World War, the Bolsheviks, the Civil War, Soviet Power, Stalin, collectivization and famine, World War II, the Shoah, and more.

He was alert, with a firm handshake. He greeted me with: "Long live Soviet power in the whole world; Israel will be under the Soviets!" and we both broke into laughter at his wonderful joke. As I opened a High Holiday prayerbook from his bookshelf, he took out his glasses and begin to chant Kol Nidrei with full voice, just like his days as a choir boy at the Brodsky Synagogue.

I distributed the gifts I had brought with me: a green kippah for grandpa, a jacket for Shimon, a gold kippah for their friend Yan, a raincoat for mother, a sweater for dad. They give me a picture of Isaac Babel. Grandpa began to recite prayers buried deep in his memory. It was very emotional for all.

Shimon's mother has prepared a meal for us: latkes, salad, fish, bread. She was surprised that I kept kosher. "But he is such a young man," she said. In Russia, only the very old still observed these traditions.

I began to speak about our trip, life in America, making aliyah, living in Israel. Yan said that he remembered me from Simchat Torah night in Moscow in 1968, a young American visitor leading the singing on Arkhipova Street. Shimon told me that *The Traveler's Guide to Jewish Landmarks of Europe*, which Libby had given him on our Moscow-Kiev train ride, had been translated into Russian and disseminated among local Jews for Jewish tours of Odessa and other Soviet cities.

I exchanged a few words in Hebrew with Shimon's father, Nahum, who had studied before World War II, but he had forgotten much since then. His mother called me "Yonatan."

I was amazed by their Jewish feeling and connections after so many years under the Communists and asked if there were other families like theirs around? "Of course," they responded. I had not known that such deeply Jewish family units had survived.

Between the menu, the music, the books, the singing, the Yiddish, and the memories, I was in a real Jewish home. There was an old-world flavor that reminded me of my own grandparents' homes in America, rather than in the heartland of Soviet Ukraine. Shimon's mother invited my parents to come and visit them in Odessa.

On my way back to town with Yan, I asked him if he was not afraid to be seen with a foreigner. With characteristic Odessan chutzpa, he smiled and asked "Should I be afraid of you, Yonatan?"

What an unforgettable evening.

Three years later I received the following note from Shimon: "Mazal tov! I am getting married on July 20 and I am sending you an invitation. My bride's name is Regina. We are now dealing with pleasant problems planning the wedding. I want to ask you a favor. Please send Regina a wedding dress."

Included was a line sketch of the style dress she wanted, and her measurements in centimeters.

That Friday evening, when I read Shimon's note out loud at Shabbat services in my New Jersey synagogue, Temple Beth O'r in Clark, New Jersey, Arnold Goldstein, owner of Starlight Tuxedos and Bridal Attire, called out in shul: "I've got a gown for you, Rabbi!" My wife Deena and I visited Arnie in his shop, picked one out, and sent it to Odessa, in time for the wedding.

The story was written up in Newark's hometown newspaper, the *Star-Ledger* (June 4, 1977), and concluded with: "Rabbi Porath's reward for his good deed is the pleasure he will give his friend in Odessa. And Arnold Goldstein had enjoyed helping a perfect stranger." We had all taken part in the mitzvah of *hachnasat kallah* (marrying off a bride) thousands of miles away.

ONGOING FRIENDSHIP AND A FINAL SHALOM

Shimon and I stayed in contact over the years. In 1989 he visited Israel with his brother Boris, and they stayed with us in Jerusalem. In 1992, I invited him to be my guide and traveling companion on a trip I made to the then post-Soviet Union, on behalf of the Wexner Foundation. I visited with Shimon and his family in Odessa a decade later, when I was working for the Joint.

We had not been in touch of late. During the COVID-19 pandemic, I contacted his brother Boris. He told me that my friend Shimon had passed away in Odessa a few years ago.

I was very saddened to hear the news. We shared wonderful Jewish adventures and dreams from our youth. His dear parents and grandfather welcomed me into their family with love and affection.

May this retelling of our times together bring comfort to the memory of Shimon ben Nahum v'Tzila. May his memory be for a blessing.

CHAPTER 11

Threats and Warnings

A MOST INHOSPITABLE WELCOME

In the summer of 1973, the travel agent divided USY into two separate travel groups for the Soviet portion of the trip. I led one and Rabbi Arnie Turetsky the other. Since this was our fourth summer with Pilgrimage, we felt confident that, security-wise, this would be a safe and uneventful trip, like all of the previous ones.

We were sorely mistaken.

We departed Warsaw on different flights and met the following day at the Hotel Ukraine in Moscow. Arnie's group had undergone a particularly traumatic encounter at customs. They were thoroughly searched and nearly a hundred items were confiscated, including books and mezuzot. They demanded that Arnie sign a Russian-language "receipt" for the items, which he refused to do, instead writing a statement in English, which he signed before walking away. The USYers were scrutinized one by one, item by item. It was a frightening event, which some carried with them for years to come.

Upon arrival at the Moscow hotel, Arnie was warned by Intourist that his group had been caught trying to smuggle forbidden items into the Soviet Union, and was cautioned against any future "provocations."

It soon became apparent that both of our USY groups had been "marked" and placed under surveillance, which only intensified over the course of our stay and weighed very heavily on us.

The next morning at shul, as the USYers were mixing with the older men and giving out gifts, Libby overheard a phone conversation by one of the gabbais: "If you come right now you will see everything." With that, we immediately left the shul and returned to the hotel.

Two of our USYers had accused the hotel staff of searching their room and of taking some of their books, and Libby had filed a written complaint with the front desk. When I went to try to "soften up" the floor lady to relieve the tension, I overheard her saying: "You know which group. It was the one from *Israel*," obviously referring to us, since Israeli tourists were not permitted to visit the Soviet Union at that time.

I met Luba, our Jewish friend and former Intourist guide. She told me that we had been targeted as "suspicious," and that we should not speak about our Jewish activities in our rooms, only outdoors, due to the likely presence of hidden listening devices. It was an act of great trust on her part to tell me and cemented our relationship. She was clearly "one of us."

I contacted the American embassy in Moscow and spoke to an acquaintance of mine there. We arranged to meet him the following day for an update and a security briefing.

The following morning, Libby and I were summoned to a meeting with the director of the hotel's "Service Bureau," the official local Intourist representative. I fully expected the worst, anything from a reprimand to the threat of expulsion. He asked how we liked the hotel, and I replied "very much." He then referred to the written "complaint" that had been submitted about some missing items. I said that it was undoubtedly "a mistake," and with that, he demonstratively tore up the page in front of us, to his relief and ours. Neither of us wanted any trouble.

It turned out that we had come to Russia at a very sensitive time in US-Soviet relations, which was to become clearer after we met with the Americans.

We were welcomed by Marty Wenick, the Second Secretary of the US embassy in Moscow, whom I had met on a previous trip. Marty was then a young diplomat with the Department of State.

Over the course of his career, he became an outstanding Jewish public servant, serving as the executive director of the National Conference on Soviet Jewry and then as the executive director of HIAS.

I updated him privately on what we had experienced so far during our stay, and he then spoke to the USYers.

SOVIET, JEWISH AND AMERICAN POLITICS COLLIDE
After a brief US-USSR political update, he focused on the current Jewish situation:

- The last Soviet census recorded 2.1 million Soviet Jews, but the real number may be as high as three million Jews. They were highly urbanized and educated.
- Aliyah to Israel was picking up. So far 60,000 had left for Israel, at a rate of about 2,500 per month.
- There were about sixty to seventy shuls still functioning in the USSR, alongside private, semi-official minyanim.

- The Jewish activist movement existed, but in limited numbers. He confirmed that there were Soviet Jews who wanted to leave. Some were desperate and would try anything to get out, while others were waiting to see what the official response would be. Many did not want to depart, having already made their own accommodations with the system.
- Soviet Jews were viewed with increasing suspicion, especially since the 1967 Six-Day War, but they still occupied important professional positions in Soviet society.

He was especially pointed about how foreign Jewish tourists should behave from the perspective of the American government, clearly intending to caution and discourage us.

The negative reports in the West about Soviet Jewish activists being denied visas, losing jobs, being harassed, and being imprisoned, definitely bothered the government, and they were monitored very carefully. Marty recommended not to accept any materials for transmission out of the country, such as requests for visas, articles, open letters, and other public statements.

He advised us not to meet activists, but if we did so, only very discreetly, in a limited way, and never alone. We should weigh the risks against the gains, and he was not sure if the benefits were worth it.

He warned us that "customs formalities" leaving the country could be more stringent if, while monitoring our group here, they saw us in contact with activists.

He added that, personally, he did not think that visits to activists helped, as they were in constant telephone contact with the West and listened to Voice of America, BBC, and Voice of Liberty broadcasts. They gather on Arkhipova St. after 11:00 a.m. on Saturday mornings. He suggested that we devote a greater part of our time to those older folks inside of the shuls and not linger too long with the activists.

It turned out that our summer's trip came right in the middle of a major US foreign policy debate on the Jackson-Vanik Amendment, which had been introduced in Congress only a few months previously. That proposal tied US foreign trade to the emigration and human rights policies of the Soviet bloc, including the USSR. Marty articulated the official position of the Nixon administration, which was that denying Moscow Most-Favored Nation status would be a mistake and harm US-Soviet relations as well as the Soviet Jews themselves. The Jews would be blamed for souring international relations. It was conceivable that the harassment we had been experiencing was due to the current state of US-Soviet relations. The law was finally signed by President Ford in January 1975.

Marty explained that Intourist and the KGB were working at cross purposes. The latter saw all foreigners as potential subversives. Intourist guides were responsible for our actions and reported to their higher-up about our activities. Intourist got blamed if things went wrong. He said that we should consider all of these outcomes if we wanted to make any public protests or anti-Soviet demonstrations during our visits. That was both his view and also that of the Soviets. Neither they nor the Americans needed a "provocation."

He was giving us the "official" US governmental line, which did not necessarily match the reasons for our visit. We had come to meet Soviet Jews and encourage them, and to convey to them that they were not alone. We would often have to "tiptoe" between the official guidelines and our self-appointed mission. Still, we took his security warnings very seriously.

We were learning the operative "ground rules" for visiting Soviet Jews. No protests, slogans, or demonstrations would be permitted. "Private" and low-key religious visits were allowed. We kept his words of warning in our minds as we departed the embassy for the remainder of our journey.

We had one more stop to go on our 1973 trip: Kiev. They were waiting for us there, as well.

Our "Official Welcome" in Kiev

As soon as we arrived in Kiev, we got word from our local Intourist guide that "they" already had their eyes on us. When my friend Shimon came to visit me at our hotel, the director of the restaurant targeted him as a possible black marketeer, or so she labeled him. "For a group like yours, you have to be careful," our guide told me, refusing to elaborate.

We made our way to the old Jewish section of Kiev, the Podol neighborhood, and entered the shul courtyard.

They were expecting us. I had noticed a man following us from the hotel, and as we got off the bus, he made a phone call, obviously warning the shul officials that we were coming. As we moved inside, I told the USYers to "cool it." We were being watched and should behave accordingly.

About thirty men were waiting for us. We were shepherded to the front rows of the shul, with our girls in the back, like in a large "choir box," with us in the center. They turned on all the lights for tourist pictures. They were well accustomed to visitors and adept in dealing with us. A number of the gabbai's "helpers" kept us under guard. It was all done quite politely, of course, but we knew fullwell who was in charge. There would be no opportunity to mingle with the locals and give out gifts, that was for certain.

It was, in a way, a "vacation" for me. We weren't rushing around taking pictures and meeting people. We could daven in peace for a change. I told the officials that we conducted a daily Torah class, asked permission to teach and the gabbai agreed. We opened to the section of the Amidah prayer that begins "*Modim anachnu Lach*" (We thank You) and really understood, perhaps for the first time, the words: "For our very lives which we entrust into Your hands." We were all very keenly aware that only divine providence was keeping us safe from the KGB and others who sought to do us harm.

I asked if I might say a few words to the congregation, and the gabbai refused my request. One of our USYers, Mordechai, opened up a Talmud to show a page to one of the men. They were very impressed that a teenager felt so much at home in the ancient text.

On our way back to our hotel, we went looking for the former great synagogue of Kiev, the Brodsky Shul, and following an old map, found our way to the location, the current State Puppet Theater. It was constructed at the end of the nineteenth century for the well-to-do "downtown Jews" by the sugar magnate and philanthropist Lazar Brodsky. In 1926 it was closed down by the Soviets, barely survived the Nazi occupation of Kiev, and was then turned into a government theater.

Entering, we met a local Jewish woman who confirmed that this, indeed, had been the shul for the rich; the common folk davened on the other side of town. We conversed in Russian and Yiddish.

She told us that she was very content living in the Soviet Union. The stories about people wanting to leave were all "anti-Soviet propaganda." Libby challenged her, but she held her own. She was the granddaughter of a rabbi, she said, but she had had a vastly different education and life experiences. There was a shul in Podol, which we had just visited, for those to choose to attend, but not for her. Her children just happened to marry Jews, but it made no difference. After spending so much time around shuls and activists, it was easy to forget that she was far more representative of the masses of Soviet Jews who grew up under Communism and for whom the Soviet Union was their home.

Not all Soviet Jews shared our dreams for them, of leaving the USSR.

OUR FINAL SHUL VISIT
The following day, we returned to the Podol shul for our last visit, and they were ready for us. Things had unmistakably tightened up since we had been there the day before. We were all hustled to the front, no talking or conversations permitted. They told us, quoting from the High Holiday prayerbook, that the only purpose to being in services was "to listen to the prayers."

I asked if I could conduct our daily Torah lesson, and they said no.

"Why not?"

"The law of the land is the law," they shot back, quoting a famous Talmudic principle. The authorities had forbidden it. I appealed to the chief gabbai, and he responded "Absolutely not!" ("*Loi!*" in a heavy Ashkenazic Hebrew pronunciation). He later told me privately that the people from the "Cult," the state religious authorities, had vetoed it.

We were caged in, and we felt it. The local Jews were not allowed to speak to us. When the services were over, we were hustled out of shul. We had gotten a real taste of what Soviet Jews experienced all the time.

We greeted many daveners outside of shul, said we would bring their heartfelt wishes to Israel, and received many blessings in return. As we left the courtyard, I gathered the USYers in front of the entrance for a brief Torah lesson. If the synagogue authorities wouldn't allow us to study Torah inside, then we would do it here instead, in the street.

So ended our "official" visit to the Jewish Religious Community of Kiev. They would have been just as happy had we not come.

We still had one more stop to make before departing Kiev and the Soviet Union for Israel, Babi Yar.

At Babi Yar

We had been traveling and mourning in the footsteps of the Shoah for the entire summer of 1973: concentration camps, ghettos, Auschwitz. Now we were on our way to Babi Yar.

What was left for us to see that we had not already seen? To feel that we had not already felt?

As we approached the site, an anxious stillness filled the bus.

We made our way towards the Ukrainian stone marker, which announced, rather laconically, that a memorial would be erected to "those victims of Fascism" who had perished here. In classic Soviet-style, there was no mention of the seventy thousand Jewish victims who were murdered in this ravine only because they were Jews. There were two large intersecting jagged cracks across the face of the stone, almost resembling a swastika.

As we approached, I spotted an older woman and her teenage daughter who had been standing there, quickly turn and walk away, obviously reluctant to be seen in the company of tourists or foreigners. I caught up with them and greeted them with a *shalom aleichem*.

She responded with a *shalom* and started to move on. I invited her to stay for a memorial Kaddish. She said that I was not wearing a kippah, so I took mine out of my pocket. She asked if I would recite a memorial prayer, and I assured her that I would.

We gathered together near the monument and I began to read aloud from a handwritten copy of Yevgeni Yevtushenko's epic 1961 poem "Babii Yar," which I had brought with me for this moment.[1]

Standing at the sacred site, the poet's intense and haunting words penetrated our very hearts and souls:

No monument stands over Babii Yar.
A drop sheer as a crude gravestone.
I am afraid.
            Today I am as old in years
as all the Jewish people.

…

The wild grasses rustle over Babii Yar.
The trees look ominous,
                        like judges.
Here all things scream silently,
                        and, baring my head,
slowly I feel myself
                turning gray.
And I myself
                am one massive, soundless scream
above the thousand thousand buried here.
I am
        each old man
                here shot dead.
I am
        every child
                here shot dead.
Nothing in me
            shall ever forget!

…

---

1. Yevgeny Yevtushenko, "Babii Yar," in *The Poetry of Yevgeny Yevtushenko,* trans. George Reaves (London: Calder and Boyars, 1966). Now available as *Early Poems* by Yevgeny Yevtushenko (London: Marion Boyars, 1989). Quoted with permission.

> In my blood there is no Jewish blood.
> In their callous rage, all antisemites
> Must hate me now as a Jew.
> For that reason
>   I am a true Russian!

There was absolute silence. I recited the El Maleh Rachamim memorial prayer for the Jews of Kiev and the entire Soviet Union, and we said the Mourner's Kaddish together. I wanted to add a few heartfelt words out of respect for the local Jewish woman standing with us. As I looked up at her eyes, red from crying, and her tear-filled cheeks, I completely broke down as well, sobbing and weeping. I saw in her the faces of all the Jewish mothers who perished here.

We separated, and our USYers began walking into the fields, forests, and overgrown brush of Babi Yar. The Intourist guide summoned us back to the bus with the honk of a horn, but I waved her away and continued walking and crying.

We moved deeper and deeper into the park. A few locals cut through the woods on their way to work. We saw a man eating his lunch, picnic-like, on the grass. I imagined that had I, or my family, been living in Kiev back then, we, too, would have been murdered here, and perhaps some tourist would today be treading over the place of our deaths.

One of our USYers, Sue from Boston, suddenly burst out sobbing. She had found a baby's white shoe. We knew it could not have been from those terrible times over thirty years ago, the leather would certainly have rotted away, but it was so evocative. We could imagine families suddenly trapped and running in an attempt to escape, with a child's shoe falling off.

We returned to the bus and attempted to comfort each other, but ultimately, we could only sit alone, each absorbed in their own feelings and thoughts.

It was a most fitting conclusion to our visit to Kiev and the Soviet Union.

CHAPTER 12

My Final Trip to the Soviet Union

PASSING THROUGH MY BUBBIE'S HOMETOWN

We were traveling from Warsaw to Leningrad by train and were scheduled to make a brief stop in Bialystok, Poland, where my Bubbie (my father's mother) had been born nearly ninety years before. She and my grandfather had passed away several months earlier, and they were very much on my mind. We all come from somewhere, and for me, that place was here. If this was her "*alter heim*" (hometown), then it was mine, as well.

I shared with the USYers my excitement and anticipation at stopping off there, even for a few minutes.

The train slowed down as we pulled into the station, early on a Monday morning. I anxiously stepped onto the platform, wanting to get a picture with the name of the town, just so I could prove to myself that I was there, but I couldn't find one. I began to run down the length of the train, looking all around for a sign.

Suddenly, on the rooftop of a large building overlooking the tracks, I spotted "Bialystok," took a picture, and quickly ran back to my carriage, so as not to miss the train, which was about to pull out of the station. One of the USYers took a picture of me taking the picture, understanding how significant a record of my brief stopover was to me.

In my diary for that day, I recorded: "Just passed through the town of Bialystok. I've come home to you, Bubbie; your grandson has come home. I wish I could have told you in person that I was here. I am so sorry that I can't."

It was 1974 and we were on our way on an ofttimes exhilarating as well as dispiriting trip to Russia and Ukraine. I didn't know it then, but it was to be my final visit to the Soviet Union. The next time I would return, almost twenty years later, the USSR was no more.

A HEARTFELT SHALOM IN LENINGRAD

We entered the weekday shul in Leningrad and were greeted very warmly by the old men. They recalled our visits from previous years and were very excited to see our group once again. Aaron, one of our staffers, had thoughtfully brought with him pictures he had taken of last year's visit and began distributing them. As we broke into song, Reb Nechemyah requested a rousing tune and we all joined in. We davened Minchah, studied, and were having a wonderful time, across the generations. All agreed that our teenagers were, indeed *"sheine kinder"* (lovely young people).

Suddenly, the chief gabbai, Moshe (also known by the nickname "The Commissar") entered the room.

Immediately, he divided us up into two groups, the USYers on one side of the shul, and the Jews of Leningrad on the other. We began to daven the evening services out loud, as we usually did, and the gabbai told us to stop. Whenever we attempted to initiate conversations, the locals said to us "the walls have ears," and we were forced to sit quietly. We sat silently through the end of the service and then departed, rather dispirited and upset.

We returned the following evening and, even though we were seated separately, were still able to hand out some pictures to the men. Trying a different approach, I offered "The Commissar" a contribution of $100 worth of rubles for the repairs of the large shul. With that, he warmed up a bit and took us on a tour of the shul complex.

We visited the kosher slaughterhouse in the basement, where they butchered about twenty chickens and two or three larger animals every week. Perhaps fifty families out of a quarter of a million Jews still kept kosher. The adjacent mikveh (ritual bath]) was only used by a handful of people. It was the first time that most of our USYers had ever seen such facilities in person.

We returned upstairs for evening services. The gabbai permitted me to daven, but without the community singing that the old folks so much enjoyed.

It was our last night in Leningrad. As we parted, I made a point of shaking the hands of each of the old men. I wanted to thank them for their faithfulness in keeping the shul open morning and evening, and wished them a personal *shalom*. As we departed, one of them whispered "Next year in Jerusalem." It should only be; if not for them; then perhaps for their children or grandchildren.

We were not to meet again.

Sad News in Moscow

When we arrived at the Arkhipova Street shul on Shabbat morning, I was greeted by the sad news that one of my dearest Moscow shul friends, Reb Yonah, had passed away. We had first met in 1969 at the most remote of Moscow's three shuls.

In 1972 he had been forced to relocate to the main synagogue on Arkhipova Street. After the authorities had closed his neighborhood shul, it had burnt down in a fire. "Our home was destroyed," he had told me with great pain and sorrow.

I had given him my siddur as a gift, which he said he used every day. When we met the following year, he assured me that he still davened from it. We would send and receive regards through visiting American tourists.

His customary place by the window on the right-hand side of the small shul was empty. His full name was Reb Yonah Melamed – the teacher, the learned one. He was one of my Russian Jewish heroes who keep the spark of Jewish life and tradition alive under the most hostile conditions. I was honored to include him in the opening dedication of my book *Jews in Russia*: "To Some Very Close Friends – Reb Yonah from Moscow." May his memory be a blessing.

Targeted at Shul and a Joyous Havdalah

As we entered the main shul on Shabbat morning, Efim (Efraim) Kaplun, the Chairman of the Moscow Religious Community of the Moscow Choral Synagogue, and the "Man-in-Charge," ordered a group of us to be seated in the tourist "choir box" in the front, where they could restrict our movements and contacts. It was clear that my "cooperating" would allow some of the USYers to spread throughout the shul and make their own personal connections. I recognized many faces from years past, and we communicated with our eyes, a smile, or a nod.

Midway through the long morning services, I felt the need to break out. I made my way to the back of the hall, and from there to the street where many of the younger people had gathered: a young man from Ulyanovsk, Janet from Leningrad, a teenager from Tbilisi, a mother and daughter from Moscow, and many more. I met Liana, who was dressed in American jeans. I thought she was a visiting tourist but she was a local girl who had heard that we were coming to shul and came to see us.

Kaplun dispatched four of his cronies to find me, and finally, *he came out himself in person* and escorted me back inside, where he could keep his eye on me. I submitted, with a forced smile on my face, but was very upset inside. Who is this guy to tell me what to do? As I was escorted to the front, one of the old-timers gave me a look: "What can we do? That is how it is here." I felt "used," like a bit player in a cosmic performance or an actor in a theater of the absurd.

Everyone here was playing their role: Kaplun, the Jews, the younger people, the USYers, and me, as well. Clearly, after all of my visits, they recognized me and targeted our group. Maybe it was time for my trips to come to an end. Better not to come than to get cynical and upset by what was going on. This would interfere with our mission, which was to meet and touch as many local Jews as possible. Our USYers were magnificently up to that task.

When we returned to shul later on in the afternoon, people had gathered in eager anticipation of our arrival: a family from Voronezh hoping for a visa, a young man from Tallinn as well as several Muscovites. We went into the small shul, where, wanting to break out of the morning's constraints, I led an exuberant afternoon service.

Thankfully, Kaplun was not present.

As I was inside, my friend and co-leader, Rabbi Yaakov Rone, moved to the outside hall and directed the giving of gifts and Jewish items. We began to sing "David Melech Yisrael" and "Am Yisrael Chai" with great feeling: I cheered them on with words of encouragement and hope. "Thank you for remaining Jews. We have not forgotten you." We all sang the Grace after Meals with gusto and passion.

We concluded the evening with the Havdalah ceremony, followed again by singing and celebration. One of the local Jews took out a tape recorder, so he could share our Jewish spirit with others who were not present. We wanted to show the Russian Jews that they were not alone and that we were all a part of Am Yisrael.

After two and a half weeks on the road, in Budapest, Prague, Auschwitz, Warsaw, Leningrad, and now Moscow, we were focused on getting to Israel. Only one more stop to go.

OUR LAST NIGHT IN ODESSA AND THE USSR

The synagogue in Odessa was notorious for its unfriendliness towards visitors, whether locals or foreigners.

We arrived at 7:30 a.m. for the start of morning services. The shul had absolutely no external markings identifying it as Jewish: no Magen David, no Hebrew lettering, no signs. If you didn't know it was there, you would never find it. Upon entering, we meet one of the most controversial rabbinic figures in the entire Soviet Union, Rabbi Israel Shvartsblat.

He was infamous for his support of governmental anti-Israel and anti-Zionist positions and was often called a "*moyser*," a pejorative term for an informer. Surprisingly, my old-time friend from Odessa, Shimon, had very positive things to say about him. Shvartsblat, who knew Shimon's elderly grandfather, was responsible for our first meeting in the Jewish canteen in Bucharest a few years previously. He had written a letter of introduction on Shimon's behalf to Rabbi Moshe Rosen, the chief rabbi of Romania. That had gained Shimon entry into the community facility, where we met him with our USY group.

Rabbi Shvartsblat possessed a sharp sense of humor. He told us that someone inquired if there were Bar Mitzvahs in Odessa, and he answered: "Yes! After age sixty men come to shul to put on tefillin." Some people in the shul cautioned us not to speak to him, but I said that I already knew his reputation.

I had brought a movie camera with me and took pictures of the services while they were in progress. A decade later, as part of my pre-aliyah preparations, I donated the films as well as the slides of my trips to YIVO in New York City. I visited the YIVO library recently and located the "Rabbi Jonathan D. Porath Collection" in their master catalog.

We returned that evening, the last night of our trip. The president of the shul was very, very cold to us. He did not invite our young people to participate, except to take our seats. I asked permission for the kids to daven, and he refused. Our discussion got very, very heated.

We began our own evening services and he said that it was forbidden for our students to daven here. Their cantor always led services, he claimed, which I knew was a lie since I had asked permission from the cantor beforehand. I told a number of the old men present that this was not proper behavior and told our USYers that we were not welcome here.

As we departed, they hustled us out of the shul and turned out the lights.

I gathered the USYers in a neighboring park and shared my anger and frustration. Obviously, those in charge did not want us there.

On our way back to the hotel, I saw one of the old men whom I had previously befriended, Reb Nosen Noteh. He told me that the president was loyal to the authorities rather than the Jews who came to shul. I repeated the story a few hours later to Shimon, and he confirmed that whenever young people came to the synagogue, the president refused to welcome them and threw them out.

It was a fitting ending to our last visit to a Soviet shul.

EXITING SOVIET SPACE

One ordeal still awaited us.

I had always thought that entering the Soviet Union and going through customs transporting a veritable "Jewish bookstore" in hand, was the most frightening experience imaginable. It turns out that I was wrong. Our group's departure from the Soviet Union in the summer of 1974 was an "exit from hell."

After two emotional weeks of meeting Jews in Leningrad, Moscow, and Odessa, and being received enthusiastically wherever we went (except by the various shul officials), we were ready to leave the Soviet Union and to make our way to Israel. All that stood in our way was a train ride from Odessa to Bucharest, and then home. We boarded the train in Odessa and arrived at the border station at Ungheni, Soviet Moldavia at 9:30 p.m. We were scheduled to pass through Soviet customs on the train and continue two hours later into Romania.

They were waiting for us.

The border guards did not come alone. Someone from Intourist was with them, but he was clearly no mere "travel agent" or "guide." He was a member of the security services. He demanded to see all the literature we had with us as well as notes and books. They went through our flight bags and jacket pockets. They took all of our remaining Jewish books. Our group had been assigned a series of compartments on the train, and they methodically proceeded to check each and every one.

I was scared. We were trapped on a Soviet railroad, totally at the mercy of the border guards, increasingly desperate to leave this hellish scene, with a train to catch to freedom, and the clock ticking away.

Some of the group went with the Intourist man to change money in the station and we waited for them. How long did it take to put some rubles on the counter and receive dollars in return? I had my eye on the emergency brake in case the train started moving without them. I had thoughts of jumping off the train carrying my bags since we would never leave them there alone.

The guards knew exactly what they were looking for and who we were. They asked if I could speak Russian. Who had told them that?

I asked myself: Why did I choose to go through this experience once again? My anxiety and fear were palpable.

Finally, our USYers reentered the train. The guards returned the books and the things they had taken. Did they make copies? Expose the film? Find any of the refusenik addresses and contacts we had been given on the way? At that moment, none of that mattered.

We departed the Ungheni station at 11:30 p.m. and crossed the Prut River into Romania. We greeted the Romanian border guards in Iasi with great joy and relief. "*Slava bogu*" (Thank God we are here), we declared, meaning it from the bottom of our hearts. The passport and customs checks were only formalities, and we got to the hotel and went to sleep with feelings of great relief.

Blessedly, we had come through safely. As dramatic as that may sound, at that moment, that is exactly how we felt. The Soviet Union was now behind us and we were on our way to Israel.

I would not return until after the fall of the Soviet Union, more than seventeen years later.

The intensity and pressures of the trips were taking their toll. After a decade of almost annual visits to the Soviet Union, in addition to various Eastern European Holocaust sites, I was emotionally spent and wanted to proceed with the rest of my life. Deena and I were married in March 1975, I accepted a pulpit position at Temple Beth O'r in Clark, New Jersey, and we began raising a family. At the same time, USY decided to suspend the Eastern European Pilgrimage for a few years, primarily due to increasing Soviet-American political tensions.

Though I continued writing and speaking about my Russian experiences, in my mind, I was moving in a different direction. I felt that I had concluded an extraordinary chapter in my life. I never imagined that I would ever return to the world of Soviet Jewry.

PART II

Welcoming Soviet Jews Home

CHAPTER 13

Looking Back after Fifty Years

SOVIET JEWRY ACTIVISTS

As I was reviewing my diaries, stories, pictures, and memories from the USY trips to Eastern Europe and the Soviet Union, I was very curious about the long-term impact on the participants themselves. Had our visits made a difference in their lives or behavior? Was the trip significant to them? So, I decided to ask them.

What made the inquiry of special interest was that I was no longer addressing teenage high school students, but rather parents and grandparents, all presently in their sixties, with a lifetime of experiences and achievements.

I was able to make contact with about two dozen of the two hundred participants. Their responses were informative, encouraging, and inspirational.

One of the most immediate effects of the trip was their extensive involvement as activists and leaders in the Soviet Jewry movement:

- Sarrae was a founding officer of the National Conference on Soviet Jewry as the youth representative and attended the first Brussels Conference on Soviet Jewry in 1971.
- Larry, as national president of USY, also attended the Brussels Conference, and often drew on his personal experiences on the trip.
- Sid spent the next twenty plus years as a Soviet Jewry activist, returning to Russia twice more to contact and support the refuseniks, and as the executive director of the Jewish Community Relations Council in Greater Washington, he ensured that Soviet Jewry was on the community agenda.
- Susan F. traveled throughout the Northeast giving talks on Soviet Jewry and addressed a huge rally at the State Capital in Hartford.
- Paula became an activist, joined the local JCC Soviet Jewry Committee, and organized a Philadelphia March for Soviet Jewry. At the University of Arizona, she made calls to Soviet Jews and spoke at USY events.
- Pearl, also known as Puah, wrote letters, spoke at synagogues, schools, USY events, and churches, and was instrumental in bringing a Soviet Jewish mother and son to the US for medical treatments.

- The trip thrust Neil into a leadership role in USY, particularly regarding Soviet Jewry, and he was one of the Americans who would speak on international calls to refuseniks.
- At his younger brother's bar mitzvah, Phil dedicated his remarks to Soviet Jews, designating his thirteen-year-old brother as a "stand-in" for all of them, "giving strength and encouragement to ourselves and also to them." He spoke all across Philadelphia about his trip.
- As a young associate and the first female executive at the Jewish Federation of Cleveland, one of Harriet's initial assignments was to staff the Soviet Jewry Advocacy Committee. Her first-hand experiences gave her credibility and a place in community leadership.

More than a quarter of the respondents became full-time Jewish professionals in synagogues, Federations, JCRCs, the United Synagogue, Hillel, Jewish Healing, and the Masorti movement in Israel; or founded their own organizations. The trip further strengthened their own Jewish connections.

It strongly impacted the intensity of the Jewish life choices of the future rabbis in the group. Neil said that the trip "folded into a strong Jewish identity and life, and became one of the factors that produced me." Amy said that she was probably already on the path to a career in Jewish education "but the power of the experience embedded in my heart the commitment to Jewish sacred work." Andy noted that "it was the trip that led me to combine what had become my passion with a career," because it had directed him to rabbinical school and aliyah. Michael was the most categorical: "All of this happened because of Eastern European Pilgrimage." He went on to become the chief rabbi of Poland.

A LIFE-CHANGING EXPERIENCE

For many of those who did not become Jewish community professionals, the trip was no less significant. It was their first experience in intensive, full-time Jewish living. Many of them used the phrase: "The trip changed my life":

- "I became a Sabbath observer. I never took being a Jew for granted again."
- "My parents had always kept a kosher home but when I came back, I became kosher outside as well, and went to Shabbat services often."
- "To say that summer impacted me is the understatement of my lifetime!"
- "It was life-changing in the truest sense. My life took a different direction and stayed that way. I came to understand, both emotionally and intellectually, the importance of the survival of the Jewish people."

- "It had an impact on my life that I carry with me today – 24/7! After the trip I decided to keep kosher; that began with the Eastern European Pilgrimage. I returned knowing I wanted to adopt a more observant lifestyle. I became a Jew full of pride and strength, not hiding as I had felt before. I got a degree in social work and Jewish communal service, raised a Torah observant family, and after seeing four out of five children serve in the Israeli army after studying in yeshiva, made aliyah. I don't even want to look back and think what would have happened had I NOT participated in the trip."

- One thought that perhaps he was too young or immature to fully appreciate what he was experiencing, but referring to the Jews we met, he said "I was inspired by their holy souls."

- "I came from a small Jewish community, and even though I had attended Jewish camps and USY, the summer exposed me to the historical richness of Jewish life in Eastern Europe, and to Israel, which ultimately became my home. We ended up making aliyah after the trip."

- In a different style but in the same vein, one of the participants who traveled the world on his own spiritual path, recalled a pot-luck Passover Seder in a remote village in Hawaii. Asked to relate a significant personal story, he was flooded with memories from the trip. In his words: "amid tears and laughter and a kind of passion that only deep wells can reach" he shared his experiences. He now lives in Jerusalem.

ENDURING MEMORIES

Many shared stories that they carried with them for the rest of their lives.

Bob recalled giving away his bar mitzvah tefillin and surreptitiously removing his tallit katan on a packed tram in Moscow, to give it to a Jew who asked for it.

Ruchel told of communicating in shul in Russia by holding hands with an older lady and of dancing the hora in Leningrad with a young refusenik woman who began to cry as they circled together. "Why are you crying?" Ruchel asked. "You don't understand. This doesn't happen to us in Russia."

Phil never forgot his feelings at being stopped and searched at Soviet customs, of not knowing if the person next to you was a spy or not, and, in contrast, of giving away the most prized gift he had brought with him from America, a Tikkun (Torah reader's book), "something of lasting value" which could not be acquired in Russia. He recalled celebrating his seventeenth birthday in Tbilisi, Georgia. It was a blessed moment for him.

Pearl met a student named Fima, who asked her to call him Chaim, who had come to the shul in Moscow for the first time in his life. After being reluctant and visibly frightened to enter the building, he finally accompanied her inside for Havdalah, and soon felt elated and emotional. They corresponded for many years. The summer's trip culminated for Pearl with spending Tishah b'Av in Israel with Shlomo Carlebach and feeling immense gratitude for having our own Jewish state.

Harriet recalled sitting in shul one morning in Odessa next to elderly Russian Jews, where the presence of the USYers encouraged them greatly, and her subsequent heartbroken feelings when she returned later that evening, and no one would sit next to her, since the gabbai had warned the local Jews to stay away. Those memories stayed with her always.

One participant recalled a description of me, from the pre-trip orientation:

> Though only thirty, Rabbi Porath shows signs of a receding hairline. At the motel when we met him, his small red knitted kippah, suspended by a lone bobby pin, was attached to a slim strand of hair.
>
> He was describing how we should approach our upcoming journey.
>
> He raised his right hand to his chest: "Normally we live only so high." Then he raised his hand a little more, up to his eyes: "...and sometimes we live this far... But this summer..." and he raised his hand high above his head, "we will be privileged to live way up here."

I recalled that moment vividly. During those summers we all lived on the highest Jewish and spiritual planes, as if our very lives depended on it.

A number of the participants expressed amazement that their parents had allowed them to go on a trip to Russia in the middle of the Cold War, without phone contacts, not to speak of the internet, smartphones, and the like (which had not yet been invented). Even the mail took weeks and weeks. Their parents trusted them even more than they had realized.

"We were exposed to the broader world and saw antisemitism first-hand. When we took our trips, some twenty-five years or so after the Shoah, we learned a critical lesson: Where American Jewry failed their brothers and sisters during World War II, it now rose to the occasion on behalf of Soviet Jews."

"After a week on the road, you felt that this was the closest you would get to experiencing pre-Holocaust Germany and government-sponsored antisemitism. It only sank in after we departed the Soviet Union, and we sensed that we could breathe again, as if you yourself had 'escaped and survived.'"

"I understood, for the first time, the privilege of being an American, and what freedom entailed."

Many commented that, after going to the Soviet Union, they were sensitized to the needs of recently arrived Soviet Jews in their home communities in America. One of the participants created jobs for dozens of Russian-speaking immigrants who moved to her city.

One year I invited my dear friend, the noted author and teacher Danny Siegel, to join the trip as a staff member. He had felt the "undergroundness" of the trip, traveling in Communist Russia at a time when we were certain that the Soviets would *never* Let Our People Go. Recalling our visit to an off-the-beaten-track shul in Moscow to visit some older men, he commented: "It was a real 'high' for us, and the USYers were superb."

CLOSING WORDS OF TORAH

One of the USYers, now a doctor living in Jerusalem with his many children and grandchildren, quoted one of my favorite stories from the Talmud (*Bava Metzia* 85b), which I had taught the group fifty years previously.

It poses the question: What should be done if the Torah were on the verge of being forgotten by the Jewish people, very possibly as a result of governmental repression, similar to what we had witnessed first-hand on our trip? Rabbi Chiya's response was that to save Torah, you should gather younger people and children, similar to some of the Soviet Jews whom we had met along the way, and teach each one a piece of Jewish learning, such as one book of the Bible or one section of the Mishnah, and encourage and empower them to pass on whatever they had learned to someone else. "That is how I would be certain that Torah would never be forgotten by the Jewish people," he said, to which the Talmud responds: "Chiya's deeds are greatness!" or, in our words: "Way to go, Rabbi Chiya!!"

That is how activists and underground teachers taught Hebrew, Jewish history, and Jewish tradition. Whatever they had managed to acquire, they immediately passed on to someone else…"so that Torah would never be forgotten" from the Jews of Russia.

Our friend told and retold that story throughout his lifetime, and concluded with: "I can still hear your voice teaching. Like so much of the trip, it was educational, spiritual, and brought us closer to our Jewish roots. It inspired me as I entered college. I wanted to follow your example."

Kind words and very much appreciated.

The trips had a profound effect on all the participants, USYers, and staff alike. Over the next fifty years, the entire Jewish people are still reaping the rewards.

CHAPTER 14

Teaching in the Footsteps of Elie Wiesel

PASSIONATE REPORTS

We were eager to publicize what we had just seen. It soon became apparent that a youth delegation visiting the Jews of the Soviet Union was news.

The first opportunity to speak in public came soon after we arrived in Israel, on Tishah b'Av afternoon, when we divided up and met with each of the USY Israel Pilgrimage groups. Over the course of the summers, we spoke to thousands of young people from all over the US and Canada. Our personal and passionate reports were very powerful and memorable. Fifty years later, veteran Jewish educators recounted to me some of the stories they had heard as teenagers during those sessions.

The local Israeli press was very keen to report our story. Articles appeared in the *Jerusalem Post* (Michael Graetz, "From Russia with Pride," August 8, 1969) and in the popular Hebrew daily *Maariv*, three years running ("All the Jews We Met in the USSR Wanted to Come to Israel," July 31, 1970; "We Spoke about Blue and White in Red Square," August 1, 1971; and "Copies of Maariv – Much Desired at the Moscow Synagogue," July 23, 1972). Members of the group were interviewed on Kol Yisrael Israeli radio by Avraham Ben-Melech, their senior correspondent for world Jewish affairs.

We all understood that what we had experienced belonged to the entire Jewish people. We wanted to disseminate our stories as widely as possible.

Each of the more than two hundred young people who participated over the years returned to their communities and synagogues all over North America, and many were asked by their rabbis to give a report, often at very "high profile" times, such as the midnight pre–High Holiday Selichot services, or on the holidays themselves. They also wrote articles for their shul and Federation newspapers and spoke about the trip throughout the community, including their local high schools.

The participants often became community resources on Soviet Jewry and carried the messages of their visits with them long afterwards.

Over the years, I shared my experiences with tens of thousands of listeners. I continued to "update" the stories and applied them to contemporary situations. I would talk about the power of the Jewish people to connect, our shared concerns for the Jewish future, the dual calls of Jewish yearning and memory, and the importance of Jewish tradition, all illustrated and supported with examples from the summer trips. Soviet Jewish tales, about "hidden" Jews, fearful and proud Jews, joyous Simchat Torah Jews, and activist Jews, became as familiar to my listeners as classic rabbinic texts.

Even years later, in the 2010s, when I served as a scholar-in-residence for synagogues and Federations across North America, one of my most requested topics was "175 Visits to the Jews of Russia." The subject continues to engage the imagination and the hearts of audiences, both Jewish and non-Jewish.

THE CHANGING COMMUNITY RESPONSE

In my spring 1974 article "The Challenge of Soviet Jewry" (*United Synagogue Review*), I sought to place the Russian Jewish experience in a broader perspective. I asked: What has this experience taught us? What should we learn from this epic story for our contemporary Jewish life?

I wrote that the real challenge of Soviet Jewry was not only what they were doing in Moscow or Vilna or Tbilisi, but rather what its impact was on us here in New York, Chicago, or Toronto. Were we inspired by Soviet Jews to exemplify, in our own lives, that which we were demanding for them? To learn Hebrew, to proudly declare our loyalties to the Jewish people and Israel, to add more Jewish traditions and practices to our personal lives, even to contemplate making aliyah? We usually viewed this saga exclusively about ameliorating *their* conditions and allowing those who chose to emigrate. I wrote:

> Ultimately, the Jews of the USSR will teach and give the Jews of North America and Israel far more than we can possibly hope to give in return. For the past five summers, 200 young people and their leaders have visited the Jews of the USSR.
>
> Invariably, they would come asking: "What can I do for Soviet Jews?" and return, instead, impressed and strengthened by *their* courage and dedication, *their* love of Torah and the Jewish people, *their* feeling for Am Yisrael, as well as *their* sense of both *simchah* and sadness.... The test of our loyalty and devotion to Soviet Jews will be the

exemplification in our own lives of the Jewish life that has been denied them.[1]

I sent copies of the article to several public figures, and was very pleased to receive a personal response from Senator Henry "Scoop" Jackson, from the State of Washington, who was admired and revered in the Jewish community for his outspoken efforts on behalf of Soviet Jewry.

Another major essay, "Saving Soviet Jewry," appeared in *The Third Jewish Catalog: Creating Community*, compiled by Sharon and Michael Strassfeld (JPS, 1980). The three volumes of *The Jewish Catalog* series (vol. 1, 1973; vol. 2, 1975; vol. 3, 1980) were extremely popular do-it-yourself and countercultural guides to Jewish living, and sold over 500,000 copies. The essays on Soviet Jewry (including "How to Make Waves" by Glenn Richter and "Aiding Russian Immigrants" by Sharon Hammerman) were featured in the opening section of the book. The cause of Soviet Jewry had moved to the forefront of the Jewish community's agenda.

All of this paralleled another project I was engaged in, writing the first textbook on Soviet Jewry for Hebrew high schools and adult education.

THE FIRST TEXTBOOK ON SOVIET JEWRY

In those days there was no single place where a non-expert could go and learn about the topic of Soviet Jewry, let alone a younger student.

I began developing a course on Russian Jewry in the wake of the 1967 Six-Day War. It was a time of tremendous excitement and Jewish renewal. I was on the faculty of the Temple Israel Hebrew High School in Great Neck, New York. Rabbi Efraim Warshaw, the newly appointed director, encouraged me to develop the classes, especially since I had visited the USSR just two years earlier, and *The Jews of Silence* by Elie Wiesel had only recently been published.

Over the next three years, I did the research, prepared weekly handouts, and wrote a course on Russian Jewry from scratch. I was greatly influenced by my professor in Russian History at Hebrew University, Michael Confino, who first exposed me to the excitement and engagement of using original documents in translation as a window into historical events. I spent much of my year in Israel researching and collecting primary sources that would stimulate and encourage students' interest.

My draft, now expanded to a book, was published in 1973, with a second printing a year later. To the best of my knowledge, *Jews in Russia: The Last Four Centuries; A Documentary History* (United Synagogue Commission on Jewish

---

1. Jonathan Porath, "The Challenge of Soviet Jewry," *United Synagogue Review*, spring 1974, 7.

Education, 1973) was the first textbook published on Russian Jewry for Hebrew high schools and adult education. (See photos.)

The book was written from a passionate Jewish point of view. Jewish values, traditions, mitzvot such as *pidyon shevuyim* (the ransom of captives) and *zecher Amalek* (remembering the evil deeds of Amalek) were part of the curriculum. As I stated in the "Word of Direction":

> This aim of this text is to develop within the student a sense of con-
> cern and a feeling of empathy for the Jewish people throughout Jewish
> history, and around the contemporary Jewish world. Spiritually we
> should dance with the Jews of Russia at Simchat Torah; we should
> have fought with the partisans and have been at Babi Yar; we should
> "go up" to the Kotel in Jerusalem. In the words of the rabbis, we should
> feel that: *Kol Yisrael Areivim Zeh BaZeh* (The fate of the entire Jewish
> people is intertwined).[2]

Ultimately, it was as much about us, the student and reader, as it was about the Jews of Russia.

In the afterword, written in the early 1970s, I tried to peer into the future, and posed the following questions:

- Will Soviet Jews continue to clamor for emigration to Israel and the West? Will the authorities answer with additional waves of arrests, trials, and repression? Will the Jewish activists be allowed to depart, leaving Soviet Jewry leaderless?
- Will Israel prove to be the homeland that the Soviet Jews believed it would be? How will the new *olim* be absorbed into Israeli life and society?
- Will the future mood of the Soviet Jewish youth and their parents be one of hope or fear?
- What role will American Jewry play in the future of Soviet Jewry?
- In Moscow on Simchat Torah, the Jewish youth sing "Am Yisrael Chai." Will their children sing it twenty years hence?[3]

Clearly, I had no inkling that the Soviet Union would collapse less than twenty years later, that masses of Jews would emigrate not only to Israel but

---

2. Jonathan Porath, *Jews in Russia: The Last Four Centuries; A Documentary History* (New York: United Synagogue Commission on Jewish Education, 1973), xiii. Used with permission of the United Synagogue of Conservative Judaism.

3. Porath, *Jews in Russia*, 162.

to other Jewish population centers around the Jewish world, such as America, Canada, and Germany, or that successor Russian governments would be remarkably hospitable to local Jewish life and culture. I also did not foresee how American Jewry would rise to the occasion and rally under the banner of "Let My People Go." Each of the communities was destined to respond to the challenges of the next twenty years and beyond in unexpected, and often heroic, ways.

SPEAKING OUT AND TEACHING OUT

With the spread of Soviet Jewry activism, I focused my primary efforts on developing educational materials. The spring 1974 issue of the *Pedagogic Reporter – A Forum on Jewish Education*, the organ of nearly fifty boards of Jewish education around North America, was devoted entirely to teaching about Soviet Jewry, including my article "Ideas for a Soviet Jewry Course of Study."

The following year, the Board of Jewish Education of New York produced *A Master Listing on Soviet Jewry for Teachers and Principals*, which I edited and which was presented at a citywide pedagogic conference in March 1975.

The plight of Soviet Jewry was finally entering the consciousness of American Jewry and the world.

Much of the initial spark and sustaining energy of the Soviet Jewry movement was inspired by the efforts of one man, a Holocaust survivor from Sighet, Romania, whose voice was heard throughout the entire world, Elie Wiesel. He and I formed a personal relationship of nearly fifty years that tremendously influenced the ultimate direction of my life.

MY FRIEND AND MENTOR ELIE WIESEL

Elie Wiesel and I first met in the fall of 1969, when I recognized him sitting in the back row of Professor Saul Lieberman's Talmud class at the Jewish Theological Seminary. I was a senior rabbinical student; he was already a well-known author and Jewish activist. I introduced myself and told him what a powerful impact *The Jews of Silence* had on me, and how it inspired me to follow in his footsteps and travel to Moscow for Simchat Torah in 1968, to be a witness and a participant in that great Jewish celebration and demonstration. Indeed, I had written in my diary: "Wiesel was right!" but never thought I would be able to tell him in person.

I wasn't aware of it when we met, but he had felt a great regret about that particular holiday. He wrote in the *Hadassah Magazine* in October 1968: "This year the Soviet Jewish youngsters will be there again. They will sing and dance. But this year I will not be with them – and for this, I cannot but feel guilty."

He felt that he was their messenger, but as he could not be there in person, he would have to think about them from afar, and then I show up, unexpectedly, and begin telling him stories of what I had experienced during my Simchat Torah in Moscow--all because of him!

Subsequently, I understood his handwritten inscription to me in one of his books:

> To Reb Yonatan – In exchange for his warm regards and blessings from Russia,
>   From a messenger just like him.
>   Elie Wiesel

We formed a friendship that lasted a lifetime.

He called me "Reb Yonatan" and I responded with "Reb Eliezer," titles of respect and fondness.

I was creating my Hebrew high school course on the Jews of Russia, and he was very interested, even insistent, in seeing new sections as they became available. He suggested that I dramatize the lessons by focusing on individual stories of Soviet Jews and offered to contribute some of his own material as well.

I told him about the recently concluded USY trip to the Soviet Union, and he was fascinated. "Perhaps I will join you next year," he told me.

"Of all the books I wrote, the phrase 'Jews of Silence' will last, perhaps, for the next thousand years."

He said something unimaginable at the time, which proved to be prophetic. He was very *optimistic* about the future of Jewish life in the Soviet Union because of the deep Jewish feelings of the young people there.

On a more personal level, he recounted to me that he had recently spoken in Washington, DC, where he had met my parents. He spoke of me warmly to them, saying that he was encouraging me to write my textbook. I know my parents loved hearing that!

We shared many personal moments over the years. When my grandfather passed away, he sent a note of consolation; he and his wife Marian came to our wedding and gave us a Kiddush cup that we still use proudly until today; and he reached out on numerous personal and family milestones.

Many more visits, calls, and exchanges followed over the years.

It wasn't by chance that I dedicated my book *Jews in Russia* to him: "To Reb Eliezer from Sighet."

I was especially touched when he reviewed my book in the Yiddish-language *Der Algemeiner Journal*:

We Can Be Proud of Our Jewish Youth

For some time now, I have been meaning to write about Rabbi Jonathan Porath and his book, so let me tell you about a young, dynamic rabbi and his splendid work on behalf of Jewish young people in America and Soviet Russia. Many Jewish parents have him to thank that their children remained, or suddenly became, proud Jews, fiery Jews.

Every year he would lead a group of Jewish students and travel out over Russian cities, where he would warm the hearts of local Jews, who were glad to know that they hadn't been forgotten. Most important was the very fact that they had come.

Rabbi Porath's book *Jews in Russia: The Last Four Centuries* is one of the best books dealing with the condition of Soviet Jewry. It contains information, anecdotes, facts, figures, excerpts, and a great, great deal of Jewish fervor. If you would like a Jewish student to know more about the history and struggle of the heroic Jews in Russia, how the Jewish revolution has won out over the Communist one, give him Rabbi Porath's book.[4]

FINAL CONVERSATIONS

After our family made aliyah in 1984, our contacts became sporadic; besides the miles and technical difficulties, I was embarrassed. After all, he had received the Nobel Peace Prize, chaired the President's Commission on the Holocaust, and was recognized as the most famous Jew and humanitarian in the world. He was meeting with presidents, prime ministers, and other prominent and important people.

Even though whenever we met in Jerusalem, after a public lecture or appearance, or at the opening of the new museum at Yad Vashem, he would greet me by name with a smile followed by a big hug, I always wondered why I deserved such treatment. After all, who was I?

Finally, at my wife Deena's encouragement, in preparation for a trip to the States, I contacted him and received his warm invitation to come and visit with him in his office at the Elie Wiesel Foundation for Humanity in Manhattan. (See photos.)

We subsequently met whenever I came to the States, and those meetings left a deep impression on me. We spoke from the heart.

---

4.   Elie Wiesel, "We Can Be Proud of Jewish Youth" [in Yiddish], *Der Algemeiner Journal*, December 6, 1974, 4.

I showed him the funeral announcement I had printed in Jerusalem after the death of my father, of blessed memory. "We davened together," he recalled.

He expressed tremendous personal interest, almost parental concern: "And what are you doing in Israel? How are you supporting yourself?" Equally important, he would ask: "What Torah did you study today?"

We shared our mutual experiences of becoming "zaidies" (grandfathers). It was, in his words, "pure nachas" (total pleasure).

When I told him that my mother, whom he knew, was planning her ninety-ninth birthday party at the Waldorf-Astoria Hotel in Jerusalem, he responded that if he were in town he would certainly come. She would have loved that!

He inscribed a copy of his latest, and ultimately, final work *Open Heart* to me as follows (translated from his Hebrew):

> To Reb Yehonatan Porath,
>   Who brings great satisfaction to all who learn with him or from him.
>   With warmth and affectionate blessing,
>   Eliezer ben Sara

In May 2014, at what proved to be our last visit together, I felt that I was taking too much of his valuable time and tried repeatedly to excuse myself, but he wouldn't let me leave. He did not want to say goodbye.

As we were about to part, I told him that I was thinking of writing a book about my lifetime experiences with Soviet and Russian Jews, to which he responded: "Do it! Do it!" This present volume is, in part, in response to that conversation. His final words of encouragement reverberated very deeply within me and continue to do so today. Clearly, our souls had touched.

Elie Wiesel influenced many people around the world and inspired many messengers to spread his words and deeds. I was privileged to be one of them. His personal and loving attention, and his charge to me of over half a century ago not to forget the Jews of the Soviet Union, impacted greatly upon the direction of my life, for which I will be forever grateful. May his memory be a blessing.[5]

---

5. A version of the preceding text was published as "Remembering My Teacher and Friend Elie Wiesel," *Jerusalem Post*, June 26, 2019, https://www.jpost.com/diaspora/remembering-my-teacher-and-friend-elie-wiesel-593764. Used by permission of the *Jerusalem Post*.

CHAPTER 15

The Russians Are Here!

THE RUSSIANS COME...SLOWLY, SLOWLY

We knew the feeling ourselves, firsthand. Our family, my wife Deena, myself, and our four children (then ages seven, five, three, and one) landed in Israel on July 3, 1984, as *olim chadashim* (new immigrants). We lived in an absorption center in Jerusalem's Gilo neighborhood and half a year later moved to our own apartment in the capital's northern Ramot suburb. I was fortunate to cobble together seven part-time jobs during the first year, we came with some savings, and, thank God, it all worked out.

But the immigrants who followed us did not have it so easy. In the closing weeks of 1984, during our stay in Gilo, there was a sudden tumult and excitement. A planeload of brand new *olim* from Ethiopia, who had just been airlifted from Sudan in Operation Moshe, arrived at their first stop in the Holy Land – our absorption center. All of a sudden, we were no longer the "new" *olim*. "Newercomers" had arrived. We went through our children's clothes closet, selected items, and brought them to our new neighbors. Deena baked cakes and prepared chicken soup to nourish them. It was a heady time, faced by every generation of immigrants to Israel. We had been given our first opportunity to "pay it forward" following our own aliyah.

But from the Soviet Union, back in those days, there were almost no newcomers. The same year that we arrived, in 1984, there were only 335 *olim* from the Soviet Union, 348 the following year, and 206 the year after that. The numbers grew to about two thousand a year until 1989, when all of a sudden, nearly thirteen thousand Soviet Jews made aliyah, and from that point on, the floodgates burst. In the early 1990s, over half a million Jews from the Soviet Union arrived in Israel, plus an additional quarter of a million who went to the US, Germany, Canada, and elsewhere.[1]

Our first hint of this future wave of immigration came when Shimon, my friend from Odessa, and his brother Boris, arrived in Israel in September 1989,

---

1. Based on figures from the Israeli Bureau of Statistics and Petrus Buwalda, *They Did Not Dwell Alone*, 221–24.

just before the High Holidays. They came, surprisingly enough for us, as tourists and not as *olim*, and were received as genuine heroes. Live Soviet Jews who came to visit! They were hosted by politicians and public figures, spent several weeks with us, and then returned home. Something was clearly changing.

We didn't quite realize it at the time, but their coming was one of the earliest indications that the Soviet Union had decided to let the Jews leave.

Over the next few months, a few individual Soviet Jewish families began to arrive in our Ramot neighborhood, quietly, with a minimum of fuss. One of our neighbors, Dr. Avraham Shafir, who himself came from the Soviet Union to Israel as a child in 1949, and I began to consider how we could help the newly arriving *olim*. We decided that we would collect used furniture for their empty apartments. Fortunately, I had recently purchased a used decommissioned ambulance with a high roof as our family car. It proved to be ideal for hauling beds, shelves, and other oversized items. Avraham and I would get leads and go out on collections.

It was extremely fortuitous that then we were both more than thirty years younger since I know we could not have managed it today. One particular call stands out. We were picking up a couch in Kiryat Moshe, one of Jerusalem's religious neighborhoods. A large photograph of Rabbi Avraham Kook, the first chief rabbi of Mandatory Palestine, recognized as a saintly and revered figure all over the Jewish world, was prominently displayed in the apartment. Both of my grandfathers had Rabbi Kook's picture in their libraries in America. I commented to the lady of the house how familiar the portrait of Rabbi Kook was, to which she responded: "Rabbi Kook was my grandfather!" I am certain that her esteemed grandfather would have been very pleased.

They're Here! Welcoming the *Olim*

And then, suddenly, it was as if all the dams broke on the same day! In mid-May 1990, my friend Avraham called, rather frantically, to say that half a dozen cabs had just arrived from the airport, pulling into our neighborhood and disgorging some two dozen newly arrived Soviet Jews, with all their bags. They were being taken to apartments that had been rented for them, only the rooms were empty. When I asked: "What do you mean by empty," he responded: "There isn't a table or a chair or a bed or a refrigerator. They're lying down on their suitcases." That's definitely empty.

After making some calls, we somehow located a truck that was moving furniture from one Hebrew University dorm across town to another and made a long-term "loan" of the items. Maybe they were sent from Heaven!

Soon, our Neve Orot neighborhood in Ramot Alef was home to some two hundred Russian *olim* of all ages, in over thirty apartments, and we had to get organized. Under the aegis of our neighborhood synagogue, Avraham and I called a meeting of the neighbors, and we began dividing up tasks. We were blessed with dozens of volunteers, a mixture of Israeli-born and *olim* families. Those of us who had only arrived recently in Israel could personally identify with the feelings and challenges being faced by our new, Russian-speaking, neighbors.

We called ourselves Keren Klitat Aliyah-Neve Orot – The Neve Orot Neighborhood Absorption Project, and it became the organizational umbrella for all of our efforts.

These were very exciting as well as demanding times. The numbers were staggering. In 1990 and 1991, the final two years of the Soviet Union, over 330,000 Soviet Jews made aliyah, 450 new arrivals every single day for twenty-four months![2] From 1992 through 1995, an additional 250,000 arrived. They had to be housed, fed, employed, schooled – everything.

After being cut off from the Jewish people for over seventy years, the Jews of the Soviet Union had come home, and we were at center of the action. We felt a personal part of the miraculous renewal of the Jewish people.

HELPING OUR NEW NEIGHBORS

The work of Keren Klitat Aliyah became an all-encompassing passion, especially during 1990–92, as the first wave of Soviet arrivals moved in, got settled, learned Hebrew, found employment, and slowly but surely became increasingly independent and able to fend for themselves.

The younger people either found work in their previous specialties or retrained for new jobs in Israel. One of our neighbors, a former policeman, worked in a bank, another became a dental assistant. It was more difficult for the seniors to find their place, and it became an almost daily occurrence to meet professors or doctors working as watchmen, babysitters, or housecleaners. It was standard for multi-generational families to pool their governmental housing allowances and to share an apartment. The retired grandparents continued in their previous Soviet roles of being responsible for childcare, so the parents could go to ulpan and, ultimately, to work.

In those early years, I was spending up to five or six hours a day visiting apartments, organizing activities, and planning and publicizing projects. For example, when we scheduled a community Friday night or pre-holiday program, I would prepare a flyer in English to publicize the event, ask our new neighbor Sveta, who had been an English teacher in Moscow, to translate it into Russian, make copies, and go walking throughout the neighborhood and the nearby shopping

---

2.   Based on figures from the Israeli Bureau of Statistics and Petrus Buwalda, *They Did Not Dwell Alone*, 221–24.

center, posting the signs. That was our only means of communication. It was real community outreach.

Many of our Ramot neighbors took very active roles in "adopting" newly arrived families, welcoming them into their homes and assisting with their absorption. The relationships formed often lasted for decades. My friend Avraham and I, who had begun our involvement by picking up used furniture for the *olim*, now found ourselves attending weddings, conducting shivah (mourning) services and joining in at circumcisions and other special occasions, such as when the newcomers received medical licenses or packed up to leave for their own permanent homes.

We had two major concerns for our newcomers: their physical welfare and their Jewish well-being; after all, they were coming to their Jewish home, even though almost none of them had any idea what that meant.

We presented each new family with two arrival gifts: a used refrigerator and a mezuzah. We wanted them to feel comfortable both physically as well as spiritually. Even if they had never seen a mezuzah before, it was the sign of a Jewish residence, and they were now at home.

Few of them knew anything about being Jewish. They were aware that they were Jews because that was what the "fifth line" of their internal Soviet passport said, but as to what that meant in positive terms, they had no idea. Where they came from, to be called a "Jew" was a term of derision.

Our newly arrived next-door neighbors were four generations of Russian Jewish women: great-grandmother Bella, grandmother Paulina, daughter Svetlana, and great-granddaughter Ola. There were no men. Either their husbands had died, or they were divorced from their non-Jewish partners. They arrived two days before Pesach, and we invited them to search for chametz with us and to join our Seder, which was their very first.

CARING FOR THEIR PHYSICAL NEEDS

Since there were no direct flights from the Soviet Union to Israel, they all had to travel via Europe, and often their bags were delayed or lost in transit. Many arrived only with the clothes on their backs.

We opened a neighborhood clothing warehouse, filling it with donated items, including children's toys and home furnishings, and invited *olim* to come and take what they needed, at no cost. We hired Bertha, a lovely lady from Minsk who had been a pharmacist, to take charge. The shelves were always impeccably organized, only this time with children's outfits rather than medicines. Often tourists and other visitors would bring donations of clothing with them for the *olim*. (See photos.)

We distributed fifty used refrigerators, 175 room heaters, 350 winter blankets, bamboo bookshelves, beds – whatever we thought our new neighbors needed at that time. Upon their arrival in Israel, they had received an initial financial grant from the Ministry of Absorption. They enrolled in an ulpan and began learning Hebrew, but none of them was yet able to join the Israeli job market. We wanted to help them stretch their modest allowances as much as possible. Later we opened an employment service and began offering interest-free loans.

We hired the new *olim* as translators and gardeners and to run summer camps; we purchased musical instruments for unemployed musicians. We organized concerts, with the proceeds going to the musicians, and even had to schedule multiple performances because of the demand.

We helped with medical equipment, hearing aids, chemotherapy treatments, ambulance costs not covered by Israeli medical insurance, dental care, and established an "eyeglass fund."

Over time, we expanded our programs and target populations to include summer camps and afternoon activities for Russian and Ethiopian children, textbooks and subsidies for class trips, books from Yad Vashem for Holocaust Memorial Day, Israeli flags for Israeli Independence Day, visits to Israeli army bases, purchase of tombstones for deceased family members, weddings for *olim*, and other forms of support.

We organized *brit milah* (circumcision) celebrations, took elderly *olim* to the Kotel for their first visit, officiated at funerals, and organized shiva services. We gave out more than two thousand kippot, provided tefillin for bar mitzvah boys (the first twenty-five with the help of the Ministry of Religious Affairs), whatever was needed. The Ministry of Absorption published a booklet in Russian entitled *How to Create a Jewish Home in Israel* written by our synagogue's Rabbi Aaron Adler, which was translated, illustrated, and produced by community members.

We received the following note from local teachers and Sherut Leumi (National Service) volunteers helping Ethiopian families: "Thank you for your generous contribution which enabled us to organize a bat mitzvah celebration for young women from Ethiopia. From the funds, we were also able to purchase school Bibles for them, an extremely useful and needed item. May you and the members of Keren Klitat Aliyah-Neve Orot continue to help new immigrants to Israel."

EXPANDING THE CIRCLE OF SUPPORTERS

The funding for these projects and activities was all private and came from generous donations both from our neighbors and abroad, especially Danny Siegel's ZIV Tzedakah Fund, Hands-On Tsedaka in Miami, the Phoenix Tzedaka Cooperative, and a range of individual supporters from all over the US and Israel. Periodically,

I would send out updates and reports as well as invite people to participate, and I always received a warm response. In addition to giving via Federations and organizations, many were looking for ways to help new *olim* directly, which was precisely what we were doing.

Our largest benefactor was Howard Lewis from Teaneck, New Jersey, who gave us ongoing grants for many years, and after whom we named our project the Howard T. Lewis Center for Klitat Aliyah-Neve Orot. Mr. Stanley Amsel from Teaneck, father of Rabbi Nahum Amsel from our neighborhood, introduced Howard to our project. Stanley was extremely gracious with his time and support and was key in helping us to qualify for US 501(c)(3) tax-exempt status.

By the Summer of 1993, we had raised over $137,000, nearly 99 percent of which went directly to fund programs and help *olim*. Our only unavoidable administrative costs, which totaled about $2,000, paid for bank charges and xeroxing. We were very proud of the fact that all other expenses, including postage stamps, telephone, and clerical services, travel, and the like, were donated. All work was performed by loving volunteers.

AN OUTSTANDING LADY VOLUNTEER

One person, in particular, deserves special mention: Mrs. Regina Mansdorff.

Regina was an extraordinary woman with an inspirational life story, who taught all of us by her example.

She was born in Kolbuszowa, a small town in southeastern Poland, in 1919 and was one of five children. Half of the town's three thousand inhabitants were Jewish. She attended the Orthodox Bais Yaakov School for Girls, whose principal was the legendary Sara Schenirer, the founder of the entire Bais Yaakov school system. She was raised in a tradition of tzedakah and *gemilut chasadim* (helping others). Her mother would always send Regina to collect for the needy before the holidays.

When the Germans invaded in 1939, she and her family escaped the ghetto, fleeing to Soviet-occupied Lvov. They were then sent to Siberia, where she survived for five years. In 1945 Regina returned home to find that all the three hundred Jewish families of her town had been wiped out. Only she and her immediate family had survived.

In 1947 they immigrated to the United States. She married Meir, and they had two sons. She had a dress store in Brooklyn and loved to embroider Jewish religious items, such as ark covers and tallit bags. She was active in the local Young Israel synagogue, president of the sisterhood, and very involved in the Soviet Jewry protest movement.

Their goal had always been to make aliyah, and in 1982 they settled in our Ramot neighborhood when she was already in her mid-sixties. When the *olim* from Russia began arriving, she threw herself into the center of the work, aided enormously by the Russian she had learned during her years in Siberia. She always expressed deep gratitude towards the Russian people for saving her family during the Shoah.

She greeted each newcomer with a welcome cake, invited them for Shabbat meals, and sent food for the holidays. She arranged numerous Jewish weddings in the shul with Rabbi Adler and kashered homes. Even after the *olim* left the neighborhood, she continued to care for them.

She inspired not only the Russian *olim* but the Israelis and Americans as well. She was the "heart and soul" of our Keren Klitat Aliyah; in Danny Siegel's wonderful phrase, a "Mitzvah Hero." When our neighborhood threw a huge festive post-Simchat Torah celebration in honor of the Russian *olim*, she was a featured honoree.

As she was approaching ninety and gave away her beloved sewing machine to her neighbors, we knew that she felt her time had come. She passed away beloved by all.

After her funeral and shiva, we returned to Jerusalem's Har Hamenuchot cemetery for the unveiling of her headstone. It was a stormy Friday morning, as if the heavens above joined with their tears – both of sadness at her loss, and of joy at what she had accomplished and taught us during her life. As the mourners huddled, shivering, under umbrellas, I expressed our feelings about Regina in one emotion-laden sentence: "She loved us and we loved her; she knew it and so did we." Nothing more needed to be said.

In addition to all of the physical help we provided, our new neighbors from the Soviet Union not only moved to a new country, they also returned to the Jewish people.

CHAPTER 16

Rejoining the Jewish People

OUR FIRST BAR MITZVAHS

For nearly all of the *olim* who arrived, everything Jewish was new to them: the calendar, holidays and ceremonies, Zionism and Jewish history, synagogues, and religious services.

They brought with them a deep thirst and desire to learn and experience what it meant to be Jews, and that encouraged us to expose them to as much as we could. The newcomers showed us how to see Jewish life anew. It was a remarkable and inspirational time for all.

When we met our new Russian Jewish neighbors, we realized that there were many young men, who, not surprisingly, never had a bar mitzvah in the Soviet Union. We gathered a group of four boys between the ages of thirteen and sixteen, organized classes with Rabbi Adler, and prepared them for the ceremony. Three of the boys from Ukraine underwent circumcisions as well. The young man from Azerbaijan already had a *brit milah* in the Soviet Union.

We posted open invitations in Hebrew and Russian throughout the neighborhood. There was tremendous excitement and anticipation. Ladies baked cakes and would-be sponsors offered to pay for the reception.

Shabbat morning arrived, June 23, 1990. The bar mitzvah boys were dressed in their new suits and a crowd of four hundred locals and guests gathered to celebrate the morning's events, including over one hundred and fifty Russian *olim* who had never been to a bar mitzvah before. There was real excitement and expectation in the air. We wanted to demonstrate to the newly arrived Soviet Jews what Jews do and what being part of a Jewish community was all about.

The young men, Emanuel, Yair, Aryeh, and Chayim (formerly Émile, Yevgeni, Leon, and Fima), performed their parts beautifully. It was my turn to address the families and the congregation in Hebrew and Russian:

> Dear boys. Dear brothers and sisters,

Who could have imagined only a few months ago, in Baku, Kharkov, and Khmelnitsky, that today you would be celebrating your bar mitzvahs in Jerusalem?

You and your families prepared very seriously for this day. You took classes with the rabbi, had your *brit milah*, but your most momentous preparation was making aliyah to Israel.

Our synagogue, even if it is still unfamiliar to many of you, is also your home.

You have come home! Welcome home!

Pent-up emotions exploded as the crowd broke out in sobs, cheers, and applause. An event that had seemed unimaginable not so long ago, the bar mitzvah of newly arrived Soviet Jews in Jerusalem, was taking place in front of our very eyes. We felt a part of Jewish history, and our new neighbors felt a part of the Jewish people.

CREATING JEWISH EXPERIENCES

We organized a series of educational events open to the entire Russian population of Ramot.

Every few weeks, we held a Friday evening Oneg Shabbat in our shul sanctuary attended by hundreds of *olim*. We sang "Shalom Aleichem" and other songs, many of which they were hearing for the first time, from a songster I had prepared in Russian transliteration. We made Kiddush, heard a *d'var Torah* (Torah teaching) from the rabbi, and spoke about upcoming Jewish and Israeli holidays and events.

We gave out Jewish books and materials, which had been generously donated by the Hochstein Foundation and the Israeli Ministry of Religious Affairs. They were especially eager to receive a copy of the Hebrew Bible since in Russia the word *Bibliya* always referred to the Christian Bible. Many never knew about the "original," which had led to confusion in Russia, with some Jews converting to Russian Orthodoxy since they thought it was virtually the same as Judaism!

For the newcomers, it was like attending Hebrew or Sunday School for the very first time, only as willing and eager adults. All was new, interesting, and exciting.

One Friday night, after speaking about kashrut in the Jewish home, I asked, almost as an afterthought: "Who would like to keep kosher?" Twenty hands shot up! The next week, Regina brought a crew of Chabadniks, kashered their kitchens, gave them sets of dairy and meat dishes, and they were on their way!

I asked one of the women, Bella from Ukraine, about her background. She told me that she had been a member of Komsomol and the Communist Party, and now she was setting up a kosher kitchen.

"Where did that come from?" I inquired.

"That was all we knew back then. Now that we have come to Israel and it's my choice," she replied. "I want a kosher home."

These were Jews who were eager to reclaim their lost heritage but weren't always exactly sure what that was. In the middle of the summer, one of the *olim* presented Regina with a bouquet, in honor of "that great upcoming Jewish holiday – Tishah b'Av!" They hadn't yet learned that it was the saddest day in the Jewish calendar.

We celebrated the Jewish holidays with mass happenings. The shul was packed, often with over five hundred attendees of all ages, including large numbers of children. On a Saturday night, we would open with Havdalah and invite all of the young people to join us around the flickering candle. We heard the blowing of the shofar before Rosh Hashanah, dressed in costumes and gave out hamantaschen for Purim, and distributed colorful explanatory booklets in Russian about each holiday.

The response was overwhelming. For our first Chanukah event, in 1990, which was attended by more than six hundred *olim*, we distributed two hundred Russian booklets for adults and seventy-five for children, and we could have given out double that amount! The following year, under the banner "Meet a Genuine Jewish Hero," we invited Natan Sharansky to speak to the newly arrived olim. (See photos.)

On the evening of Yom Ha'atzmaut (Israeli Independence Day), the neighbors would block off the street in front of our apartment complex, set up tables and grills, and have a nighttime cookout. It was glorious family fun as well as a public demonstration of how much we felt "at home" in Israel.

As the evening unfolded, I realized that I had forgotten to invite our new Russian friends, and quickly ran from door to door, encouraging them to join us. They came and were flabbergasted! In their former lives in the Soviet Union, perhaps some had gathered in front of their local shuls on Simchat Torah, but to celebrate Israeli Independence Day in public, and to close off the street with fellow Jews would have meant certain arrest! All who took part – whether born in Jerusalem, Moscow, or America – reveled in the celebration.

Pesach provided wonderful opportunities for first-time, hands-on, Jewish experiences. In an April 1991 letter to supporters and donors, I described the recently concluded holiday:

Immediately after Purim, we devoted our Friday evening Oneg Shabbat program to the topic of Pesach. We taught the 150 assembled *olim* some of the songs from the Haggadah, with specially prepared sheets in Hebrew, Russian and Russian transliteration.

To most Soviet Jews, Pesach had meant, at best, a piece of matzah, so everything was new. We invited them to a follow-up session on the topic "How to Keep a Kosher Kitchen for Pesach" and were planning on supplying them with new kosher-for-Passover dishes. We expected some thirty or forty *olim* to attend.

Monday evening came, and we were greeted by more than two hundred Soviet Jews who had come to learn about the holiday, as well as to receive the new tableware. We distributed guide books, and a long-time Russian-speaking Israeli spoke about cleaning, kashering, and choosing kosher-for-Passover products in the store. We gave out knives, forks, spoons, hard plastic plates, soup bowls, glasses, coffee cups, and frying pans (all in both meat and dairy versions) to nearly two hundred families, over 825 sets in all, in addition to packages of wine and matzah. I led a model Seder at the local ulpan. We reached over two-thirds of the *olim* in Ramot Alef via our Pesach projects.

On Pesach evening, we sponsored a community Seder for a hundred newly arrived *olim*, which was hosted by forty Israelis and led by Rabbi Adler.

Following the conclusion of the Seder at midnight, a group of twenty *olim* were on such an emotional "high" that they walked the empty Ramot streets until 2:00 a.m.

One of the participants, Dr. Oleg Savelson, from Saratov on the Volga, told me that not only was this the first Seder he had ever attended in his life, but that until that evening, he had never even heard the story of the Jews leaving Egypt! It was particularly meaningful to him since he had come to Israel himself only a few months previously.

YIZKOR ON YOM KIPPUR: THE SPIRITUAL PEAK

For the High Holidays in 1991, we invited the *olim* to join the main services in our neighborhood shul and set up extra chairs, but it was a step too far for most. On Rosh Hashanah, we conducted a smaller, separate minyan in Russian and Hebrew, attended by seventy-five people, and wanted to try something different for Yom Kippur.

We announced a special Yom Kippur Yizkor memorial service in Russian, which would take place in the main synagogue during the afternoon break, from 2:00 to 3:00 p.m.

The response was overwhelming. Hundreds of *olim* flooded the synagogue. Many came dressed in white and wearing tennis shoes. It was their time to participate in Yom Kippur services, and they were eager to take part.

It was a spiritually powerful gathering. Rabbi Adler set the mood. We opened the ark and stood for Avinu Malkeinu (Our Father Our King) and Al Chet (the roll call of Sins), which we recited responsively in Russian.

It was very important to me that we recite a Yizkor memorial prayer that included Soviet Jews, but no text existed, so we adapted our own in Russian and Hebrew:

> In memory of our brothers and sisters, Jews from the former Soviet Union, who died as victims in the Shoah, fighting in the Red Army and the partisans, in the Gulag and from Soviet terror, and who perished before being allowed to make aliyah to Israel.

The silence and intensity were deafening. For the first time, as citizens of Israel, these Soviet Jews were mourning their loved ones in synagogue on the holiest day of the Jewish year, together with all the other Jews around the world.

After their private prayers for their personal loved ones, we memorialized IDF soldiers and terror victims.

We concluded by reciting the Mourner's Kaddish out loud, word-by-word. They repeated after me, ever so slowly and deliberately: "*Yitgadal...ve'yitkadash...shemei...rabbah...,*" building to a crescendo: "*Oseh...shalom...ve'imru...* Amen."

Most had never been to services before, and barely knew how to read the Hebrew words, but they davened with such holy intensity. It was a privilege to be in their presence.

COMMUNITY AND NATIONAL RECOGNITION

Our activities were reported in the *Jerusalem Post* as well as the Hebrew and Russian press. I was interviewed on Radio Reka, Israel's official Russian-language station. Articles also appeared in the *Miami Jewish Tribune* and *Hadassah Magazine*.

We were included in a feature article in the February 1992 issue of *National Geographic*, "The Great Soviet Exodus," by Tad Szulc. After spending an afternoon with us in Ramot, he decided to use Keren Klitat Aliyah as an example of neighborhood absorption. He interviewed one of our oldest *olim*, Chaim Shatz from Ukraine. Chaim told us that there were thousands of Jews in his home town of Starokonstantinov (today Khmelnitsky), but no synagogue. Now he attends our neighborhood shul in Jerusalem. He was even given the singular honor to open the ark for Kol Nidrei on Yom Kippur eve. Tears came to his eyes as he described the scene.

We were awarded the Ramot Community Prize for "an outstanding communal project in the absorption of Russian Jews in the Ramot neighborhood." The Yeshiva University Alumni Association honored our communal efforts and our spiritual leader Rabbi Aaron Adler at its annual award dinner.

We also received the Israeli government's National Prize of the Ministry of Religious Affairs for our work, which was presented at the Knesset.

OUR MOST IMPORTANT PRIZE

The greatest and most meaningful acknowledgment we received came from our Russian neighbors themselves.

In 2000, ten years after they first arrived, we held a reunion, attended by many of the *olim* who had taken their first steps in Israel in our neighborhood and who had since moved to their own apartments.

It was a very emotional evening, the Saturday night before Rosh Hashanah. For many, it was our first meeting since the day they had left our neighborhood and struck out on their own. The local residents remembered them when they arrived from the airport a decade ago, and how settled and established they were now. They had learned Hebrew, were employed, and looked just like us. Perhaps their Russian accents were even more "authentically Israeli" than the English-accented Hebrew most of us spoke.

The surprise of the evening was the presentation of a letter from the entire group, which they all signed. (See photos.) It read as follows (in their original English):

> Dear Yonatan,
>
> All those present from the Former Soviet Union had the good luck to start our aliyah in the Neve Orot neighborhood. We are sure, there is no place and such people as here.
>
> From the very first days, we felt ourselves to be part of the family. You've lent a helping hand in all our problems.
>
> We all had come to an alien country, to an unknown language, to new traditions, to another culture. It was absolutely a new world to us, that we had to start and build all over again right from the beginning.

Thanks to your help we say now: We are at home!

You have created this unprecedented atmosphere and extraordinary relations that gave us support and encouragement and taught us to love Eretz Yisrael.

All of us will remember your noble labor.

Thank you for giving us today the opportunity to be here and express our feelings toward you all.

SHANA TOVA

Within a decade or so of their arrival, the bulk of our neighborhood Russian *olim* were now independent and could move out on their own.

We could not have asked for anything more.

An Ongoing Mitzvah

One project of Keren Klitat Aliyah-Neve Orot did continue under the radar, for the next fifteen years. It was coordinated by an extraordinary community activist, Eleanora Shifrin, originally from Novosibirsk, Siberia, and a long-time Ramot resident. She was one of the select group of "Mitzvah Heroes" who exemplified *chesed* (compassion).

She and I had a wonderful arrangement. I would receive checks from people in the US who wanted to give direct help to needy Israelis, whether Russians, Ethiopians, victims of Arab Terror, or others, and she would be in personal contact with the intended recipients, make assessments, distribute the checks, and monitor the use of the funds.

I would call her and say: "Eleanora, I just received a check from a donor for $500 or $1,000," and she would always respond: "Thank goodness, Yonatan, I have some people in mind just today who really could use help." From 2008 to 2016, we distributed over $56,000 in direct grants, including to the chronically needy, aged, or infirm, many of whom we first came to know as new *olim* twenty or more years previously.

In 2020, after thirty years of activity, Keren Klitat Aliyah-Neve Orot finally closed. The Russians had moved on, and so had most of the neighbors.

It was one of the peak experiences of my life, an extraordinary mitzvah, as well as a privilege. The neighborhood volunteers felt that the Russian *olim* had given us far more than we could possibly have given them.

I would sometimes imagine, that after a hundred twenty years, when I would be standing in front of the Heavenly Court and would be asked: "*Nu*, Jonathan, what makes you think that you merit the World to Come?" I would answer quietly but confidently, "The Russians," and the response would be: "Well done. Welcome."

ENDINGS AND BEGINNINGS

On the night of December 25, 1991, at 7:32 p.m., Moscow time, the red hammer and sickle flag was lowered over the Kremlin for the last time, and the following day, the Union of Soviet Socialist Republics, which had been in the process of dissolution since 1988, finally ceased to exist.

Five months later, I was back on a plane traveling to the Russian Federation, about to enter a brand-new world.

Why did I go, and what would I find?

PART III

Post-Soviet Jewry

CHAPTER 17

Back in the Post-USSR

THE UNEXPECTED OFFER

I had last been in Russia and Ukraine in 1974, with no plans to ever return, so when the call came in March of 1992, just a few months after the dissolution of the Soviet Union, it was a total surprise.

It was from Rabbi Nathan Laufer, an old friend who was, at the time, the vice president and director of programs at the Wexner Heritage Foundation. I had been on the foundation's Israel summer faculty for a number of years, and Nathan knew of my prior Russian experience. The foundation was exploring the idea of bringing the entire Wexner student body, past and present, on a study mission to the former Soviet Union (FSU). Would I be interested in traveling there, checking things out, and reporting back? My visit would coincide with the upcoming meeting of the Vaad, the umbrella body of Jewish organizations in the FSU, that May in Kiev.

I accepted immediately.

I didn't quite appreciate it fully at the time, but as I was soon to learn, the door had opened to an entirely new world, both for me and post-Soviet Jewry.

My first task was to familiarize myself with as many of the current "players" on the scene as I could. From Rabbi Laufer's initial contact on March 12, until I departed for Russia on May 10, I spent more than fifty hours in meetings with the organizations then operating on the ground in the FSU. They included the chief social service and welfare agency (JDC), the Israelis (the Jewish Agency and Lishkat Hakesher), the religious movements (Reform, Conservative, Orthodox, and Chabad), and a major independent player (Rabbi Adin Steinsaltz), in addition to numerous specialists in Russian travel.

Once in the field, I was to meet with Vaad members, representatives of the National Conference on Soviet Jewry, the Cummings Foundation, and Wexnerites who were originally from the Soviet Union who had moved to the US.

The trip proved to be an emotional and exhilarating experience and rekindled my long-dormant desire to be a part of this unprecedented Jewish story. Even though I was very active in assisting newly arrived Jews in Israel, being able to impact them in Russia was beyond my wildest dreams, and now I was reentering that world.

The memories of my prior Russian visits decades earlier had become so much a part of my DNA that it was difficult to imagine the changes I might discover on my upcoming journey, but I was excited to find out.

My diary opened with the following entry:

> Moscow, Monday, May 11, 1992
>
> It is an uncanny and even eerie feeling returning to Russia after an absence of nearly eighteen years. So much is familiar: the long wait in customs, the wide boulevards, the Kremlin and Red Square, yet a once critical ingredient is missing: what used to be called "Soviet Power."
>
> Absent were the ubiquitous flags, banners, posters, and signs proclaiming the "Victory of the Proletariat" or "Long Live the Soviet Union," the huge ever-present portraits of Lenin, and the larger-than-life placards exhorting the masses to "Follow the Communist Party of the USSR to Victory."

I saw, however, that it had been replaced by a pervading sense of unease among the entire population. The economy was on the verge of collapse and was to get much worse. Many food items were in short supply and poverty was rampant, especially among the elderly. There was also a widespread sense of cynicism about the West and democracy, which were seen as hovering nearby and eagerly awaiting the dissolution of Russian society. The disintegration of the Soviet system was accompanied by a collapse of morale. The myth that had endured for seventy years, even though it had long ago ceased to be relevant, suddenly vanished, and nothing had appeared to take its place.

There were more ominous signs as well. Local nationalism and antisemitism were on the rise, as was a reinvigorated Russian Orthodox Church. Each of the former Soviet Republics had spun off into its own country, and things were breaking down. The joy and celebration felt in the West were not widely shared in Russia.

Undoubtedly, the pervasive uncertainty propelled many to leave. From 1990 to 1995, 800,000 Soviet Jews and their family members emigrated, 75 percent to Israel, and the rest mostly to the US, Germany, and Canada.[1]

---

1. Based on figures from the Israeli Bureau of Statistics and Petrus Buwalda, *They Did Not Dwell Alone*, 221–24.

However, from a purely Jewish perspective, also gone were the constant fear and anxiety that had been an integral part of Soviet Jewish life, which I had personally witnessed and experienced over the years. *For the first time in generations, Jews were no longer afraid to be Jews in public.* Not all, to be sure, that would take time, but the direction was clear.

I asked Sveta, our Russian neighbor and friend from Ramot, about those days. She said that a huge void had been created. They had been given freedom but didn't know what to do with it. When she had the opportunity to leave, she grabbed it. She added, a bit nostalgically, that she was still very grateful to the Soviet system for providing her with outstanding English-language skills, which she took with her to Israel. She also reported that, with the collapse of the Soviet system, *"Jewishness returned to Soviet Jews."*

I invited Shimon, my long-time friend from Odessa, to accompany me on the trip as my local guide and companion. I did not always feel safe being alone, and it was very good to have someone at my side. During our journey, I introduced him to some very common "Western" experiences that he had never seen before, such as using credit cards, spending US dollars, writing checks, shopping at foreign currency shops, drinking Diet Coke, and eating kosher ice cream at Moscow's new Baskin-Robbins franchise.

Odessa Scenes and Surprises

Odessa was my first stop. I checked in to the Hotel Londonskaya, an aging, classic Soviet-style hotel. It was widely known as "the first hotel in Odessa," and it looked it. Isadora Duncan, Sergei Eisenstein, and many others had stayed there, and now it was my turn. The rooms were cavernous, rather shabby, without TVs, and not particularly inviting. It seemed that after seventy years, the whole country needed refurbishing.

I spent an evening with Shimon, his wife Regina, and their daughters, Irena, thirteen, and Elena, eight. They prepared a special kosher menu: fish, potatoes, salad, and Georgian bread. I recalled with great fondness my previous visit with his family nearly twenty years earlier: being welcomed by his parents, singing Kol Nidre with his grandfather, and sending Regina her wedding dress from America. When we parted then, we never expected to be meeting under such relaxed and familial circumstances, where Israel, aliyah, and the future of Jewish life could be discussed without fear.

We attended a Jewish performance at Migdal-Or, the newly organized JCC in Odessa. Performers included a local Jewish student singing group and a jazz musician from Siberia. I met members of the local Jewish leadership, including Rabbis Shlomo Baksht and Shaya Gisser. Ukrainian and Israeli flags were proudly

displayed on stage in public. As I returned to the hotel, the local Ukrainian chan-
nel on the lobby television was airing a report about the event. What a change! It
was finally acceptable to be Jewish in public.

One of the most powerful experiences of the entire trip took place when we
met with Ludmilla, the director of the Hotel Londonskaya, to discuss the possibility of accommodating the Wexner group there. She reported that the hotel was
soon to be renovated by a Swiss company. They currently had 107 rooms, plus
two deluxe suites that had been used by Armand Hammer, the American-Jewish
businessman known for his close ties to the Soviet Union.

Trying to be as off-the-cuff and casual as possible, I asked her if anybody in
her family was Jewish, to which she replied: "My father!"

Shimon and I leaned forward on the edge of our chairs and listened intently,
as Ludmilla told us her story. During World War II, when Odessa was occupied
by Germany's Romanian allies, Ludmilla's non-Jewish mother had gone to the
city archives and destroyed her daughter's birth records. Ludmilla had hidden her
Jewish identity for years; only her closest friends knew that her father was Jewish,
and now she was sharing it with us. I gave her a booklet in Russian about Israeli
Independence Day and told her of my visit to a Pioneer Camp in Kiev in the
1970s, when Maria, the Jewish nurse, gave us her parting blessing: "God knows
that you and I are one."

In a moment of candor, Ludmilla had shared with us her innermost secret,
her hidden Jewish parentage. Shimon and I left her office literally shaking, overcome by emotion.

MOSCOW RENEWAL AND CONTRASTS

In Moscow, visiting one of the newly established yeshiva high schools, I told the
boys how proud we were of them, and how significant it was for the entire Jewish
world that they were studying Torah here, for if Jewish learning lives in Moscow,
it can flourish anywhere. Imagine, young people learning Torah in the capital of
the former Soviet Union; it was beyond belief!

I stopped by the Choral Synagogue on Arkhipova Street. Signs had been
posted on the outside of the shul in Russian and Hebrew announcing daily services and other events. In Soviet times, the Jewish character of the building had
been deliberately obscured. There was a Hebrew verse above the door, but there
were no Jewish symbols, such as a Magen David or menorah, on display. To the
unsuspecting passerby, it could have been one more office building or city archive.
Now, even the shul was able to proclaim in public that it was a Jewish institution.

Inside, the main sanctuary had been turned into one enormous makeshift
open classroom, with teachers and groups of students spread out all over the huge

space, both downstairs in the men's section and upstairs in the women's gallery. Perhaps eight or ten separate classes were meeting concurrently. The room was filled with a cacophony of voices, ringing with the sounds of Hebrew and Torah. I never dreamt that I would ever see the shul packed with so many Jewish children.

We visited with Swiss-born Rabbi Pinchas Goldschmidt, who had been in Russia since 1989 and would soon be appointed the chief rabbi of Moscow. He was very welcoming and presented me with a newly printed list of all of the Jewish institutions in Moscow: religious, social, welfare, and educational. For a country where all communal life had been repressed and forbidden for generations, it was an amazing declaration of Jewish renewal.

But there were contrasting images as well.

Walking along Old Arbat Street, the mile-long pedestrian shopping mall in the heart of Moscow, local peddlers as well as pensioners, especially World War II veterans, were hawking their personal memorabilia, including army hats, uniforms, medals, and Soviet relics, such as busts of Lenin and Stalin. It was very sad to see a country selling off its past. For foreign tourists and visitors, it was souvenir heaven: imagine, genuine Soviet army medals; but for the locals, not so much.

In a stinging "in your face" contrast, this poignant scene of old people forced to sell their precious mementos to buy food was being played out within sight of the Arbat Irish House. This newly opened luxury shopping center was filled with up-to-date appliance stores and fashionable clothing shops, a fancy bar, and packed with nouveau riche customers.

Life could be very harsh in the "New Russia."

Shabbat at the Mayor's Guest House

Already in 1988, Rabbi Adin Steinsaltz had been granted permission by the Soviet authorities to open an "Institute of Jewish Studies," and he had begun to organize programs all over the USSR.

The home campus of the Institute was located in the Kuntzevo section of Moscow and had formerly served as the mayor's guest house. Shipping containers with kosher supplies and provisions for camps, seminars, shuls, and the like were scattered all over the site.

On Shabbat and holidays, it became a magnet for young Jews, a home away from home, especially for the newly observant on their way to Israel. I had arranged for Shimon and me to spend Shabbat there. Some forty university-age students and adults were also guests for the weekend.

Chaim Aharon Feigenbaum was in charge and supervised the hands-on aspects of the work. He knew all about the latest developments in Jewish life across the FSU and was the main supplier of kosher food in the periphery, where our Wexner groups might visit. One of the goals of the Shabbat was to meet him and see if we might work together in the future.

When we sat down together, by way of introduction, I had brought along photos of our Jerusalem neighborhood Russian absorption project. As we opened the album, he became very animated: "That young man delivering a used refrigerator to new *olim*; he is our son-in-law Dov!" What a small world! We instantly bonded. We were to work together on many projects in the years to come.

Between the kosher meals, the singing, the Jewish spirit, the learning, and the social contacts, it was very easy to forget that the Soviet Union had collapsed only five months earlier and that spending such a Shabbat together in Moscow was unprecedented. Shimon was blown away by the experience. He never imagined that such a Jewish world existed in the former Soviet Union.

One of the other guests was a very knowledgeable local Jew, Leonid Poppel, who proposed to be our guide for an excursion to "Jewish Moscow Today." We eagerly accepted.

It proved to be an eye-opening visit into contemporary Russian Jewish life as well as a glimpse into the potential Jewish Russia of the future.

REIMAGINING POST-SOVIET JEWRY

It was intoxicating visiting Moscow and Kiev in those days; suddenly, all had changed. Jewish life was emerging from the shadows of Soviet rule in previously inconceivable and wondrous ways.

During my earlier trips to the Soviet Union, from 1965 through 1974, I had become well-practiced at identifying "hidden" Jews but I was not prepared for the experience of meeting Jews living openly and freely as Jews.

As our Moscow friend and guide Leonid took us from location to location, I was overwhelmed by the profusion of Jewish initiatives that had blossomed. All were in the very early stages of development and had uncertain prospects, yet they expressed a desire to create a vibrant Jewish future. Truly, Am Yisrael chai, post-Soviet Jewish life had come alive!

Shimon and I went to the Israeli embassy on Bolshaya Ordinka Street. Standing outside was a long line of people waiting for visas, many proudly holding small Israeli flags in public. (See photos.) I showed my Israeli passport to the security guard and was immediately admitted. I recalled that in Soviet times, foreign tourists were permitted to go to the front of the line in Red Square to enter Lenin's Mausoleum, jumping ahead of endless crowds of often sullen and resigned Russians. These days, the mausoleum was almost deserted, while the Israeli embassy was packed.

I met with a member of the Israeli diplomatic staff. He told me that if our prospective Wexner group really wanted to experience current Jewish life, we should not limit ourselves to Moscow, Leningrad, and Kiev, but needed to visit the Jews in the periphery, outside of the capitals. There we would meet "real" Soviet Jews. I did not know it at the time, but when I would be working for the JDC in Russia during the next fifteen years, the periphery was precisely where I would be going, from Murmansk and Arkhangelsk in the far north, to Tyumen and Tomsk in Siberia, to Brest in Belarus, and more than fifty cities and towns in between.

To contextualize our visit, Leonid took us on a drive-by of Soviet Jewish historical sites, many with a very dark and checkered history: the former offices of the Jewish Anti-Fascist Committee, Stalin's willing "front men" during WWII until they were purged by the system they so admired; the Soviet Yiddish Theater headed by Solomon Mikhoels, before he was murdered on Stalin's orders; the homes of Jewish physicians unjustly accused in the so-called 1953 "Doctors' Plot," the former embassy of Israel, which had been turned over to the PLO.

At the synagogue on Bolshaya Bronnaya Street, we met Rabbi Yitzchak Kogen, a legendary figure of the underground Chabad movement, originally from Leningrad. After many years as a refusenik, he made aliyah in 1989, and a year later, was sent back to Moscow by the Lubavitcher Rebbe.

We were greeted by the scene of a half-a-dozen men and boys seated on couches, all expectantly, as well as a bit anxiously, waiting to be circumcised. Strongly discouraged, condemned, and even outlawed by the Soviets, it currently seemed to be all the rage for local Jews, as well as for those who were planning aliyah and did not want to "stand out" during their army service. Following the procedure itself, which took place in the rabbi's office, the men got dressed, rested a bit, drank a l'chayim, had something to eat, and went on their way.

Rabbi Kogen invited me to participate in the ceremony by giving Jewish names to two of the newly circumcised men. Getting into the spirit of the event, I asked him at the mitzvah meal that followed: "When should we dance – now or later?" to which he responded, "Tamid!" (Always!). Rebbetzin Leah and their eleven-year-old son joined in.

Proceeding to Cantor Alexander Pliss's Jewish Art School, we exchanged some of the Israeli flags we had brought for their posters. We visited the Sunday school sponsored by Midreshet Yerushalayim of the Masorti (Conservative) movement in Israel, with classes in Hebrew, Jewish history, and art, and passed by a local movie house advertising a Jewish Film Festival.

Lev Gorodetzky, head of the emerging local Zionist organization and founder of Banim Banot (Boys and Girls), hosted us at his apartment facility. He was running Sunday schools, camps, and educational programs. They were planning a meeting of the country-wide Russian Zionist Congress in June.

Alexander Filzer's modest and jam-packed one-room studio was filled from floor to ceiling with depictions of Russian Jewish life. Grandly titled the Museum of Modern Jewish Art, it housed an outstanding exhibition of mounted photographs of Jewish life in Moscow and across Russia as well as a collection of his own paintings and works of art. I thought we should certainly invite him to display them for the Wexner group.

The following morning, we continued with a visit to the National Jewish School in Moscow, with two hundred children in first through tenth grade. Gregory Lipman, the director, took me around and introduced me to the older classes. There was a wonderful Jewish learning environment and spirit in the school. Over the following years "Lipman's School" as it was known, became one of the mainstays of Moscow Jewish education.

From there we stopped at the Migdal Or Yeshiva High School, officially Moscow Jewish Middle School #1313, with excellent science, physics, and chemistry instruction, a fine English language laboratory, plus Russian language and Jewish studies. As they davened, the boys swayed back and forth as if they had been enrolled in yeshivot their entire lives, although the school had only opened only a few months earlier.

Our final stop in Moscow was a visit to Col. Uri Sokol, the head of the Moscow Jewish Cultural-Educational Society, whose apartment housed the first independent Jewish library in the city, founded by the former Prisoner of Zion and activist, Yosef Begun in 1987. The society hosted lectures, particularly about the participation of Jews in the Soviet army as well as Jewish holidays and celebrations. Uri and his wife Leiba were charming and elegant hosts. In parting, I presented a book I had brought with me and signed it: "To Uri Sokol – Colonel in the Red Army; General in the Jewish Army." (See photos.)

Was this to be the Jewish future in Moscow in the coming years? Although not all of these pioneering programs would survive, Jewish life, especially in the larger cities, would grow in previously unimaginable directions. Over time, international as well as local partners would make major investments in Jewish infrastructure that would have unprecedented and previously unimaginable effects. Even at this point, at the initial stage of creating a public face for post-Soviet Jewry only five months after the fall of the USSR, it was extraordinarily impressive.

Certainly, based on what I had known and experienced from my prior visits a generation ago, it was exhilarating, a veritable "Jewish Disneyland."

WALKING THE OLD JEWISH NEIGHBORHOOD OF KIEV

Kiev was no less exciting. The city had retained its intimacy and tangible Jewish flavor, albeit muted, under the Soviets. During my previous visits in the early 1970s, as well as today, you could hear Yiddish in the streets – particularly in the Podol neighborhood surrounding the shul – and were ever aware of the overpowering unspoken presence of Babi Yar.

Shimon introduced me to his friend Vita, a sparkling twenty-five-year-old Jewish young woman, absolutely fluent in Hebrew, who gave us a Jewish walking tour of Kiev. We were amazed to see Hebrew billboards displayed on the city's main Khreschatyk Boulevard advertising Migdal, the Israeli insurance company, as well as Jewish Agency placards, announcing direct flights from Kiev to Tel Aviv. Imagine…seeing Hebrew signs on the streets of the capital of a former Soviet republic!

We made our way to Podol, where a kosher canteen had recently opened. Although the menu was very modest, offering kasha and a piece of salami, to be able to order kosher food was a whole new world.

We met the director of the Jewish school, Rabbi Shaul Averbach, a warm and wonderful Jew from Jerusalem. He was particularly impressed by Vita's Hebrew. He spent hours speaking to her and offered her a position as a teacher and as his translator. It took an American-Israeli visitor with his friend from Odessa, to introduce a local Hebrew-speaking young woman to the Israeli head of the Jewish school! Obviously, that was why we were supposed to be here.

During Soviet times, the Kiev Synagogue on Shchekavytska Street was notorious for its tight supervision and inhospitality towards visitors, which I had personally experienced on many occasions. Now, the entire shul sanctuary was filled with hundreds of students from the boys' yeshiva praying together out loud and moving their bodies back and forth. The scene was overpowering.

We moved on to Ukrainian State Jewish School #299 – the girls' yeshiva. What a pleasure! I went from class to class telling stories of what it was like to be Jewish "in the old days," contrasting it with the flowering of Jewish life today.

I told the first-graders about Simchat Torah in Moscow twenty-five years ago, and the young lady I met who did not recognize the word *shalom*. I asked the children if they knew what the word meant, and they gleefully called out the translation.

In second grade, I spoke about my own five school-age children in Jerusalem. Esther, the local principal, knew Yiddish as well as Soviet Jewish history. She noted that the last state-run Soviet Jewish school in Kiev was closed down in 1938, and here we were, over fifty years later, learning once again.

I joked with the fifth-grade girls' class. We were approaching the festival of Lag b'Omer, associated with the battles of Rabbi Akiva and the Romans. I asked: "Did you know that Rabbi Akiva was a Ukrainian Jew? His name was: 'Rabbi A-Kiev-a!'" We laughed and laughed. "*Kharasho*, Yonatan, *kharasho*" (That's a good one, Yonatan)!

I posed the following question to them. "Last year you were studying in a Ukrainian state school; now you are in a Jewish school. Which do you like better?"

"*Zdes*" (Here), they called out.

"Why?"

"*Me fse yevrei*" (We are all Jews).

That phrase encapsulated for me the essence of my visit. For the first time in generations, they could gather together as proud Jews. I quoted the girls' precious words as the title for this book.

Klara Vincour, a Shoah survivor from Ukraine and a member of the Babi Yar Society, took a group of us to the newly created Jewish "Menorah" memorial at the actual Babi Yar killing site. She distributed pictures of some of the children murdered there. The "official" Soviet memorial remembered "all of the Soviet citizens," with no mention of the Jews.

On my visit to the Jewish community offices, I met David Ayzenberg, the only remaining male survivor of Babi Yar. He showed me dozens of long narrow library file drawers, containing the names of previously identified victims of Babi Yar. Even today, the identities of most of the martyrs are unknown. It was obvious to us both that the drawers would never suffice to hold all the more than a hundred thousand names.

I went roaming around the building, noting the names of the Jewish organizations on the doors, knocking, and introducing myself. One room, in particular, the office of The Union of Jewish Students, was bustling. Half-a-dozen *chevre* (members of a close-knit group) were meeting and planning activities. Organizations like this would eventually develop into Hillels, JAFI clubs, and other student programs all over the former Soviet Union.

TIME TO GO HOME

A serendipitous experience greeted me at the Moscow airport as I awaited the 3:00 a.m. return flight to Tel Aviv. New immigrant families began to enter the international waiting area, from Georgia, Ukraine, and other places across the former USSR. They looked tired, disoriented, anxious and a bit withdrawn. There were grandparents with canes and their little grandchildren; a couple with three sons; a mother, daughter, and granddaughter traveling together; two young men in their upper teens. (See photos.)

I introduced myself all around and welcomed them warmly and emotionally. They were surprised and pleased at being greeted en route on their way to their new home. There was an airport Baskin-Robbins stand selling kosher ice cream still open at 2:00 a.m. and I invited them to "be my guests" for a special pre-flight treat, in honor of their making aliyah.

When we disembarked a few hours later at Ben Gurion Airport, I approached each of them and wished them all the best. "May God bless your journey."

I was moved by the sacredness of the moment and by the privilege of accompanying these former Soviet Jews on their way home to Israel. All who worked with the Jews of Russia felt it.

I concluded with the following entry in my diary: "They are ready to leave all that is familiar to them and everything they grew up with, for a hope and a dream. What a great honor it was for me to have been sent to meet Russian Jews. I must return to see and learn even more."

Ultimately, the Wexner Foundation decided not to send the trip to Russia, but for me personally, it was a transformative experience on multiple levels: I was present in the former Soviet Union at a time of historic change and participated, however vicariously, in the beginnings of future post-Soviet Jewish life. I also reestablished my professional contacts with the Jewish organizational world. That, in turn, led to the next great journey and mission of my life, working for the JDC's Russian Department for fifteen creative, exciting, and challenging years.

CHAPTER 18

Joining the JDC
Russian Department

A New Role

In August 1993, Asher Ostrin, the Jerusalem-based director of the American Jewish Joint Distribution Committee's Russian Department, invited me to join the Soviet Union Team. I eagerly accepted.

During my prior visits to Russia, I had gone either as a private tourist or as the leader of a high school group. I was one of Elie Wiesel's proverbial witnesses and messengers. I initiated contacts with whomever I could identify as a Jew, distributed Jewish items, and sought to raise their spirits and sense of connection to the Jewish people. The interactions were often unpredictable and by chance.

Now, I would be representing a major international Jewish organization and, with my colleagues, would be able to initiate systemic programs and projects in the field across the former Soviet Union. We could reach out to every Jew, especially the needy and the elderly, and reconnect them to the Jewish people. All of this was previously unimaginable.

The JDC was the "gold standard" of the Jewish organizational world. "The Joint," as it is commonly called, was one of the most well-established, highly respected, and world-class Jewish organizations in existence. Founded in 1914, it had a past, present, and future, a rich history, a sterling reputation, deep community support, budgets, and a Jewish vision for itself and the future. The JDC took its mission very seriously, and the staff understood that we were working in the service of the Jewish people worldwide.

Ralph and Stanley and the JDC Ethos

Among the extraordinary strengths of the Joint was the longevity and continuity of its professional leadership. Two figures from my time especially stand out: Ralph Goldman and Stanley Abramovitch. You can read their stories in their own words (*I Seek My Brethren: Ralph Goldman and "The Joint,"* by Tom Shachtman,

Newmarket Press, 2001; *From Survival to Revival: A Memoir of Six Decades in a Changing Jewish World* by Stanley Abramovitch, Gefen Publishing House, 2008).

Ralph and Stanley were the most gracious of gentlemen, ever open and accessible, especially to younger colleagues like myself. When I began working at the Joint, I was forty-eight-years old, and they were from my parents' generation; Ralph was born in 1914, Stanley in 1920. Although both were thoroughly "Americanized," they came from the Old Country, Ralph from Tsarist Russia (today's Belarus) and Stanley from Poland. Each, in his own style, exuded a deep sense of intrinsic Jewishness and love for the Jewish people. They were also outstanding mentors, wellsprings of knowledge and wisdom, which they were always willing and happy to share.

Part of my organizational orientation was learning that my predecessors at the Joint included legendary World War II figures and genuine Jewish heroes, such as Joe Schwartz (1899–1975), director of JDC's wartime European operations; Gisi Fleischmann (1892–1944) in Slovakia; and Saly Mayer (1882–1950) in Switzerland. In times of crisis, I would ask myself how my predecessors would have handled this situation. I recall specifically being inspired by the example of Laura Margolis (1903–1997), who, against all odds, cared for Jewish refugees as the JDC Representative in Shanghai during WWII. When there were Jews in need, it was our job to do whatever we could to help them.

In August 1998, when I was serving as JDC country director for Belarus, there was an economic crisis in Russia. In one month, the ruble lost two-thirds of its value, inflation rocketed to over 80 percent, and many banks closed. We received reports that the JDC Hesed Community Welfare Centers in Minsk and throughout the country were out of cash and were about to shut their doors.

I imagined an elderly Jewish woman coming to the JDC's soup kitchen at the Dauman Street Synagogue in Minsk for her daily hot meal, only to be told that there was a banking crisis and that the facility was closed. Her response would be, "But I'm hungry." That was unacceptable to me. It was unconscionable that we would not do everything in our power to ensure that needy Jews were properly cared for.

Since I was the only one in the JDC Jerusalem office with a valid visa to Belarus, I told our financial department that I wanted to fly to Minsk the following day, carrying $40,000 in cash on my person, which I would declare legally at customs, to keep the local Hesed solvent. The office gave me the money, I delivered it the next day, and our local programs continued uninterrupted.

The JDC culture was very strong. There were institutional values that had to be learned and internalized. Ralph continually reminded and challenged the staff with the words from the Bible (Exodus 2:14) "*Mi samcha?*" (Who appointed you [to tell us what to do]?). Empowering the locals was a core principle, which often distinguished us from other groups operating in the field. Imagine citing the story of Moses to demonstrate how we should act, representing the Joint, over three millennia later.

THE JDC'S UPDATED MISSION IN RUSSIA

The Joint had a rich and complex history of working in the Soviet Union, from disaster and humanitarian relief in the wake of the Russian Civil War through setting up the Agro-Joint in 1924 (until the program was terminated by the Soviets in 1937).

It was also a favorite target and scapegoat of the Kremlin, most notoriously in the infamous 1953 "Doctors' Plot," which accused a group largely of Jewish doctors of attempting to murder members of the Soviet hierarchy. The doctors were arrested and imprisoned, and many were tortured. The front pages of the official Community Party newspaper *Pravda* spewed with righteous indignation about the identity of the culprits:

> Whom did these monsters [the Jewish doctors] serve? The terrorist group of doctors was enlisted by a branch of the American intelligence service – the international Jewish bourgeois nationalist organization "Joint." The dirty face of this Zionist espionage organization concealing its foul work under a mask of charity has been completely exposed. Now all can see what charitable friends of peace hide under the "Joint" letterhead.[1]

It was only Stalin's death a few months later that saved the Jews of the Soviet Union from disaster.

In 1988, fifty years after the JDC was expelled from the Soviet Union, Ralph negotiated with the Soviet authorities for its official reentry. Following several visits to Moscow and extensive meetings and negotiations with Konstantin Kharchev, chairman of the Council of Religious Affairs of the USSR, the Soviets proposed that the JDC return to the Soviet Union to reestablish the Agro-Joint in the form of Jewish farms to produce kosher meat and kosher wine. Politely but firmly, Ralph refused the offer. *This time the Joint had come for a different purpose: to Judaize the Jews.*

Minister Kharchev ultimately agreed to an entire package, including the establishment of kosher restaurants, meal-on-wheels programs for the elderly,

---

1.   *Pravda*, January 13, 1953, 1.

the importation of books on Jewish history as well as the teaching of Hebrew, the establishment of a Jewish choir, and public Jewish concerts.

The JDC's new mission was: "*To return the Jews of the Soviet Union to the Jewish people.*" To implement this grand vision, they established the Soviet Union Team, which Asher had invited me to join.

Working for the Joint in the FSU, especially in those early years immediately following the dissolution of the Soviet Union, was a great honor and opportunity, and presented enormous challenges as well. After more than twenty-five years of involvement with Soviet Jews – as a student, tourist, guide, author, educator, public advocate, and activist in Israeli absorption – I would now share, together with colleagues, in the task of helping to rebuild and recreate Jewish life in the former Soviet Union.

We were confronted, in the prescient words of my friend and colleague at the Joint, Seymour "Epi" Epstein, with two critical needs: "hunger and thirst." There were pressing, often desperate, physical needs – the "hunger" – and no less, a "thirst" for Jewish spiritual connections.

Masses of the elderly were impoverished, the local economic and social safety nets had collapsed, unemployed adults could barely take care of themselves not to speak of their aging parents, all against the background of mass aliyah and emigration. Who would be left to care for those remaining? And who had the resources or vision to plan for the middle generation, not to speak of the children? There were barely any schools and virtually no trained teachers. It all seemed, on the face of it, overwhelming.

No less important, how actively and enthusiastically did the Jews remaining in the FSU want to rejoin the Jewish people? Had the negative self-image of Soviet Jews, which was constantly reinforced by the "fifth line" in their internal passports, eradicated any hopes for creating a new Jewish reality at this moment in Jewish history? Would my colleagues and I, even with all of our best efforts and well-meaning intentions, succeed in making that so-called "Jewish revival" come about? Were our hopes and expectations real or illusory?

I vividly recall sitting in a taxi en route from the airport to my hotel in August 1993, in the middle of the Moscow rush hour, on my first trip back to Russia for the Joint. The city was so busy and lit up, obviously occupied with itself and its newfound freedoms and opportunities. How in God's name could I possibly hope to make a difference or have an impact on what was going on? The country was so vast, the history so deeply rooted, the mission was so great.

I was challenged as well as heartened by Rabbi Tarfon's words in *Pirkei Avot*: "The day is short, the assignment is overwhelming, the workers are barely up to

the task; despite that, the reward is great, and the Master of the House is insistent"
(Ethics of the Fathers 2:20).

And so I embarked on the first of my 165 trips to the former Soviet Union on
behalf of the Joint.

HEARTFELT EXPRESSIONS OF JEWISH RETURN

Wherever I traveled in post-Soviet Russia, I met Jews who were eager to rejoin
and identify with the Jewish people. The Jewish yearnings I had seen on my 1992
visit immediately following the collapse of the Soviet Union were real and deep,
and widely felt by Soviet Jews. I encountered them in the most unexpected settings, including in movie theaters and the middle of the Siberian winter.

It was May 1994 and I was sitting with great anticipation in a Moscow cin-
ema, waiting for the picture to begin. It was to be the unforgettable premiere of
a film the likes of which no one in the audience, myself included, had ever seen
before.

It was one of the first screenings of *Schindler's List* in Russia.

The audience, largely Jewish by their responses, sat transfixed. They saw
images most of them had only heard about or perhaps recalled from before
World War II, if at all.

The opening of the movie depicted a Jewish mother lighting Shabbat candles
and her husband making Kiddush over wine; hearing the word *yevrei* used over and
over again – by the Jews as a term of familiarity and community and by the Germans
as one of derision; the Red Army soldier arriving on horseback at the gates of their
labor camp in Czechoslovakia and telling them they are free, and when they ask him
"Where should we go?" responds, "Don't go east – they don't want you there!" as all
of us in the theater were sitting "there – back east." Those scenes were electrifying.

I will never forget the closing panorama when the black and white of the film
was transformed into glorious color as the "Schindler Jews" and their children
and grandchildren gathered at his grave at the Mount Zion Christian Cemetery
in Jerusalem. As the sounds of "Yerushalayim shel Zahav" filled the theater, the
audience began to sway to the music and hum along. The movie ended. There
was total silence. And then…a thundering explosion of applause and an outpouring of tears.

Everyone in the theater felt totally drained and emotionally exhausted. We
didn't merely see a movie; we saw ourselves. Jewish history, the Jewish people, the
Holocaust, and Israel were portrayed in a manner that Soviet Jews had not been
permitted to experience in generations.

As soon as I got back to my hotel room, I called Asher in Jerusalem and told
him what I had just seen. The movie was to open in twenty theaters across the

Russian Federation on June 22, the anniversary of the start of the German-Soviet War in 1941. I urged us to acquire distribution rights, provide free tickets, and prepare a Russian dubbing (the movie was subtitled), in order to show the film to as many Jews as possible.

The emotional evening echoed a similar event that had taken place in Kiev in 1945, right after the end of the War, at a performance of the Ukrainian State Jewish Theater:

> The theater, stalls and gallery, were full to overflowing…the audience: writers and poets, doctors and painters, workers and artists, people of many professions; the space was hushed. A black curtain was raised and in glowing white letters were the words in Hebrew: "The People of Israel live" [*Am Yisrael chai!*].
>
> Suddenly, the audience rose as one to its feet, the thunder of applause shook the theater building. With the applause rising like an electric current passing through the audience came the cry: "The People of Israel live" [*Am Yisrael chai!*]. The applause is unceasing, people choked back sobs, women weep, and men's eyes well up with tears.[2]

Even in those times, notwithstanding their loyalty to the regime, there were many Soviet Jews who had never severed their deep connections with the Jewish people; emotions were suppressed but never forgotten. Now as well, with the dissolution of the Soviet Union, the time had arrived when they could openly express in public the innermost feelings of their hearts. If I had harbored any doubts or reservations before, they were being dispelled. *Soviet Jews wanted to return to the Jewish people.*

STUDENTS OF ALL AGES

It was early September 1993, and I was sitting at the dais of the festive opening of the Touro College Moscow program. I was initially skeptical as to the appeal of an Orthodox-sponsored American college program in the post-Soviet reality and was therefore both astonished and impressed at the scene in front of me. Over four hundred Russian Jews were eagerly sitting in the audience preparing to start classes, including many in Jewish studies. The bulk of the students were of adult age, with a solid core in their late teenage years and early twenties. They were serious, enthusiastic, motivated, and were clearly looking forward to the

---

2.   Altshuler, *Religion and Jewish Identity in the Soviet Union*, 52. Excerpts reprinted with permission.

experience. They had come out on a rainy and dreary Moscow afternoon to the distant Touro campus.

Speakers included representatives of the Russian Ministry of Education, the Jewish Agency, and the Israeli ambassador, Chaim Bar-Lev, who spoke with great emotion about Israel as the only place where a Jew can be 100 percent Jewish.

This was my first time appearing publicly in my "official" capacity, as a representative of the JDC. I began to understand how we were perceived by the local Jews as well as by the other players operating in the field. I was no longer just "Jonathan Porath from Jerusalem," but rather I was speaking on behalf of the American Jewish Joint Distribution Committee, the arm of the American Jewish community tasked with responding to Jewish needs around the world. In their eyes, I was "Mr. Joint."

I spoke about my visit the previous year to the newly opened Jewish girls schools in Kiev, which I have often recounted here. When I had asked the children why they liked being in a Jewish school, they responded enthusiastically: "Because here we are all Jews."

A tremor went through the Touro College crowd as I related the story. They began to applaud and cheer. Clearly the story had touched something very deep within them. They, too, were eager to be with fellow Jews, to learn where they came from and where they were going.

Similar scenes were reenacted all over the former Soviet Union, even in the most far-flung locations.

IN THE HEART OF THE SIBERIAN WINTER

I landed in Tyumen, Russia, one thousand miles east of Moscow, in December 1995, and exited from the overheated plane into the frigid Siberian winter. It was twenty-five degrees below zero Fahrenheit. What would bring me to such a place at this time of the year? It was the annual "Chanukah in Siberia Festival," whose oversized placards were posted all over town. (See photos.)

Word about the festival, now in its fourth year, had reached the West and Israel, but it remained a mystery: Why was such an event taking place in such a remote location? The city of half a million was not known for its Jewish connections.

Our heroes were two local Jewish boys, Ilya Pestrikov and Pasha Feldbloom, both twenty-five-year-old pre-med students at the Tyumen Medical University.

Ilya's story was as follows.

My mother was born in Belarus in 1935 and was the eldest of three children. When the Nazis invaded in 1941, her parents took the children in search of a safe place and moved to their close relatives in a nearby shtetl, where they immediately found themselves trapped in a newly established ghetto. In 1942, many Jews succeeded in escaping to the forests and spent a few months near a Soviet partisan unit.

In September–October 1942, the Nazis bombed the forests from the air and soldiers began shooting those who remained alive. Of her entire family, only my mother survived that massacre. She was a seven-year-old little girl who was completely alone. She was found alive the next morning by partisans, who cared for her until the end of the war.

After liberation in 1944, she lived in an orphanage, attended school, and continued her studies in the State Railroad Technical College in Belarus. Upon graduation, in 1955, she was assigned to work in a railroad unit in the Urals. She met a local Russian young man, they married; after a few years together without having children, he tragically drowned. Now a lonely widow, she moved from the Urals to Tyumen in Western Siberia, where she continued working on the railroad and studied in the local university. There she met my Jewish father, also a Shoah survivor, and I was born in 1970.

I didn't know anything about Judaism before the 1990s. I only saw a piece of matzah for the first time when I was a teenager. However, one childhood memory stood out. Since I was a young boy, I remembered my mother telling me every year on May 9, Victory Day, at the time of the "Memorial Minute of Silence" for all the victims of WWII, that this was very important for us, since our entire family had been murdered by the Nazis.

Growing up, I encountered occasional expressions of antisemitism when some adults or children despairingly called me a Jew. When I entered the Medical Institute in 1987, I met more Jewish students, some of whom had family members in Israel, and began becoming connected to the Jewish world. In 1991, Pasha and I, along with a few others, organized a Jewish Culture Society in Tyumen.

With the collapse of the Soviet Union in December 1991, we became active participants in the All-Russian Jewish Vaad, the umbrella organization for local communities. In 1992, the March of the Living reserved places for younger participants from the FSU (I was twenty-two at the time), and I was invited to attend. It was my first exposure to such an international gathering of five thousand young Jews from all over the world.

For me, the tipping point came with our visits to the Nazi death camps in Poland. I realized that, despite the suffering and losses to the Jewish people and my own family, I was standing on the doorstep of an incredibly great Jewish world, civilization, and heritage. The following ten days in Israel only further strengthened that understanding.

Ilya returned home, began to learn more about Judaism, and became one of the founders and heads of the local Reform community. He even acted in various rabbinic roles, such as officiating at funerals and other life-cycle events. He was among the first wave of post-Soviet local Jewish young leadership.

Ilya and his friend Pasha had an idea. "Winter Festivals" were a familiar feature of Soviet life, so they decided to organize one of their own in Tyumen, which they called "Chanukah in Siberia." It became a very popular citywide event and attracted attention in Russia, Israel, and the West.

I also went to Tyumen with something else in the back of my mind. At one of our senior staff meetings in Jerusalem, Asher raised the possibility of identifying local Jews to direct the offices of the Joint in Russia. Up until then, all of the JDC field representatives were foreigners, usually Jews from the former Soviet Union who made aliyah years earlier and had returned to Russia on behalf of the Joint. I volunteered to try to locate a community member to work for us. I had never met Ilya or Pasha, but if they could organize a Chanukah Festival in the heart of Siberia, who knows where it might lead?

As I entered Tyumen's main municipal concert hall the evening of the Chanukah Festival, I was overwhelmed to see more than a thousand people in attendance. There were more Russian than Jewish faces, to be sure, but there were Jews there as well. The performance itself was a mixed bag, with some acts resembling amateur participants from a Simon Cowell version of *Siberia's Got Talent*, and a fashion show by one of the local sponsors.

Others were premier Soviet Jewish performers. One sang ghetto songs, another gave a wonderful portrayal of a Jewish grandmother, and a third included Yiddish and Hebrew favorites (more about him later). Missing were the outward Jewish signs of such events, so familiar to us in the West. There were no Jewish symbols on stage, no greetings from the local synagogue (the only one in town was in ruins) or the rabbi (they didn't have one), and no lighting of Chanukah candles.

However, there was no mistaking the Jewish character of the evening. It was clearly in honor of "Chanukah," whatever that was, and the audience was participating in a Jewish celebration.

I learned that, earlier in the week, the local Jewish community did have some holiday events, including a party for the Jewish children in town, and unsold festival tickets had been distributed for free to local elderly Jews.

From my vantage point, the highlight of the evening, the real "happening," was yet to come. At 10:00 p.m., following the public event, the leading Russian Jewish cultural figures, including singers, playwrights, television stars, musical artists, and critics, who had come to Tyumen for the festival, gathered at the local hotel, the five-star Tyumen Quality Inn, for a banquet, organized by Ilya and Pasha, our hosts. The Russians love to party, and they are very good at it!

A Soviet Jewish super-star performer was also in attendance, Yosef Kobzon. Not being familiar with him, I asked one of my staff how famous Kobzon was, and he replied that he was called "the Frank Sinatra of Russia." Yosef Davidovich Kobzon came from a Jewish family in Ukraine and was one of the most popular singers in the USSR. He had also been involved in a "Jewish" diplomatic incident in the mid-1980s when he was expelled from the Communist Party on the charge of "political short-sightedness," for daring to sing Jewish songs during an international friendship concert, which had resulted in the Arab delegations leaving in protest, but he was restored to the Party the following year.

Ilya called on me to speak. I figured that was my chance, so I invited the guests to join me in the lighting of the Chanukah candles that I had brought with me from Jerusalem. The flickering lights and the sounds of "Maoz Tzur" evoked from the participants a torrent of Jewish stories, reminiscences, toasts, and public confessions. There was something about the event that had touched their Jewish souls. The post-show party had been transformed into a genuine "Chanukah in Siberia" Jewish happening. Although the story of the Maccabees and the miracle of the oil was unfamiliar to most of them, we were sharing a profoundly "Jewish moment."

The evening continued in a festive mood, with musical games, such as singing Soviet sacred songs to mismatched tunes, like a children's holiday song to the tune of the Soviet anthem, akin to singing "I Had a Little Dreidel" to the Star-Spangled Banner. I was among the first to depart at 1:30 a.m., while one of our loyal staff, Leonid, brought up the rear, well into the early morning hours. A great Chanukah evening was had by all.

I subsequently met with Ilya and offered him the position of coordinator for the local JDC Urals office, which he accepted. Following a training program in Russia and Israel, he was appointed the first local Jewish representative of the JDC. He served with distinction for many years and was a source of great community pride.

NEW JEWISH LIFE IN THE RUSSIAN HEARTLAND

Among the earliest JDC-sponsored educational programs was the Public University of Jewish Culture of Central Russia and the Volga, which offered lectures on a variety of Jewish topics. The program was directed by an outstanding organizer and educator, Dr. Semyon Avgusteivich from Samara, Russia.

This was an especially ambitious undertaking, since none of the lecturers had any formal Jewish educational background, save perhaps for a few from the Baltics who had been evacuated to the Russian interior more than half a century previously.

Semyon invited me to participate and I prepared some talks, including: "The Life and Death of Rabbi Akiva: A Hero for Our Time" and "Faithfulness to the Principles of Jewish Life: Rabbinic Responsa from the Kovno Ghetto." They were subsequently published in Russian by the Association of People's Universities of Jewish Culture, with the support of the Joint.

Semyon and I would go out on the road, and I would speak in different Jewish communities in the Russian heartland, including Samara, Saratov, Penza, and others.

I received some very insightful, as well as humbling, feedback to my first presentation, on the topic "Shabbat in the Jewish Home." Inspired by the children's play set "Shabbat in a Sack," I brought with me a bag filled with Shabbat paraphernalia, such as Shabbat candles, candlesticks, a Kiddush cup, a cover for challot (Shabbat loaves), and a Havdalah set, and showed the audience how we use them. I also carried with me Shabbat candlesticks for distribution to interested attendees.

Here is how Semyon described that 1995 presentation:

> Rabbi Jonathan Porath's topic "Shabbat in the Jewish Home" is not new. What was new was the lecturer's approach to the subject. He did not instruct the listeners how they should observe Shabbat; he did not recite slogans. He just lived Shabbat, infecting the listeners with the joy of ending a week of work and anticipating the joyful day. It was not even a lecture, but more exactly, an improvised performance, with plenty of commentary.
>
> He reflected the Jewish national way of life. Elderly participants remembered anew the warmth of their childhood when the Shabbat reigned in many Jewish families. Those with no such recollections of the past were glad to meet the Shabbat, together with a speaker of outstanding personality.
>
> The audience was carried away by the presentation, where everyone became both a spectator and a participant in the Shabbat feast, which went by so quickly during the hour-and-a-half meeting.

After the talk, the listeners were slow to leave. Many of them approached Rabbi Porath to thank him and to share the thoughts and feelings which he had aroused.

I was present at all of those lectures, and I saw the audience as well as myself burn with the joy of reviving our traditions.

Most interesting to me was Semyon's analysis of what had occurred in Soviet times, taking the Shabbat as an example of what the Jews had lost, and what the implications were for the future:

> There were many reasons which prevented Jews from observing the Shabbat in Soviet times: the obliteration of our national traditions, the deeply rooted habit of being ashamed of ourselves and our nationality, and, as a result, of our national culture.
>
> But it seems to me, that the main reason remains our *spiritual orphanhood*. It was created when we stopped believing in the idols called "Soviet culture," and rejected them, some with joy and others with pain, and acquired no new guidelines to replace the old ones.
>
> And this absence of confident and reliable leadership, which combines intellectuality, spirituality, and a strong sense of Jewish identity, produces passivity. There will be a Jewish revival today only in those communities which have such leaders.
>
> That was why the lecturer impressed the listeners so much. They saw in him a model of the kind of person who exemplifies the future renewal of Jewish life. It is good that Rabbi Porath spoke in those clubs, where a new generation of Jewish intellectuals is growing up, which will produce new leaders.

The path to "returning the Jews to the Jewish people" was not going to be an easy one. Providing exciting lecturers, showing evocative and powerful films, holding public festivals, publishing numerous books, even reopening or reinvigorating long-closed synagogues and Jewish schools and providing trips to Israel would not suffice. The changes had to be internal as well, in the minds and perceptions of Soviet Jews, and that would take much more thought and effort, and became the basis for my opening assignment at the JDC.

CHAPTER 19

Academic Jewish Studies: SEFER

OVERCOMING THE LEGACIES OF THE SOVIET PAST

In the wake of the Bolshevik Revolution, and particularly since Stalin's time, religion in general, especially Judaism and all things Jewish, were ridiculed, distorted, or suppressed. These attitudes had permeated deeply into the Soviet Jewish psyche. Dr. Victoria Mochalova, who was to become the future director of the JDC's academic initiative SEFER, explained:

> Being Jewish was shameful for so many years; a negative identity – a secret illness. We were forbidden to speak about it, we were treated like criminals. It was politically incorrect to mention our national niche.[1]

They were indeed "spiritual orphans," in Semyon Avgusteivich's apt phrase.

To address and overcome this, Ralph Goldman believed strongly that utilizing the influence and prestige of local academics and intellectuals, both Jews and non-Jews, would be key to transforming how post-Soviet Jews saw themselves. Academics and intellectuals counted in Russian and Soviet life. Echoing the impact of major figures such as Tolstoy from years gone by, a man of Nobel Peace Prize laureate Andrei Sakharov's stature could influence and change Soviet society, even when operating at variance with the official rhetoric and pronouncements. Intellectuals set the tone for civic standards and values.

Helping to develop a cadre of serious academics and thinkers who could advocate for the legitimacy, validity, and value of Jewish studies as an important part of world culture would be a critical component. It would help to shape a positive Jewish self-image and provide outreach to Jewish intellectuals who had been distanced, drawing them into the community, expanding the pool of local leadership, and exposing students to Jewish role models in addition to connecting them to the Israeli academic community. An indispensable step in making that happen would be in revitalizing, or rather, creating from scratch, the entire

---

1. Tom Shachtman, *I Seek My Brethren: Ralph Goldman and "The Joint"* (New York: Newmarket Press, 2001), 236. Quoted with permission.

field of academic Judaica in the post-Soviet Union, the study of Jewish subjects on the highest levels of scholarship by both Jewish and non-Jewish researchers.

That became my first task at the JDC. An entire worldview had to be transformed.

Jewish studies had been proscribed in the Soviet Union, branded as cosmopolitan and Zionist. Only one major academic institution offered such subjects, the Moscow State University, known by its Russian initials "EmGeU." It was considered to be the Soviet academic equivalent of Harvard or Oxford but was totally subject to the control of the ruling Communist Party. The courses offered, including Hebrew language and Middle-Eastern/Israel studies, were designed primarily for the needs of the KBG and the foreign service and were effectively closed to Jews.

EARLY EFFORTS AND THE KREKSHINO CONFERENCE

Since 1990, Professor Moshe Davis of Hebrew University's International Center for University Teaching of Jewish Civilization had sponsored a series of academic workshops in Jerusalem for scholars from the Soviet Union, with the support of Ralph and the JDC. It was a pioneering effort to create a nucleus of academicians in the field of Jewish studies. Participants, Jewish and non-Jewish alike, came from "crossover" fields, such as history and sociology. The Jewish aspects of their subjects would be presented and supplemented by Hebrew University faculty.

In addition, around the time of the fall of the Soviet Union, a few pioneering programs had been founded, such as the Jewish Universities of Moscow and St. Petersburg and the Jewish Theological Seminary of America's Project Judaica at the Russian State University for the Humanities. Others were in the initial stages as well, including Touro College and Maimonides State Academy. Individual Jewish studies courses were also being developed through the Russian Open University and the Open University of Israel, with the active involvement of the Joint. Additionally, as we were soon to learn, interest was not confined only to the capitals. Plans were afoot all over the FSU.

In late 1993, Ralph and Professor Nehemia Levtzion, the director of the International Center for University Teaching of Jewish Civilization, decided to convene a gathering in Moscow of the forty or so graduates of the Hebrew University workshops, as an initial foray into exploring the current status of Jewish studies in the post-Soviet Union.

Our expectations were modest; after all, how many scholars would have even contemplated going into Jewish studies in Soviet times? Often, those who had wanted to pursue the field had to find some kind of camouflage or subterfuge, such as specializing in Polish Ethnic History, Ukrainian Folk Culture, or Ancient

Semitic Languages, which is why the grassroots response to the invitation was so stunning.

On February 4–8, 1994, over 110 scholars and academics from all over the former Soviet Union – some from as far afield as Tomsk in Siberia, Tbilisi, and Vilna – gathered together at the Krekshino conference center near Moscow and declared that they wanted to revive Jewish studies across the former Soviet Union.

Everyone present felt the uniqueness of the moment.

I opened my official welcome on behalf of the JDC as follows: "*Hineh mah tov...* [How good it is (for brothers and sisters to gather together)]. Who would have imagined only a few years ago, in Soviet times, that we could convene such an open and public gathering dedicated to the teaching of Jewish studies in universities across the former Soviet Union?"

I felt a tremor of emotion throughout the entire room.

I emphasized, in particular, the uniqueness of the opportunity, coming as we did from many nationalities, faiths, and beliefs, to share in a subject that was dear to us all. However, it soon became apparent that those in attendance were not only engaged in a shared academic mission but in a spiritual quest as well. People had been waiting for such a gathering for a long time, perhaps even for generations.

The participants networked all the time, at meals, in between sessions, at the book displays, during the breaks, and late into the night. The interest was so intense that we stayed up until 3:00 a.m. meeting with local delegations from St. Petersburg, Rostov, Kiev, Donetsk, and Tbilisi.

We were honored by an official visit from Israeli ambassador Chaim Bar-Lev and the newly appointed cultural attaché Shamai Golan.

The distinguished professor Nikita Tolstoy, the great-grandson of Leo Tolstoy, was the keynote speaker at the conference. His participation was of particular importance since it gave an "official sanction" to the Krekshino event. The study of academic Judaica was not just of sectarian interest but had much broader appeal.

I asked Academician Tolstoy what had brought him to the gathering. He responded that Jewish studies, which had been forbidden under the Communists, sparked tremendous interest now that they were permitted. In addition, the Pravoslavac Church was bursting with renewed enthusiasm since the fall of Communism, and they, too, were deeply engaged in Jewish and Old Testament studies. On a personal note, he mentioned that his great-grandfather had studied Hebrew with a local rabbi and was able to read the Bible in the original. Something about the event spoke to his soul.

He became a key supporter of Jewish studies at the highest levels and intervened with the leadership of the Russian Academy of Sciences (RAS) to allow local Jewish academics to open the future SEFER office in the RAS building. That became a statement both to the Jewish community and the general academic world that academic Judaica was not only permitted, it was encouraged.

VISITING THE FIELD AND FOUNDING SEFER

At Krekshino, we learned that Jewish studies programs had been started or were planned all over the former Soviet Union. During the next several months, I traveled to Moscow and St. Petersburg, Yekaterinburg, Tyumen, and Tomsk, Kiev, Donetsk, and Dnepropetrovsk, Minsk, Kishinev, and Tbilisi to make initial contacts and to see these new developments for myself. I met the professors, sat in classes, and spoke with university administrators, staff, and students.

On the one hand, I found tremendous interest, enthusiasm, and a heartfelt desire, almost desperate at times, to teach Jewish studies across the former Soviet Union. But on the other, there was a near-total shortage of resources, funding, trained faculty, textbooks, and curricula, not to speak of recruiting and training students, summer and winter schools, and graduate study.

Everyone I met wanted to do something but had no idea how to go about it.

In addition, the many pioneering projects already active in the field were operating independently of each other, isolated and alone. There was no contact or communication between them.

Following the Krekshino gathering, Ralph, Nehemia, Asher, Epi, and I met in Jerusalem and formulated the JDC approach for developing and expanding academic Judaica in the former Soviet Union. Our proposal was to establish a central address in Russia to plan joint projects, collect information from the field, publish a newsletter, hold an annual conference, organize academic seminars, engage in publications, develop curricula, set up a speaker's bureau, and encourage student programs.

Equally important were two parallel practical decisions: that the future Moscow Center would operate in concert with the International Center for University Teaching of Jewish Civilization in Jerusalem, with Professor Levtzion functioning as the academic "mentor" and "advisor," and that this organization, soon to be named SEFER, would become a project of the JDC Russian Department, with the support of the Joint. It was to be my staff assignment.

Epi knew of an outstanding Jewish academic, teacher, and personality, Dr. Leonid Matzich, who was interested in becoming involved. Dr. Matzich, originally from Kiev and living in Israel, was fluent in Russian, Ukrainian, English, French, and Hebrew, had a charismatic presence, and a love for Jewish studies. Professor Levtzion hired him with JDC backing, and Leonid became the coordinator and field person.

In keeping with the JDC commitment to local empowerment, my task was to organize partners on the ground to direct and manage the new organization. I invited Professor Rashid Kaplanov and Dr. Victoria Mochalova, both graduates of the Moshe Davis Hebrew University summer workshops, to lead the project – Professor Kaplanov as the head of the Academic Council and Dr. Mochalova as the director. They were to provide outstanding leadership over the years, Rashid until his untimely passing in 2007, when he was succeeded by Professor Mikhail Chlenov, and Vica into the 2020s. (See photos.)

At the end of the summer of 1994, Nehemia and I traveled to Moscow for the official founding of SEFER – The Moscow Center for University Teaching of Jewish Civilization.

Two key strategic decisions by Rashid, Vica, and the local academic counsel set the tone and direction for the future success of the project. By naming it by the Hebrew word *sefer* (book), they publicly identified it as a Jewish organization, a very significant and even courageous step for those times. And locating it at the Russian Academy of Sciences, the premier academic address in the Soviet Union, gained it immediate academic credibility and prestige.

The establishment of SEFER raised the bar as to what the future of Jewish life in the former Soviet Union could aspire to. In addition to the familiar Jewish communal frameworks such as synagogues, schools, and welfare programs, Judaism had something to say to the wider world as well. Jewish culture and knowledge were no longer "shameful," as they had been perceived under the Soviets, but were now worthy of respect and a source of pride.

Over the years, I participated in hundreds of SEFER meetings, activities, and projects. The high point of the year's programming was the annual international academic conference.

CELEBRATING THE SEFER COMMUNITY

The SEFER gatherings, held every year in the heart of the Moscow winter, were highly anticipated festive events, similar to college homecomings. They were marked by intense feelings of camaraderie and community. In Vica Mochalova apt phrasing, we were an "academic *mishpachah* [family]" whose members gathered from all over the FSU, as well as from abroad.

In 2000, for example, the JDC brought delegations from across the FSU, including seventy participants from Kiev and twenty-five from Belarus; from Khabarovsk in the Far East to Brest on the Polish border; and from Central Asia, the caucasus, and the Baltics. They were augmented by nearly forty foreign guests from Israel, the US, the UK, Germany, and France. The chief rabbis of Russia attended, as well as the Israeli cultural attaché, the head of the Jewish Agency delegation in Russia, the presidents of the All-Russian Vaad and the Russian Jewish Congress, plus representatives from Yad Vashem, Kibbutz Lochamei HaGeta'ot, the Open University of Israel, the Hebrew University, ORT, and others. SEFER became the central address for academic projects and activities in the post-Soviet Union.

Some of the world's outstanding scholars of Jewish and Russian Jewish studies also attended over the years, including Professors Mordechai Altshuler, Yom Tov Asis, Yisrael Bartal, Michael Brown, Yossie Chajes, Edward Feld, Herzl Fishman, Ernest Frerichs, Zvi Gitelman, John Klier, Nehemia Levtzion, Ada Rapoport-Albert, Antony Polonsky, Avi Ravitzky, Moshe Rosman, Lawrence Schiffman, Aliza Shenhar, Shaul Stampfer, Mervin Verbit, Yair Zakovitch, Bernard Zelichov, and Rabbi Adin Steinsaltz. (See photos.)

The meetings became a genuine international Jewish happening. We all sensed that something unique and unprecedented was taking place. The discussions and reunions between far-flung colleagues seemed that much more fervent against the background of the previous decades of isolation and fear. The lectures of the international academics seemed fresher and more contemporary than at similar events in the West or Israel. The students' excitement was greater, and feelings of wonderment and awe, with perhaps a touch of uncertainly for the future, were ever at hand.

One of the most exciting SEFER-related developments over the years was the growth of student involvement. By the year 2000, five years into the SEFER undertaking, over one hundred students in Judaic studies attended the annual conference. A Student's SEFER had been formed with its own Student Executive Council; the first Judaica Winter School had been held in Moscow; twenty students were taking part in "Eshnav," a month-long intensive study program at the Hebrew University in Jerusalem; and there were two summer schools in St. Petersburg and Kharkov. A ten-person delegation attended an International Conference of Judaica Students in London, and the first issues of a student academic journal entitled *Tirosh* (Young wine) were being distributed. (See photos.)

In addition, individual graduates were studying at Oxford, University College London, New York University, Brandeis, and other outstanding departments of Judaica, largely through contacts made via SEFER. Many of the foreign academics who came to Moscow for the conferences met students, were very impressed by their abilities, and helped them to continue their advanced studies abroad.

One of my roles at the Joint was to generate support and partnerships for many of these projects. For example, for the programs at Hebrew University, the JDC would cover the participants' travel from Russia to Israel, and the Hebrew University and the Jewish Agency would provide the land portion. The fact that the Joint was prepared to "put money on the table" for SEFER and academic Judaica was a powerful incentive for others to join, which they did eagerly.

Ralph and I met with potential American sponsors, several of whom ultimately braved the Moscow winter to attend conferences and became ongoing supporters, such as Herb and Stephanie Neuman and Michael and Joan Schneeweiss, who took ownership of the "SEFER Mentoring Project."

As part of the JDC's efforts to expand SEFER's international connections, I attended gatherings of the Association of Jewish Studies in Boston and invited leading Russian Jewish academics to join me. We organized a reception at the AJS conference for the Americans to meet their SEFER colleagues.

Dr. Victoria Mochalova was invited to speak at a JDC Board meeting in New York and subsequently hosted guest delegations from the Joint in her Moscow apartment, something that the visitors particularly enjoyed. The academicians shared their compelling stories about the role of the Joint in renewing Jewish life in the post-Soviet Union.

THE AMBASSADOR'S TALMUD LESSON

One of SEFER's favorite and treasured guests was Professor Aliza Shenhar, the Israeli ambassador to Russia during the formative years 1994–97, who was also a professor of Jewish Folklore at the University of Haifa.

In one of her most memorable conference presentations, in 1996, she retold and analyzed the famous Talmudic tale of poor Hillel (*Yoma* 35b), who nearly froze to death in the middle of a snowstorm, while listening to a Torah lesson from the skylight, since he could not afford the tuition to enter the academy. She derived the message that if one devotes their total efforts to study and scholarship, they will ultimately succeed.

At that, Dr. Moshe Lemster from Kishinev rose and posed the following: "How could Hillel have endangered himself to study words of Torah?"

I responded from the audience that, not long ago, every person in this room, all of those engaged even in private Jewish scholarship under the former regime, made the same choice: they placed their careers and, at times, even their freedom, at risk, for the sake of those very same principles.

Suddenly, the ancient tale of Hillel took on renewed relevance and meaning for us all.

A Jewish atmosphere infused the event. When you entered the conference halls, you felt as if you had been transported from the cold and wintery streets of Moscow to an entirely Jewish world; not quite Jerusalem, but not so far away.

The main entryway featured a book fair, presented by Gesharim press, with SEFER student-volunteers giving out free copies of recent publications, including

Proceedings (in 2000 that consisted of four separate volumes totaling well over 1,110 pages) and the most current *Academic Directory of Jewish Studies in the Former Soviet Union.*

The evening programs were often Jewish cultural events, such as a Festival of Jewish Music and Song, featuring the twenty-voice Hassidic Section of the Moscow Choir singing rousing songs in Yiddish and an ancient Georgian Jewish hymn. Another event was a Shlomo Carlebach "happening," led by Dr. Yossie Chajes, a faculty member at Haifa University, who had also been a backup musician for Reb Shlomo for many years. The students were dancing in the aisles!

One year, the conference evening program was a student performance of *Fiddler on the Roof* in Russian, performed by a cast from the Kiev Hillel. The scenes in the play, which were pure nostalgia for the visiting Americans, were living history for the local audience.

The conferences were staged under the ever-present blue and white SEFER banner, in Russian, English, and Hebrew, with the symbol of an open book in the center.

SEFER: AN APPRECIATION

The creation of SEFER was a unique and unprecedented component in the rebuilding of post-Soviet Jewish intellectual and academic life. Its genesis was in Ralph Goldman's vision, and I was fortunate to have played a part in making it all come about.

What made the creation of SEFER so unique and why was it so successful?

- It was born out of a culture and memory of state suppression and had to overcome the fears and legacy of that past in addition to the need to create, virtually from scratch, the institutions and structures for reviving Jewish studies.
- It responded to the unique character of Russian and post-Soviet Jewry, with their deep intellectual commitment; it had no outside political agenda and was led over the years by an outstanding group of local academics and scholars.
- It became one of the keys to the personal identity of its members. To many, it was their primary Jewish statement and affiliation. One professor would carry a kippah in his briefcase – just in case! As I would explain to foreign visitors: "You may think they are lecturing, but they are davening, only they are not familiar with the Hebrew words. This is how they express their identification with the Jewish people."

- SEFER became the collective home to many intellectuals and scholars of Judaica from across the former Soviet Union, of all nationalities, with over ten thousand academics and students participating in its programs over the years. In the words of Professor Arkady Kovelman, head of the Department of Jewish Studies at Moscow State University, SEFER matched the classical meaning of the word *sinagoga*, a *beit knesset* or place of gathering.
- Even politically, SEFER affirmed faith in the future of the Jewish community in Russia and reached out to common allies. After a hiatus of generations, it was permitted once again, and accepted, to publicly declare one's interest and allegiance to Jewish life and learning. That was a revolutionary statement.

My personal hopes for the future of SEFER are contained in the familiar High Holiday blessing: *Katveinu b'Sefer Hachayim* (Inscribe us in the Book of Life), which can also be rendered as: "Inscribe us with a SEFER of life" – a living, vibrant SEFER, filled with length of years, friendship, and learning.

I was honored when, some years after I had finished my work at the JDC, SEFER published a full-color display-size wall calendar, which featured the individual photos of over sixty academics, students, and supporters from over the years, and very graciously included my picture among them. Even though I was physically far away, I was neither out of sight nor out of mind. That touched me very deeply.

We were, and remain, family.

The goal of restoring Jewish pride and creating an academic and intellectual home for post-Soviet Jews and their friends and allies, which we accomplished via SEFER, was paralleled within the Jewish community by the establishment of a network of Hillels for Jewish students across the FSU.

CHAPTER 20

Bringing Hillel to the FSU

BEGINNINGS

The story of Hillel in the FSU has been told in detail by my dear friend and colleague Rabbi Yossie Goldman in his critically acclaimed book *Let My People Grow: Hillel and the Jewish Renaissance in the Former Soviet Union* (Gefen Publishing House, 2020). The following is my personal perspective.

On my first day working for the JDC in Russia in September 1993, I visited the recently established Jewish University of Moscow, then about to begin its second year of operation. I met with the president, Dr. Misha Grinberg, and the rector, Professor Arkady Kovelman. They had been hard at work launching the school. They had students and faculty, an office staff, and a budding library, and were very eager to develop extra-curricular student life. Misha had been in the States during the summer, and he showed me the pictures of his trip, including one of him standing in front of California's Stanford University Hillel Foundation.

As we looked together rather longingly at the scene, Misha said to me: "I would like one of those in Moscow as well." It was almost a futuristic thought. Hillel in Russia? It seemed then like a very distant dream.

More than any other memory of the visit, that picture of Misha at the Stanford Hillel remained with me. In my report to Asher and Epi on the visit, I mentioned the concept of a "Hillel model" at the Jewish University as a future goal.

Rabbi Yossie Goldman, the director of Hillel at Hebrew University, who had visited the Soviet Union in the late 1980s, had independently reached the same conclusion. We met in Jerusalem to explore the possibility of collaboration between Hillel and the JDC in the field. With the blessings of the JDC's Asher Ostrin and International Hillel's Richard Joel, Yossi and I planned a trip together to Moscow and St. Petersburg for the end of December, to explore if bringing Hillel to the FSU was really a possibility at that time.

During a November visit to Kiev, I visited the newly opened International Solomon University (ISU). I spoke with one of the senior administrators, an old-time Marxist, still sporting his Soviet medals. When I said that I worked for "The Joint," he noted that the name was familiar to him. "You used to be spies," he said. Despite this questionably warm welcome, I was struck by the tangible Jewish spirit on campus. Some of the students were wearing kippot and a number inquired about the Jewish studies program. Here was a student body eager to identify as Jews.

I was particularly impressed by the director of student life at ISU, a young man named Yosef Axelrud (called Osik), who had outstanding people and organizational skills. His father had been the director of the local "October Club," a Soviet-era cultural center, and Osik had inherited his knack for community organization.

I recalled a quote often attributed to Stalin that we frequently cited, a bit sardonically, at JDC Russian Department senior staff meetings: "Cadres are everything." Finding the right staff is the key to any successful project, and I filed Osik's name away.

Yossie subsequently hired Osik as director of Kiev Hillel, and he became one of the longest-serving and most successful Hillel directors anywhere (twenty-eight plus years and counting), ultimately overseeing all of the Hillel programs in the former Soviet Union outside of the Russian Federation, including those in Ukraine, Moldova, Belarus, Azerbaijan, Georgia, and Uzbekistan.

When Yossie and I arrived in Moscow in December, Aryeh Goichman, the head of the Moscow JDC office, introduced us to a new staff member at the Jewish University, recently returned from studying in Israel, Jenya Mikhaleva. She had a particularly compelling story.

Raised in a totally secular Moscow Jewish family, Jenya saw herself as a budding Soviet academic who happened to have "Jew" in her internal passport. As an honors student, she applied for a doctoral program, certain that there would be no problems with her admission. Consequently, she was particularly shocked when her advisor rejected her application out of hand, asserting that it "was not possible that a Jew could ever fully appreciate the depth and richness of Russian literature." Jenya was crestfallen and angry. She was looking for rational answers where there were none.

To understand what her antisemitic professor said to her, she went to the Arkhipova Street Synagogue and began exploring her Judaism for the very first time by taking some clandestine courses. That sparked her interest into pursuing a career in Jewish education. She learned Hebrew, participated in the Hebrew University's Melton Program for Jewish educators, had recently returned from Israel, and was working at the Jewish University leading their theater workshop program.

Yossie spent two hours interviewing her and subsequently invited her to be the founding director of Moscow Hillel.

Both Osik and Jenya were members of the pioneering generation of post-Soviet Jewish professionals who paved the way for new "cadres" to begin filling the positions of Jewish leadership. Slowly but surely, they would augment and replace the former Soviet-raised and trained managers. Such young leaders would proliferate, with time, across the entire former Soviet Union.

OPENING MOSCOW HILLEL: A SURPRISE ENDING

It was at the end of September 1994, and I had flown from Israel to Moscow to participate in the opening event of Hillel in Russia. It was attended by over 150 students, including a group of visiting Israelis. Very ingeniously, Jenya and her friends had distributed flyers at the Arkhipova Street synagogue on Simchat Torah, announcing the program. There was tremendous enthusiasm. This was something new to the Jews of Russia: Jewish students gathering as Jews to celebrate their long-suppressed and often hidden identities. There was singing in Hebrew and Yiddish and then at 8:20 p.m., just when the excitement was building, the fire alarms went off!

We all rushed outside and huddled together in the cold Moscow evening. Even though fire trucks pulled up, no one knew then if there was a real fire or whether all of this was a false alarm or provocation, although, in the end, it turned out to be a real fire.

Jenya was very distressed. She felt that all of her planning and work had been for naught. Meanwhile, the students were having a grand time meeting, schmoozing, and socializing. There was a wonderful feeling of being part of an extended Jewish family. Jewish kids were meeting other Jewish kids under the stars.

The entire scene conjured up a twenty-five-year-old memory, when I had spent a Simchat Torah evening in Moscow on Arkhipova Street, not far from where we were presently standing, at the same age as these Moscow Hillel *chevre*. It all seemed so familiar.

As the evening's camaraderie continued, Jenya was buoyed, even more so when the following morning at 8:30 a.m. (a very early time for students), twenty of the group returned to help.

It turned out to be an auspicious and unforgettable launch for the first of many Hillels that were soon to be established in the former Soviet Union.

HILLEL GATHERINGS AND CELEBRATIONS

A few months after the post–Simchat Torah opening event, Hillel organized its first week-long seminar outside of Moscow. Over a hundred students attended from Moscow and beyond.

Yossie invited me to speak to the group on Shabbat afternoon. I sensed the moment. I was about to address a new audience of Jewish young people, who were meeting their Jewish selves for the very first time. I wanted to emphasize what a unique occasion we were all experiencing: Shabbat, with a group of Jewish students, in the heart of Russia, after the fall of Communism – something totally unimaginable by their parents' and grandparents' generation.

"I remember your parents at your age," I began, and told them about my visits to Soviet Jews back in the 1960s and early '70s; how fearful Jews were then to express their Jewishness, with the exception of one night during the year, Simchat Torah. "Just imagine what a privilege it is for us to be here together today, and to celebrate Shabbat as free and unafraid Jews. How fortunate we are."

As Yossie recorded: "The students of the 1990s were enthralled by the comparisons between their own search for a Jewish identity and that of their parents' generation."[1]

By early 1997, only two years later, Hillel had already expanded to include Moscow, St. Petersburg, Kiev, Minsk, and Yekaterinburg, with additional groups on the way. They anticipated opening twenty Hillels across the FSU; by 2004, there were twenty-seven. (See photos.) The weeklong winter seminars had grown into full-fledged Hillel Winter Congresses, with hundreds of participants (in 1999 over six hundred attended), and were preceded by a Pesach Seminar (called a "Pesach University") to train students how to run seders as well as a Student Leadership Conference for local Hillel staff. Attendees came from as far away as Khabarovsk in the Russian Far East and Tbilisi, Georgia, and from dozens of cities in between.

As I got up to address the hundreds of students at the 1997 Winter Congress, I felt the energy of the crowd. I wanted to highlight how far they had come in just the past few years.

"How many of you were in the Young Pioneers?" I asked, and all of the hands went up. "How many were in Komsomol?" I continued, referring to the teenage and young adult version of the Community Party, and most of the hands were raised as well. And then I delivered the punch line: "And how many are in Hillel today?" and all the hands shot up! "Is that how it was supposed to be: Pioneers, Komsomol…and Hillel?" We laughed and laughed, in joy, and also with more than a touch of relief.

We were in the middle of a modern-day Russian revolution; all the old norms had collapsed, and they had the opportunity to rebuild their Jewish lives from

---

1.   Rabbi Yossie Goldman, *Let My People Grow: Hillel and the Jewish Renaissance in the Former Soviet Union* (Jerusalem: Gefen Publishing House, 2020), 28. Quoted with permission.

scratch. What a unique and magnificent opportunity; for them, Hillel was the driving force.

The timing could not have been better. Rabbi Goldman had invited Rabbi Moshe Shur, director of Queens College Hillel in New York, to lead the singing and generate *ruach* (Jewish spirit) at the Winter Congress. Moshe, who himself had been an outstanding teenage leader (we went to camp together in the early 1960s), was also a world-famous Jewish composer, a member of the Diaspora Yeshiva Band, a close friend of Rabbi Shlomo Carlebach, and a natural tummler. Rabbi Goldman described the scene as Moshe began to play:

> Something suddenly clicked. Around us, an eruption of Jewish spirit burst forth, as the students began banging on tables and stamping their feet. Clapping and dancing, they sang along as best they could, not even knowing the words of the songs. Students jumped up onto one another's shoulders and began dancing wildly. Nowhere had I ever been part of such a display of frenzied feeling and energy. The music awakened an inner core within the students. What was Moshe Shur's take on the *ruach*, the spirituality through singing? "The mike barely functioned and one of my guitar strings broke, but none of these insignificant details hampered the ecstatic singing and dancing. The songs and spirit took on a life of their own."[2]

I was present in the room that evening. An atom bomb of Jewish energy had exploded. It was beyond unbelievable. I am certain those present will never forget that moment as long as they live. I certainly will not.

They had never been part of anything like this before. The previous Soviet Simchat Torah celebrations were a once-in-a-year event. But now, thirty years later, these Hillel *chevre* were just one element of a much larger Jewish movement, which was expanding throughout the country, with programs on a weekly and monthly basis. They were part of something and it was a part of them.

Am Yisrael chai was being realized, in front of our very eyes.

Moscow Hillel Deja Vu

A generation later, in November 2019, Yossie Goldman and I traveled to Moscow to attend the twenty-fifth anniversary celebration of the founding of Moscow Hillel. Guests had flown in from Israel, the US, the UK, and from all over Russia.

There was a tangible feeling of accomplishment. In attendance were many students past and present as well as members of the Moscow Hillel Advisory

---

2. Goldman, *Let My People Grow*, 56. Quoted with permission.

Board. Each of the board members was contributing financially to make the program self-sustaining, something we could only have dreamt about years ago.

The high point came when former students, Hillel alumni who were now adults, came up to Yossie and me, introduced themselves and their spouses, and told us about the Jewish families they were raising, thanks to Hillel. One man from Yekaterinburg, now in his mid-forties and a father of two, recalled meeting me as a teenager. Knowing that what we had pioneered decades ago had borne fruit was a wonderful feeling.

One droll exchange highlighted how the passage of time has a way of obscuring past events.

On our way to the evening's program, Yossie and I were sitting in the back seat of the taxi with a younger member of the International Hillel staff from America in the front. As we began to reminisce among ourselves about "the old days," she turned and asked us incredulously: "Do you mean to tell me that you two guys started Hillel in Russia?" It was all news to her and a good lesson in life for us both. We smiled and didn't feel the need to respond. (See photos.)

LET MY PEOPLE GROW

After many years of work, Yossie Goldman published his book *Let My People Grow: Hillel and the Jewish Renaissance in the Former Soviet Union* (Gefen Publishing House, 2020). It is filled with memories, history, insights, and photographs recalling what it was like to launch and direct FSU Hillel during those formative years.

Yossie decided to present his book on Zoom in December 2020, just after Chanukah, and invited me to participate with him in the program. I was deeply honored to be a part of the event, for it allowed me to express my deep personal regard for Yossie and for what he had accomplished. I was also very inspired by his publication, and it greatly influenced my decision to record my own story.

I opened our conversation that evening with the following question: On the face of it, hadn't the Soviets, over the previous seventy years, been successful in eradicating all Jewish spirit and feeling? Why even attempt such an obviously futile task, such as trying to establish Hillel in Russia under such conditions? Why waste your time?

In response, Yossie evoked for us the powerful image of lighting the Chanukah candles. "We light one candle at a time," Yossie reminded us," and then a second and then a third. Just because a project may appear to be overwhelming and even hopeless at the outset does not exempt us from taking the first step, from doing our part, and if we continue one step at a time, with hard work, and God's help, we will succeed." Of course, he was absolutely correct.

Even though the book was ostensibly about the Jews of the former Soviet Union, it was really about each one of us, how we approach and overcome life's challenges.

It was particularly moving when Osik Axelrud, the founding director of Kiev Hillel, who had joined us on Zoom from Ukraine, expressed with great emotion his thanks to Yossie for all he had done in bringing Hillel to the FSU, as well as for himself, personally. Yossie was really "his" rabbi. One of the former students, Dasha, who had since made aliyah to Israel, also spoke about how Hillel and Yossie had changed her life.

Many of us had grown up during the epic struggle for Soviet Jewry. We had attended rallies, protested, even been arrested, as Yossie had been, for chaining himself to the gates of the Soviet Consulate in San Francisco many years before. Others had visited the Soviet Union in person, to bring support and supplies to the activists and refuseniks. Yossie's story was ours as well.

At the same time as we were opening Hillels in the FSU, many others were also actively involved in reviving Jewish life in the post-Soviet world, notably Rabbi Adin Steinsaltz from Jerusalem, whose words and wisdom were a beacon to us all.

CHAPTER 21

Restoring Jewish Pride and Jewish Feeling

SHABBAT WITH RABBI STEINSALTZ

I spent a Shabbat at Rabbi Steinsaltz's Moscow yeshiva in Kuntzevo in May 1994. Being in the presence of the rabbi himself was an unforgettable experience.

I was surprised and humbled when, after introducing myself to him, he knew exactly who I was! He was familiar with my grandfather's writings and had spoken at my father's shul in Chevy Chase, Maryland.

Rabbi Steinsaltz had an extraordinarily sweet and welcoming manner. He exuded a genuineness and Jewish authenticity that were tremendously compelling and drew you into his circle. He was a great "people person" and loved schmoozing.

It was already midnight on Friday night. I was exhausted from my travels and could barely keep my eyes open. As I was making my way to my room to collapse, I wished the rabbi what I intended to be a parting *Shabbat Shalom*. He said to me: "You're not going to sleep so early, are you?" with the clear implication that he was ready for conversation. How could I refuse such an invitation? We sat until 2:00 a.m., exchanging stories, anecdotes, and words of Torah. Finally, reluctantly, but blessedly, I retired.

The rabbi was the real pioneer in outreach to Soviet Jews. In 1988 he had received official governmental approval to open an "Institute of Jewish Studies," which was really an academic yeshiva, and began instituting educational programs all across the Soviet Union. Ralph Goldman had immediately contacted him, offered him the support of the JDC for his work, and ultimately invited him to serve on the JDC Board. The rabbi traveled extensively across the FSU and reached out in particular to Jewish intellectuals. Chief Rabbi Shayevitch gave him the title of "*Dukhovny Ravin*," the "spiritual rabbi and mentor" of Russia.

Late on Shabbat afternoon, the guests, including local Jews, Israeli educators running programs in Moscow, and visitors like myself, listened with rapt attention as Rabbi Steinsaltz spoke about the unique challenges of this particular moment in Jewish history, and what it demanded from each of us working in the field. His words were bold and electric:

> To be born a Jew in Russia was like being a hemophiliac. They were suffering but could not help themselves.
>
> My father fought in the International Brigades in Spain at the side of the communists against the fascists, around when I was born. He didn't come from a kosher home but had a desperate need to show that he was a Jew.
>
> We need to return Jewish pride to the Jews of the former Soviet Union. We must try to "change the music" from one of apology – "What can I do? I was born a Jew" – to one of self-esteem and dignity: "I was born a prince – look what I can do!"
>
> It is like someone who was born into poverty who learns that his parents had a hidden treasure; like the branch of a tree that was cut off – either it regenerates itself, or it dies.

I was deeply stirred by his words and I asked myself: What could I do to restore the pride and self-worth of Soviet Jews? As I traveled into the vast hinterland of the Russian periphery, I would find and create many opportunities.

AT THE MENORAH ARTS SCHOOL IN YEKATERINBURG

As JDC country director for the Urals (1995–97, 2001–08), whenever I made a field trip, I would meet with the heads of the community organizations and see their programs in action. It was a wonderful opportunity to visit with the local Jews, as well as to honor their efforts.

Sundays were the busiest days since the Jewish schools were open. One particular weekend in 1996, I was accompanied by a guest, Rabbi Joe Schoenwald, from Jerusalem. We stopped at the Menorah Arts School in Yekaterinburg, known in Soviet times as Sverdlovsk, directed by Freida Kletz, one of the pioneers in community programs. They offered classes in art, music, dance, basic Hebrew, tradition, and Jewish history.

We did our "rabbi thing." We entered the classrooms with a big smile, greeted the children with a hearty *shalom*, shook every child's hand, gave out kippot, which we plopped on the little boys' heads, and, to their delight, dramatized stories from the Bible. How many visitors from Jerusalem came to town and were so eager to see the children?

After class, I asked to meet with the teachers. I wanted to congratulate and encourage them in their holy task. They were, after all, fulfilling the words of the

Shema (Deuteronomy 6:7): "You shall teach your children." They seemed so at home with the material that it poured out of them. One wouldn't have known that almost none of the faculty had ever attended a Jewish school in their lives. They were mostly art and music specialists from Jewish backgrounds, doing their very best; from what we saw, they were working with all their hearts and souls.

I asked them if, when they were teaching a subject that they had never seen personally or experienced as children, did it nonetheless seem somehow familiar, a part of them? Their heads nodded in enthusiastic agreement.

I then posed to them a question from the Talmud (*Niddah* 30b): What does the fetus do inside the mother's womb? Obviously, it studies Torah! So why don't we all know Torah? Because God doesn't want newborn infants divulging all of the hidden secrets and wisdom of the universe, hence, as we are born, an angel appears, lightly taps our upper lip, and says "shhhhhh…" and we forget all that we had learned. And to prove that, I asked them to place their fingers under their noses, in front of their lips, and to feel the groove, called the "philtrum." "There it is! The mark of the angel!" We all laughed together.

Then I asked:

> What is this story telling us? That once, all of us, the entire Jewish people around the world, knew all the words and the lessons of the Torah, but over time, we forgot them or they were taken from us (as happened under the Soviets) but they are still deep within us. So, when we stand in front of our beautiful children in Yekaterinburg on Sunday mornings and teach them how to be Jewish, we are drawing from the deepest parts of our souls and recalling what we had once known, but had forgotten, and that is the essence of the Jewish experience in these post-Soviet times. We are reclaiming our teachings lost over the past seventy years. And that is what brought us here this morning from Jerusalem: to thank you, dear teachers, for all that you are doing for our children, and for our people.

We all were overwhelmed by the emotion of the occasion.

A Pre-High Holiday Experience

I was in Moscow just a few weeks before Rosh Hashanah in 2000, in a room filled with lecturers from the Association of People's Universities of Jewish Culture, from all over Central Russia and the Volga, the Urals, Moldova, Ukraine, Belarus, and Georgia. Their inimitable director, Semyon Avgusteivich, had brought them together for a pre-holiday seminar and invited me to come from Jerusalem to speak to them.

It was a unique opportunity. I wanted to convey to them the profound message and relevance of the upcoming High Holidays in a manner that would leave a lasting impression.

I didn't want to just speak "about" the holidays. I wanted to create and share a pre-holiday experience.

To convey the seriousness of the moment, I took out my tallit and put it on, something I had seen my own rabbi in Jerusalem do before speaking on special occasions. I blew the shofar that I had brought with me and spoke from the heart.

> Two things deeply concern me in particular at this time of the year. According to Jewish tradition, we are about to go on trial for our very lives. Each of us will be summoned to a Heavenly Court and our fate will be decided, for life or death, and none of us knows the ultimate verdict.
>
> But even more troubling is that no one here has any inkling, any conception, of what I am talking about. Trials? Courts? Living and dying? What does this all have to do with me?

With that, I opened a High Holiday prayerbook and quoted the text of the liturgical climax of the Days of Awe, the Unetaneh Tokef prayer, with the poignant and evocative words: "Who shall live and who shall die...who *by water* and who by fire?"

I cited the recent disastrous and heart-rending sinking, just a few weeks previously, of the nuclear submarine Kursk, the pride of the Russian fleet, with all one hundred and eighteen hands on board, an event that had shaken the entire country to its core. The prayers for the High Holidays suddenly came alive, leaped across the centuries, and took on personal meaning. Their recent national tragedy found a place, a resonance, in the ageless words. One woman broke out in tears.

God willing, they would feel a part of the upcoming High Holidays as well.

SHABBAT IN THE URALS

It was 1997 and I was preparing to spend my first Shabbat in the field, at a JDC welfare seminar in a hotel outside of Yekaterinburg. Previously, when I had been in Russia for the weekend, it was in a "protected" urban setting, near a synagogue, eating Shabbat meals with the local rabbi and his family, or at Rabbi Steinsaltz's yeshiva in Moscow.

This Shabbat, however, would be different. Since almost none of the participants had ever experienced a traditional Shabbat before in their lives, I knew I would have to bring Shabbat with me. I packed up my challot and my Shabbat "dressing coat," which I wore at our home during Shabbat meals, and set out for the Urals.

We gathered on Friday evening around a table set with white tablecloths, the Jerusalem challot, Shabbat candles, and bottles of Israeli wine. Everyone came dressed for the special occasion. We lit candles together and sang "Shalom Aleichem."

I spoke about our forefather Jacob's blessing to his grandsons which we quote on Friday evenings [Genesis 48:20] "May God make you like Efraim and Menashe," and asked: Why Efraim and Menashe and not any of the other grandchildren, Reuven, Shimon, Levi, and all the rest? Because only these two were raised in Egypt, in a foreign land, not in the Land of Israel, and yet they still maintained their Jewish loyalty and identity and were an integral part of the Jewish people.

In our days as well, I continued, the true test was not whether you could be Jewish in Jerusalem or Brooklyn or even Moscow, but rather in the heart of the Urals or Siberia or wherever they came from. Since most of them had spent their entire lives away from the large population centers, I sensed that they felt inferior to the "big city Jews" from Moscow and St. Petersburg, so I exhorted them: "We are not second-class Jews, and should never think of ourselves as such."

I assured them that nowhere in the world today was there a more ardent desire to be Jewish than in the former Soviet Union, especially in the periphery. That is what brought us together that Shabbat, to expand the Jewish circle and to serve even more members of our communities.

They had invited Professor Abraham Konstantinovich Kikoyin, an esteemed and beloved local academician, who had taught physics at university to many of the participants, as their Shabbat guest. He astounded the group by reciting the Kiddush over wine fluently, from memory. No one knew that he was such a storehouse of Jewish knowledge.

The head of the Jewish community from the town of Tobolsk in Siberia, three hundred miles to the east, with a population of some one hundred Jews, said it was the first time in his life that he had ever experienced Shabbat in person.

I spoke about the future challenges to be faced: creating not only Jewish organizations but Jewish communities; responding to the spiritual and religious needs of our people – even if those feelings had been suppressed and unarticulated over the years; and considering making aliyah. Without a doubt, I said, Israel was the best place in the world to be a Jew. Most of them had Israel connections. I asked for a show of hands: a third of the group had already visited Israel, and more than 60 percent had family there!

We spent Shabbat afternoon meeting with each of the delegations and discussed starting or expanding JDC Hesed programs in their communities. To preserve the Shabbat spirit, we did not take any written notes.

We approached the end of Shabbat with the customary Third Meal, complete with toasts of *l'chayim!* They were very complimentary to me, declaring "Porat equals Shabbat," calling me "*Nash rebbe*" (Our *rebbe*), and saying: "Yonatan, you are a true Diaspora rabbi – you understand us." I was very moved by their comments.

We finally made Havdalah and ended Shabbat at midnight. We had all felt the Shabbat spirit, even in the wilds of the Ural Mountains.

The JDC also organized and supported large community-wide and regional events, all aimed at restoring Jewish pride and Jewish meaning to the lives of post-Soviet Jews.

THE WEDDING OF A LIFETIME

It all began, quite unexpectedly, as I concluded my "Shabbat in a Jewish Home" presentation in the Russian city of Ufa, about 750 miles east of Moscow. I was approached by Inessa, one of the local ulpan teachers, with a request. She was getting married to Boris, a Jewish young man, and wanted to know if the Joint could help organize her wedding. I said we don't do private affairs, but if you would be willing to invite the entire community to the event, it would be our pleasure. She readily agreed, and with that, we were in the wedding business!

I contacted the nearest rabbi, Rabbi Rafi Rosen, in the town of Perm some 350 miles away, and arranged for him to speak to the couple. He reported back to me that he was not able to confirm their Jewish status from the call, so I turned to Rabbi Pinchas Goldschmidt, the chief rabbi of Moscow, and asked him to inquire. He spoke to Inessa and they arranged a phone call with her maternal grandmother, her mother's mother.

In the course of the conversation, it came out that one of Inessa's great-great-grandfathers had been drafted into the Tsarist army, and, upon completion of his service, was allowed to settle outside of the Pale of Settlement deep in the Russian interior, far away from any existing Jewish population center. The family, including the grandmother, had been raised with no Jewish upbringing whatever. The rabbi then asked her if she spoke Yiddish, and she responded: "*Gei in drerd!*" (Go to hell!).

"She's Jewish!" said the rabbi, and the wedding was a go.

A date was set for June. Rabbi Rosen would come in from Perm to officiate, and I would join from Jerusalem.

My JDC colleague Seymour Epstein wisely noted that a wedding must have live music, so we invited the Klezmer group Simcha from Kazan, twenty hours away by train, to perform.

How do you have a Jewish wedding when no one, except for the rabbis, had ever seen one? After all, there had not been such an event in Ufa in more than fifty years.

At the JDC office in Jerusalem, we created a decorative four-page pink wedding booklet in Russian. I divided the ceremony into a dozen brief paragraphs with explanations of the wedding day, the ketubah (marriage contract), the *badeken* (veiling the bride), the chuppah (canopy), and Sheva Brachot (wedding blessings), and brought enough copies to distribute to all.

At the same time, Azriel Weissman, the head of the local community, was making preparations. He arranged for hotels, transportation, and food, and secured a large hall in the Municipal Palace of Nationalities. Ilya Pestrikov, from our office in Yekaterinburg, brought a JDC-designed Russian-Hebrew ketubah for the ceremony and helped us with the documents and the arrangements.

Rabbi Rafi and Chaya Rosen arrived from Perm by train the night before the wedding at 11:00 p.m., and Inessa insisted on going to a mikveh at once. At half past midnight, the two women went to the local river for the ceremony. Chaya was deeply impressed by the bride's spirituality and lovely disposition, as were all who knew her.

Once we arrived at the wedding hall the following day, I assumed my familiar role as rabbi/master of ceremonies/stage director/cheerleader. We had set up the chairs in the large hall in a three-sided open square surrounding the chuppah, which consisted of my tallit held up by four makeshift poles. The room was filled to overflowing with hundreds of participants: old and young, grandparents and little children, students and teenagers, future brides and grooms, people in their thirties and forties. (See photos.)

Also present were guests from the city administration, the Department of National Minorities, and a representative of the Chief Mufti of Russia, who resided in Ufa. They had been invited by Azriel Weissman, who wisely saw the event as a "neighborly" opportunity to reach out to the local authorities and to enhance the standing of the Jewish community.

As we proceeded with the ceremony, I signaled for the band to stop playing and announced the number of one of the paragraphs in the booklet: "*Nomer sem* [Number seven] – placing of the ring!" and I read the description into the microphone, so all could follow.

We sang and danced, joked and cried, for hours and hours, and made a Jewish wedding in the Russian heartland.

It was really "awesome," best captured by the Yiddish word *moyradig*, filled with joyous trembling to the depths of one's soul. We had to stop several times because of our tears of happiness.

The community members were active participants. Ilya had brought hundreds of kippot from the JDC office in Yekaterinburg so that the locals could "dress" for the occasion. When I asked them at the *badeken* veiling ceremony to affirm that the bride was indeed lovely, they all called out "*Da, da!*" After every blessing I said "Say Amen!" and they did so with gusto!

The ceremony was followed by a kosher reception consisting of vodka, JDC Pesach grape juice, fruit, and Coke. Afterward, there was a sit-down meal for the immediate family with Israeli salami and kosher bread from Perm. We concluded with the traditional Sheva Brachot blessings. Nechama, Inessa's Israeli friend and ulpan supervisor, came from Yekaterinburg for the event, and couldn't get over the *simchah*. She, a native Israeli, had never been part of such a traditional Jewish wedding.

We were all glowing at the end. We had exposed an entire community to something so authentic and so Jewish that it would remain with them for a long time, perhaps forever. I noted to the guests that when a future historian writes the story of Jewish life in Ufa, they will undoubtedly include "The Wedding."

We presented the couple with JDC gifts I had brought from Jerusalem: Shabbat candlesticks, a Kiddush cup, and a mezuzah, along with a mazal tov telegram from Asher.

The following day we received the good news that the municipality had granted permission to turn over a piece of property to the Jewish religious community, where they could establish a synagogue, a Hesed Community Welfare Center, and classrooms. It gave us the feeling that the previous evening's event was not a one-time affair, but was the catalyst for continued growth.

A few days later, Ilya and I arrived in Yekaterinburg where we would be spending the weekend. On Friday afternoon, we visited the local Menorah Club's Oneg Shabbat program, and I showed the wedding video we had made in Ufa. It was a wonderful lesson in how to build a Jewish community in the post-Soviet Union. What was most striking was that the event was taking place in Russia, and not in Israel or America. Hopefully, some other local couples would be inspired to organize something similar for themselves.

Looking back, this 1996 wedding was one of the most powerful experiences in all my many visits to Russia. It was remarkable for its "normalcy," and held out the hope and conviction, that, over time, the Jews of Russia could once again rejoin the Jewish people as full-time and equal partners.

Twenty-five years later, in 2021, I had the pleasure of speaking with Inessa, now living in Israel. She and Boris and their parents had made aliyah in 2015. She changed her name from Inessa to Esther and was doing here what she did in Russia: teaching Hebrew to Russians, now in an ulpan in Rishon LeZion. They have three children, twenty-four, twenty-one, and fourteen, and are very, very happy.

It was, indeed, "the wedding of a lifetime."

"ELUL IN OMSK"

It was an audaciously breathtaking proposal.

I was the newly appointed JDC country director for the Urals, and Seymour Epstein was the country director for neighboring Siberia and the Russian Far East. "Let's have a leadership seminar for our two regions," he proposed, and when I inquired "Whom should we invite?" he answered, "All of them!" I quickly looked at the map and gasped. From Izhevsk, west of the Urals, to Vladivostok, on the Pacific Ocean, was 3,500 miles and spanned eight times zones. Just for comparison, from Maine to California is about 2,800 miles, and the entire Continental United States is only four time zones.

It was 1996, barely four years after the collapse of the Soviet Union, and Jewish life was reviving across Russia, but at varying levels and paces. The Jews of the Urals and Siberia were very isolated and had no one else to turn to but themselves...and the Joint.

How would we organize and gather participants from isolated communities all over the Russian periphery, assemble faculty and staff, and arrange kosher food and programming? It was a very big idea. It reminded me of one of Epi's other farsighted dreams, of holding a Jewish Woodstock Music Festival for fifty thousand Russian Jewish kids in Crimea! It never happened, but it showed the scope of his vision.

In retrospect, it is difficult for us to imagine what it was like growing up as a Jew in the Soviet Union. Basic things, such as hearing the shofar on the High Holidays, attending a Pesach seder (though they knew about matza), visiting a synagogue, fasting on Yom Kippur, having a *brit milah* or bar or bat mitzvah, not to speak of Jewish schools or learning Hebrew, were either strongly discouraged, prohibited, or foreign to them. This was especially true in the deep periphery of Russia, east of the Urals and across Siberia, which was isolated from outside Jewish contacts and visitors.

Epi and I wanted to take maximal advantage of our time together to flood the participants with Jewish content and experiences, as well as to generate local community momentum in preparation for the upcoming programming year. We decided to call the seminar "Elul in Omsk," though I am certain that few of the participants had any inkling that the word "Elul" referred to the Hebrew month before the High Holidays. We ended up creating much more than we had envisioned, both for them and us.

Each of the staff members came with different strengths: Dr. Eugene Weiner, from Haifa and now working for the JDC in Moscow, was a Jewish intellectual and professor; Seymour Epstein was a master Jewish educator with extensive field experience in North Africa and the worldwide JDC; Dr. Leonid Matzich, originally from Ukraine and now with the International Center and SEFER, was an outstanding Russian-speaking teacher and motivator, kind of an "academic *rebbe*"; and I brought years of practical rabbinic experience.

We crammed into our four weekdays together as much as we could, from the most basic to the most profound. Seventy-five participants – hailing geographically from the Ural Mountains, through the heart of Siberia, all the way to the Russian Far East and the Pacific Ocean – took part.

"Elul in Omsk" was like entering a "Jewish time warp." Things so familiar to us were new and exciting to them.

We opened each morning with a "shofar-blowing ceremony," the daily sounding of the shofar in the synagogue during the month of Elul. I used the occasion for a pre–High Holiday introduction. On the first morning, when I held up the shofar in my hand and asked them "What is this?" most recognized it, but few had ever heard it blown, since, in most of their communities, there were no functioning synagogues. Participants approached me and said it was their first time hearing the sound of the shofar.

I spoke about multiple Jewish examples of the mitzvah of "listening": to the shofar, to the words of the Shema, to others' feelings and opinions, to our own hearts. As we stood each morning for the shofar blowing, the moment was so still and holy; we really felt the approaching High Holidays.

We had scheduled daily prayers, but our expectations were very modest. How many would come for the afternoon service? We expected perhaps five or ten, if we were lucky. On the first afternoon, nearly fifty showed up! We ran out of seats. By the last day, the numbers had leveled off to a still-respectable fifteen or twenty, only now, one of the women from Birobidzhan had replaced me as the leader, and was announcing the pages. The responsive readings in Russian came out as if they had been in shul their entire lives (Temple Beth El of Irkutsk? Young Israel of Omsk?)

The following morning, at the Shacharit services, I had one of the most pro-found prayer experiences of my entire life.

As we were about to begin, I asked one of the men from Krasnoyarsk, who said he knew Hebrew, to lead us in the opening morning prayer Modeh Ani ("Thank You, Eternal King, for restoring my soul in Your great compassion"), a twelve-word meditation that usually takes about five seconds to recite. *Only he didn't recite it that way.*

He began:
Mohhhhh…deh… [pause];
ahhhhh…ni… [pause];
leh…fah…neh…cha… [pause]…
He read ever so slowly and deliberately, letter by letter, vowel by vowel, syllable by syllable. It took him nearly five minutes to pronounce the dozen words.

I asked him where he learned to read Hebrew, and he said that in Siberia there were no schools, and there were no texts, *so he learned to read Hebrew by himself!*

I said to him: "You taught *yourself* how to read Hebrew, so you could address God directly, in His own language? I am certain that He did not receive a more wonderful Modeh Ani from *anywhere* else in the world this morning!" Our friend sat up a little straighter in his seat, with a slight, perhaps embarrassed, smile on his face. I felt honored to be in his presence.

I thought of how often many regular daveners, myself included, rush through the words, just to finish "on time."

It was a most humbling experience.

Eugene Weiner taught the book of Ecclesiastes ("Vanity, vanity…all is van-ity"; "A time to be born and a time to die…"), which he presented as the classic text for the skeptics, doubters, and curious among us, which spoke to most in the audience, who had never opened a book of the Hebrew Bible in their lives. We were all beginning anew.

We taught the practical preparations and customs for the holidays, so famil-iar to us, but new and groundbreaking for them: dipping apples in honey, holiday meals, lighting candles. I had brought with me forty sets of Shabbat candlesticks to distribute, and they went like hotcakes! We distributed copies of the newly published JDC/Machanaim Siddur, which includes explanations, customs, and songs, as well as books by Rabbi Joseph Telushkin in Russian translation.

The teaching staff, Eugene, Epi, Leonid, and I, were inspired by the inten-sity and eagerness of the participants. Among the most significant factors in the success of the seminar was our shared mutual respect. We took them seriously as Jews, and they knew it and we knew it, as well.

If the JDC vision in the former Soviet Union was "to bring Jews back to the Jewish people," to renew Jewish life and the Jewish spirit, then we had taken giant steps at events such as the wedding in Ufa and the "Elul Omsk" seminar.

We also sought out Jews in the distant corners of Russia.

CHAPTER 22

Being Jewish in the Periphery

IN THE FARTHEST NORTH

Literally at the end of the line, twelve hundred miles and forty hours northeast of Moscow by train, lies the town of Vorkuta, the coldest city in Europe (record low: minus sixty-one degrees Fahrenheit). Under the Soviets, it had been part of the Gulag labor camp prison system, and we suspected that we might find Jews there. Mr. Spektor, the mayor, had a Jewish-sounding name, and perhaps there were former Jewish prisoners, medical personnel, or administrators who were still living in town. I sent a team from the JDC to investigate.

Semyon and Yulia from the St. Petersburg JDC office and Sharon Faulkner, a JDC photographer from New York, arrived in Vorkuta in the summer of 2002 and went to their scheduled appointment with the mayor. They were told that he was out of town, but the deputy mayor was available to see them for a few minutes.

It turned out that the deputy mayor also was a Jew but was particularly "cool" to the visitors. Nothing seemed to capture his long-dormant Jewish spirit until Semyon offered him a Bible in Hebrew and Russian. He was overwhelmed by the gift and asked what he could do. They said: "Help us find other Jews," and he immediately went to work.

He began calling up the municipal agencies in town, demanding: "Are there any Jews there?" an unsettling question in any setting, but especially in the former Gulag.

When he asked Ludmilla, the director at the Municipal Palace of Youth, if she knew of any Jews who worked there, she responded: "As a matter of fact, I am a Jew myself!"

The deputy mayor was stunned: "But we have known each other for years and you never told me you were a Jew!"

"You never asked," she replied. For three generations, the Jewish women of her family had been hiding under the identities of their Russian husbands, and had our delegation not arrived, would have continued to do so into the future.

"I must see her. How can this be?" he exclaimed, and the group immediately went off to visit Ludmilla in person. His face showed sheer astonishment and hers glowed with pure joy. Other formerly hidden Jews in town began to arrive. They had known each other for years, even decades, but never as Jews.

As a result of that JDC visit, the five hundred Jews of Vorkuta organized a Hesed Community Welfare Center program, Jewish holiday celebrations, participated in seminars in St. Petersburg, and even sent some of their young people to Israel. Will there be a Jewish community in Vorkuta in fifty years? Probably not. But as a first step, for now, they had rejoined the Jewish people.

IN THE FARTHEST SOUTH

At the exact opposite end of the Ural Mountains, eleven hundred miles to the south of Vorkuta, just twenty miles from the border with Kazakhstan, lies the city of Orsk, Russia. When we landed for our 1996 visit, it was over one hundred degrees outside. The fetid smell of oil and gas production reminded me of Secaucus on the New Jersey Turnpike or the Acre oil refineries.

Orsk was one of the most hospitable communities I ever visited. The town boasted a Sunday school, a women's club, a seniors' club, a Hesed Community Welfare Center, religious services, and holiday celebrations, all based on a benevolent community infrastructure.

The key player was one young man, Vadim Freedman, then only twenty-five-years old, a graduate of the JDC's Buncher Leadership Training Program in Jerusalem. He had galvanized a whole cadre of mostly younger women and their mothers, and they were the backbone of the community. The fact that a number of them were also his cousins and other relatives did not hurt. He was their leader but in a very unassuming and quiet way.

We met with about ten of the activists, each responsible for a specific project or activity. I showed them a video of the wedding in Ufa that had taken place earlier that week, which captivated them.

I was told that the Jews in town had come originally from Belorussia and Ukraine during World War II. Even the older generation seemed bereft of Yiddishkeit (Jewishness). With the sole exception of Reb Noteh, an eighty-five-year-old who had studied at the Radom Yeshiva, they were missing even the basics. They had never heard the Friday evening Shabbat song, "Shalom Aleichem." Everything was new to them.

Out of the one thousand Jews in town, about a hundred showed up for my "Shabbat in the Jewish Home" presentation and participated enthusiastically. Reb Noteh recited the Friday evening Kiddush over wine, children held the Havdalah candle, and everyone eagerly smelled the spices from the end of Shabbat. (See photos.)

Vadim took me to the local Jewish cemetery to conduct a brief memorial service. The neighboring Muslims had been impinging on the Jewish section. The local Jews didn't attribute this to anti-Jewish motives; that was simply the nature of the situation. The Jewish community was inevitably shrinking, save for the graves.

Despite its remoteness and size, the Jews of Orsk had been very successful in creating a viable Jewish community…at least for the present. Their successes showed how small locations often retain key strengths missing in larger settings, depending on local leadership. Vadim's innate ability to bring people together for a common goal, plus professional training, really had an impact. It was an important lesson worth imparting all across the field.

IN THE MIDDLE OF NOWHERE

I'm not even quite certain how we ended up, in 2001, in Kurgan, Russia, one thousand miles east of Moscow in Western Siberia. I had been looking at a map of the Urals and noticed that Kurgan seemed to be the only city in the region that the JDC was not servicing, so I wanted to visit and meet the locals.

We set off by car in pitch-black darkness from Yekaterinburg at 6:00 a.m., arriving in Chelyabinsk three hours later. We spent most of the day visiting the local Chabad rabbi, the school, the Hesed Community Welfare Center, and the building site for the new JCC. We left town around 4:00 p.m., headed due east, arriving in Kurgan around 7:00 p.m., in time for our appointment.

It was as if we had stepped back in time, reminiscent of our initial round of field contacts half-a-dozen years earlier. The ten older men who had gathered to meet us were sitting on one side of the room and we were facing them, on the other. They were very skeptical and even dismissive. In their view, the JDC was foreign and remote, and our office in Yekaterinburg was not on their radar. I would just make promises, and they expected very little. They had been schooled and raised in the Soviet system, where directives came from above, local initiatives were throttled, and creativity was discouraged. If nothing had happened by now, what could they expect for the future?

Picking up on their tone, I thought that I would call their bluff, and said: "If that is the case, then why waste your time and mine? If I came from Jerusalem to Kurgan to meet with you and you aren't interested, no problem," and with that, I got up to leave, signaled to the staff, and headed for the door.

That got their attention. They pressed me to stay, things settled down, and we began a serious conversation. I asked why there were only ten participants at the meeting, and they answered that they only had ten chairs! With that, as an act of "largesse" of the JDC, I told them that we would be happy to purchase twenty new chairs for them as our gift! We also arranged for them to meet with our staff and said we would fund their upcoming Chanukah program. Ultimately, we opened a Hesed Community Welfare Center in town and began working with them to organize community activities.

For them to make the transition would be a hard climb. It would probably take the future involvement of a younger group to move things along. But for now, we would certainly be happy to do our part.

We departed Kurgan at 9:30 p.m. for the remaining one hundred twenty-five-mile drive to our final stop for the evening, Tyumen, on some of the darkest and poorest roads I had ever traveled in Russia. I made an especially fervent "Prayer for a Safe Journey" as we headed out. I was very grateful when we arrived unscathed past midnight at the Tyumen Quality Inn after one of my longest and most eventful days in the Russian heartland.

Opening a "Closed City"

Among the most isolated locations in Soviet times were the "closed cities," usually of military or strategic importance. One of those was Izhevsk, six hundred miles east of Moscow. It was a center of Soviet weapons production and the home of the world-famous arms inventor Mikhail Kalashnikov, creator of the AK-47. Local Jews had been part of the engineering elite of "Izhmash," the Izhevsk Arms Plant, especially during the 1930s and '40s. The local Jewish community was founded in the nineteenth century by former cantonists, Jewish boys conscripted into the Tsarist army for a twenty-five-year term of service. The only synagogue had been closed in 1930.

Despite there being less than one thousand Jews in the city, I was amazed on my trips in 1996 and 2004 to find a vibrant and organized Jewish community led by Mark Goldin, the founder of the Society for Jewish Culture. (See photos.)

They boasted a Sunday school, an ulpan, a Hesed Community Welfare Center, a library, Hillel, two religious congregations, a student singing group, a Shabbat Club, and the Izhevsk JCC! Mark knew every Jew in town, and they looked to him as their leader. For my "Shabbat in the Jewish Home" talk over seventy people showed up, mainly parents in their thirties and forties and several students as well. I had never seen such a group of active younger community people in all of my Russian field visits.

The seniors were cared for as well. Mark took me to visit two elderly Jewish women who had been evacuated from the Bialystok Home for Orphans to Izhevsk during World War II. They had been together ever since. Sisters could not have been closer. Mark and his group were caring for them with the support of the JDC Hesed Community Welfare Center program.

Writing in my diary on the night train to Yekaterinburg, I described my visit to Izhevsk as "a magical evening." It was an impressive example of what local leaders and communities were accomplishing with our help and support. I concluded with the following note: "What a great job God gave me, to help spread the words and deeds of Torah in places like Orsk, Izhevsk, Kurgan, and all the rest."

A VISIT TO THE AMERICAN MIDWEST

A decade later, while on a speaking tour of the States in 2013, I visited Waterloo, Iowa. The local Sons of Jacob Synagogue had been established in 1905 and had reached its peak of one hundred and fifty members after World War II. Since then, it had been shrinking steadily, and now a core of only a few dozen faithful families remained.

My topic for the evening was "Being Jewish in Small Communities," and I spoke about what I had seen and experienced in the Russian periphery over the years. I wanted to encourage the remaining Jews of this small midwestern town by describing what their brothers and sisters across the ocean had accomplished. I assured them that they, in America, had far greater resources than the Jews of Russia did, especially in these days when the modern internet had brought all of Jewish knowledge into their own homes and synagogue.

Ira, the congregation's past president, wrote me as follows:

> Rabbi Porath came to our small community in Iowa, and by the time he left, our pride and sense of Judaism were as tall as the corn that surrounds us. He connected with every generation in our community and reached out to the non-Jewish community, as well. He helped all of us better understand our history and customs in a way that leaves all of us wanting more. Todah Rabah!

He thanked me, but I was indebted to the Jews of the Russian periphery who showed me the way.

Moving from the periphery to the capitals, I was also country director for the JDC in St. Petersburg. There we had been working on a major project that was about to come to fruition.

CHAPTER 23

A Jewish Home in
St. Petersburg – YESOD

A PURIM CELEBRATION LIKE NONE OTHER

My heart was bursting with joy and pride as I stood on the stage at the opening event of the Yevreiskiy Sankt-Peterburgskiy Obshchiny Dom – YESOD, the St. Petersburg Jewish Community Home, in March 2006, a project sponsored and constructed by the JDC for the Jews of St. Petersburg. (See photos.)

It was the evening before Purim, and the entire building was in a festive and celebratory mood. Children of all ages were parading through the four-story-high atrium in their costumes. A banner "Purim Festival in YESOD" hung on the wall. On Purim day, a magician performed in the atrium in honor of the holiday. (See photos.)

The Jewish character was especially striking and pronounced to those who had grown up under the Soviets: the menorah design on the metal security fence; the name YESOD in Hebrew letters on the outside of the building; the mezuzah on the doorpost; the Russian, American, Canadian, and Israeli flags as you entered the atrium; the words *"Hineh mah tov..."* (How good it is [for brothers and sisters to be together]) in Russian and Hebrew displayed prominently on the main entry wall; even a shattered tile, recalling the destruction of the Temple in Jerusalem. You knew that you were entering a Jewish world.

Every detail had been purposefully and lovingly planned.

YESOD was awarded a "Gold Prize" by an International Architectural Festival, as one of the finest buildings constructed in St. Petersburg that year. The external style and beauty were a deliberate part of the design. One of the major goals of the construction was to give the Jews of St. Petersburg a Jewish home to be proud of, and we had succeeded.

I prepared a brief greeting in Russian:

Dear Friends!

I am so very happy to celebrate this holiday of Purim with you this evening, on the opening day of community programming in YESOD.

Today is a great day, long anticipated, and it has come to pass.

In our vision, YESOD is a place where all of the Jews of St. Petersburg will feel at home.

With God's help, today's opening event will be the first of many programs at YESOD, and we hope and plan on seeing you again very soon.

Shalom, Happy Purim, and Mazal Tov to all!

Many community organizations put on performances that evening. One scene that particularly stood out was the Purim Shpiel, a Purim musical play, performed by members of the Eva Jewish Charity Organization. As they portrayed the poignant tale of Queen Esther's desperate plea for the lives of her people, they played the melodious theme song from *Schindler's List*. Suddenly, the biblical story, ancient, distant, and little-known to Soviet Jews, became theirs as well.

After a festive dinner at the Lechayim Kosher Restaurant, I returned to the building at midnight just to walk around and absorb the events of the day and was greeted by a late-night Hillel student Purim party. It was worth opening YESOD, just to give the local Jewish kids a place to hang out.

I departed St. Petersburg the following day with a great sense of satisfaction and relief. I even wrote the word "triumphantly" in my diary.

CREATING YESOD

Tremendous effort had been invested into putting this entire undertaking together, consuming literally thousands of hours and starting long before I had arrived in St. Petersburg as the country director in 2001.

Based on all of our experience, it was clear to us that for the community to grow and flourish in the future, they would need their own "Jewish home" for projects and activities, rather than working out of temporary facilities spread all over town. The only remaining Jewish property in St. Petersburg after seventy years of Communism was the Great Synagogue on Lermontovskiy Street. This venerable and distinguished structure from Tsarist times, built in the 1880s, had fallen into disrepair under the Soviets and was later renovated with a generous contribution from the Safra family.

A new, modern, multi-purpose facility was needed.

Conceived of as the largest building constructed by the JDC in the former Soviet Union, it was an extremely complex project to plan and execute. The first element, of course, was finding an available location in a place where determining the legal ownership of property could be very murky. We had to identify architects, choose a construction company that could build to Western standards, set a production schedule, and ensure oversight and supervision, all against the background of post-Soviet society and a Jewish community trying to establish its own path.

Critical to the project was the engagement and input of the local St. Petersburg Jewish community, as represented by many local organizations and their leadership. They took this undertaking very seriously and, together, we devoted tremendous amounts of time and thought to a community planning process.

We brought in Dr. Jack Ukeles, a leading international Jewish community planner, to St. Petersburg several times, to accompany and help focus our discussions. The JDC took members of the planning committee to visit Jewish Federations and facilities in the US such as Palm Beach, Cleveland, the New York metropolitan area (including the recently constructed Manhattan JCC), in addition to Israel and Moscow. We commissioned a St. Petersburg Jewish community survey of over one thousand participants, conducted by Professor Vladimir Shapiro from Moscow, to identify what the local needs were and what kinds of programs should be developed as part of YESOD.

Not everyone in town shared our vision. When I invited one of the longtime local leaders to relocate his program to YESOD, I naively told him that we all would be like "one big family" under a single roof. He responded that it sounded to him too much like a Soviet "communal apartment," where everyone shared the same kitchen and bathroom, and he wanted no part of it. He preferred to remain independent rather than join us.

I came to understand and appreciate over time what a huge change and challenge a project like this was for the established organizations, and I worked very hard to allay their concerns.

Only when the building was finally completed and functioning could both the JDC and the local partners fully appreciate what an extraordinary asset YESOD would be in shaping the Jewish future of St. Petersburg.

The entire enterprise was supported, in addition to the Joint, by several very generous partners, including the Conference on Jewish Materials Claims Against Germany (the Claims Conference); the Jewish Federations of Cleveland and Palm Beach; the Weinberg and Schusterman Foundations; the president of the JDC and his wife, Eugene and Stephanie Ribakoff; Richard and Rhoda Goldman; members of the St. Petersburg branch of the Russian Jewish Congress; and many others, each of whom was deeply committed to the project. They all shared the vision of investing in the future of Jewish life in St. Petersburg.

YESOD OPENS AND HOSTS A NOBEL LAUREATE

The opening of the building was greeted with great excitement and featured a series of new programs and community "firsts," including

- the first wedding in YESOD of a couple who had met at Hillel, held in the front garden, officiated by Rabbi Pewzner from the Great Synagogue
- a series of adult education classes in Cinema-Midrash, Jewish Thought and Mysticism, Yiddish and Jewish Folklore through "Eitan," the YESOD Education Department
- a municipal Conference on Tolerance with over twelve hundred participants, including seven hundred local non-Jewish school children and one hundred teachers
- the first adult *brit milah*, for a nineteen-year-old student
- "Granatik," a city-wide children's program, featuring a Purim Pirate Party
- a book-signing by Amos Oz, the world-famous Israeli author, to mark the Russian translation of one of his works
- a giant outdoor Chanukah menorah lit by Rabbi Farbman from the Progressive congregation that was meeting at YESOD

A special high point was our hosting Nobel Prize laureate Professor Yisrael Aumann in 2007.

I had heard in Jerusalem that Professor Aumann, the winner of the 2005 Nobel Prize for Economics and a kippah-wearing Jew, was planning on visiting St. Petersburg to attend an academic conference, and I contacted him, inviting him to speak at YESOD. I told him that there were many Jewish intellectuals and scientists in the city not currently identified with any of the local Jewish organizations who would be drawn to such a gathering. It would bring them through the doors of YESOD for the first time and show them that a new Jewish address had opened up in the city. Finally, I said that this was part of the mitzvah of bringing Jewish people closer together. He graciously accepted.

Upon his arrival in St. Petersburg, he was interviewed on television and radio. It was announced at the Great Synagogue on Shabbat morning that he would be speaking at YESOD.

Despite all of the publicity, I was still a bit anxious. After all, how many would show up to hear a presentation on "Game Theory and Practical Life?" I need not have been concerned.

That Sunday afternoon Professor Aumann spoke before a full-house of over three hundred people in the YESOD Ribakoff Auditorium. It was precisely the crowd we had targeted and wanted to bring into the building: young and middle-aged Jewish academics and professionals. The presentation was carried by the Echo Moscow radio station and covered on local television.

Though personally very modest and understated, Professor Aumann had a very impressive appearance, with a knitted white kippah and a matching long flowing white beard, someone whom you would not usually see on the streets of St. Petersburg. The program began with a video of his being awarded the Nobel Prize in Stockholm. The opening shot featuring an Israeli flag fluttering over the Swedish capital.

Professor Aumann was asked during the question-and-answer portion if he found it hard to reconcile being a world-renowned scientist with being a religious Jew. He saw no contradiction: "Science is a way of perceiving the physical world. Judaism is an experience. It can be compared to playing the piano. When playing the piano, you don't try to understand the physical world. You have an experience."

Following the presentation, we held a festive reception in his honor in the library. One of the attendees told me: "Yonatan, I never felt so proud to be a Jew as I did this evening." That feeling was shared by many who attended.

Thinking back, the heartfelt response to hearing Professor Aumann in St. Petersburg that day reminded me of Rabbi Adin Steinsaltz's charge to us on a Shabbat afternoon in Moscow a dozen years before: "We need to return pride to the Jews of the former Soviet Union."

That day we had definitely succeeded.

RETURNING TO YESOD A DECADE LATER

In 2018, I accompanied thirty-five adults on a Keshet Jewish Educational Tour to Moscow and St. Petersburg as the Scholar-in-Residence, and we spent four hours visiting YESOD. It was my first time back in ten years, and it was a very personal and emotional experience for me. We were received royally, just like the visiting JDC and UJA-Federation Missions I had welcomed so often when I was the country director, only now, I was the guest and not the host.

As impressed as our group was by the imposing physical appearance of the building, it was even more attracted to the "soul" of YESOD and the renascent St. Petersburg Jewish community.

Elena Eybshits, the local representative of the JDC, greeted us and gave us a briefing. She opened by sharing her personal story:

> Our family was not Jewishly involved. I had been working for years for local and international organizations, and I felt that it was time to help my own people. I needed it for my soul.

When I applied for the job to direct the local JDC office a few years ago, and was asked to which Jewish organization I belonged, I replied: "To none – and it is an advantage! No one can accuse me of favoritism or being too parochial!"

My Jewish father, Binyamin Moiseivich Eybshits, was a three-star major general in the Soviet army, and our son, his grandson, moved to Israel and served in Tzahal, the Israeli army.

Our eyes opened wide in astonishment and awe as Elena recounted the story of the generations of her family. What she described about her father and her son – one in the Soviet army and the other in the Israeli army – was never supposed to happen. Soviet Jews were destined, so we had imagined, to assimilate and disappear, not to suddenly and almost inexplicably assert their Jewish identity and actively reconnect with the Jewish people.

Our next speaker, Masha Aryeva, the director of the YESOD JCC, told us that even though she came from a Jewish family on both sides, they were "internationalists." The only Jewish experience she knew growing up was eating a piece of matzah on Pesach. Before she came to work at YESOD eight years ago, she hadn't even known that the building existed!

Since she had been running the YESOD JCC, she had learned for the first time what it meant to be Jewish. In her words: "We danced the dance together." Her eight-year-old daughter grew up in the building and went to camp and school there. Her goal was to make all Jews feel welcome, and to this end, she partnered with as many of the organizations in the city as she could.

We met with Genia Lvova, the founder of the Jewish Family Center "Adain Lo," which had a branch at YESOD, and one of the pioneers of Jewish renewal in the post-Soviet Union. Adain Lo was created by Genia and her friends – mostly underground Jewish activists who wanted to reach out and help the many impoverished Jewish families and children who were affected by the economic and social collapse of the Soviet Union – around her kitchen table in 1991.

When I introduced her as a "Jewish hero," she responded with words of Torah, inspired by the actions of an ancient Jewish heroine. When she would arrive unannounced to ask local businessmen for money, she said that she "felt like Queen Esther," who similarly appeared unexpectedly in front of the king. "I soon realized that after five years of working on Adain Lo, I was no longer a computer programmer; I had become a Jewish professional."

She explained that many foreign visitors would ask her which "branch" of the Jewish world they identified with: Orthodox, Conservative, or Reform. Her response was "Adain Lo" (in Hebrew: *adayin lo*, "not yet"), quoting from the early twentieth-century German Jewish intellectual Franz Rosenzweig. They had embarked on a Jewish voyage of a lifetime and were enjoying the journey.

In her view, the Russian Jewish community was in transition, the leadership was aging, and many Jews were making aliyah. She wisely cautioned that while the situation has never been better for Russian Jews, this should not be taken for granted.

We toured the building, visiting an Adain Lo workshop for young adults with disabilities, and Hesed Avraham, the first and largest JDC-sponsored welfare program in the FSU. At the seniors' club, we asked how many recalled the nine-hundred-day Leningrad Blockade, and most of the hands went up. One of the women took out a picture of her underground Jewish wedding in 1954, which she always kept in her purse.

I asked one of our group members, Pearl from Philadelphia – who visited the Soviet Union with me as a USYer in the early 1970s and now returned with her husband David nearly half-a-century later – to share her feelings. She expressed how exciting and inspirational it was for her to be with them, and what an unanticipated treat it was to see how much Jewish life had changed and developed since her first visit.

As we prepared to depart the group of seniors, I said we would never forget them, and thanked them for not forgetting us. They sang "Heveinu Shalom Aleichem" in our honor as we tearfully departed.

Gathering on the steps in the atrium and posing for a group picture, we began to sing "Hineh mah tov u'mah na'im," the words that were inscribed on the wall directly in front of us in Hebrew and Russian. It was just like we were in our own Jewish home. (See photos.)

Visiting YESOD was a powerful and evocative experience. I remarked to Saul, one of our group members: "We aren't worthy to be in their presence. This is totally a place of mitzvah, of Jews helping fellow Jews."

I departed YESOD that day with deep regard and affection for all of those who had taken this wonderful project to its next level and was proud to have been one of its builders.

CHAPTER 24

A Time for Goodbyes and Farewells

MY FATHER, OF BLESSED MEMORY

On Shabbat morning, December 1, 2007, my father passed away. In the words of my eulogy, this was the essence of his life's story:

> Tzvi H. Porath, may his memory be for a blessing, was born in Jerusalem, in the old Sha'arei Zedek Hospital, on the third candle of Chanukah in 1916. He was brought to America at age six, grew up in Cleveland, became a rabbi, and served the American Jewish community for sixty years. When he was in his late eighties, he and my mother returned home to Jerusalem, to be with our family. He passed away a few days short of his ninety-first birthday, in the same hospital where he was born.

That was my father. His life had come full circle, ending where it began, in Jerusalem. He had an enormous impact on me and my future direction. I absorbed my Jewish calling from him. Serving the Jewish people was in our veins for generations. Both of my grandfathers, originally from Jerusalem and Lithuania, were also American pulpit rabbis, in Cleveland and Minneapolis. Although I was not consciously aware of it when I joined the JDC, working with the Jews of Russia was destined to be my rabbinate, in the footsteps of the generations before me.

I was now faced with an entirely new situation. I wanted to mourn my father while faithfully maintaining my professional responsibilities with the Joint. How I melded those two together was to present very interesting challenges, as well as opportunities, over the following year.

After an initial period of private mourning, I was prepared to return to the field, though not without some hesitancy. I felt more muted and contemplative and much less outgoing than usual.

My first occasion to appear at a large public event was at the Fifteenth Annual SEFER International Conference on Jewish Studies in Moscow, in January 2008. In honor of the gathering I had prepared one of the keynote presentations: "Jewish Mourning and Its Response to the Human Condition: Personal Reflections."

At the opening session, we had already planned to mark the loss of three of the most significant figures in the rebuilding of academic Judaica in the former Soviet Union: Professor Nehemia Levtzion from Jerusalem, Professor Rashid Kaplanov from Moscow, and Professor John Klier from London.

- Professor Nehemia Levtzion, the director of Jerusalem's International Center for the University Teaching of Jewish Civilization, had been the chairman of the Planning and Budget Committee of the Israeli university system, in essence, Israel's minister for University Education. He and Ralph Goldman were the intellectual "founders" of SEFER. They had the vision that academic Judaica would deeply resonate in the post-Soviet reality. All the rest of us were followers – partners, contributors, organizers – but the dream came from Nehemia and Ralph. Since Nehemia's passing in August 2003, SEFER had dedicated the opening session of the annual conference to his memory.
- Professor Rashid Kaplanov, who had passed away in November, was the founding academic chairman of SEFER and the president of the European Association of Jewish Studies, a remarkable statement about the progress and regard Jewish studies in the FSU had achieved, less than a generation after the collapse of the Soviet Union. The *Times* of London wrote of him: "One of the world's great polyglots – a scruffy, …lovable man with a prodigious memory and a mastery of 36 languages," who "did much to foster Jewish learning and culture."[1] He loved his students and colleagues and was beloved by them. Rashid, together with Dr. Victoria Mochalova, the executive director, was the heart and soul of SEFER.
- Professor John Klier, who died in September, was one of the world's leading historians of Russian Jewish studies. He was the Professor of Modern Jewish History at University College London and endowed with "a modest and beguiling charm" in the words of the *Times*. He was born into a Catholic family in Pennsylvania and relocated to London. He never failed to attend the annual SEFER conferences, bringing students and faculty with him to Moscow, and enabling undergraduates of academic Judaica in the former Soviet Union to study at University College. John's

---

1. "Professor Rashid Kaplanov," *Times* of London, January 7, 2008, https://www.thetimes .co.uk/article/professor-rashid-kaplanov-6wgrfpd5k53.

presence signaled to the international academic community that SEFER was not a "parochial" endeavor, and was worthy of support across all religious and national lines.

In memory of all of the above, as well as of my late father, I described how Jewish mourning spoke to the soul of the mourners and helped them/us to cope with and to recover from their/our loss. It allowed me to reflect on how the wisdom of the tradition applied to contemporary life, for all people, and from all backgrounds. I concluded by reciting the El Maleh Rachamim memorial prayer.

Although I did not quite realize it at the time, my appearance and presentation at SEFER was a cathartic and spiritual moment for me as well. I was now ready to go out into the field.

MOURNING ON THE ROAD

Had I spent the following year in Israel, I would have attended daily morning, afternoon, and evening prayers to say the Mourner's Kaddish and, wherever possible, lead the congregation. I knew that would be impossible on my field trips to Russia because travel schedules would not allow it, and the local communities I would be visiting, especially in the periphery, did not maintain a full schedule of daily prayer services. If they were able to meet once a day, usually in the morning, that was already a major accomplishment.

I felt that my first obligation was to be certain that Kaddish was said in my father's memory at the required times, so whenever I was about to depart for a trip, I would ask another mourner at our daily minyan in Jerusalem to include my father in his prayers and offered to do the same for him, whenever needed. No matter what transpired on the road, I would have fulfilled my basic responsibility.

But that was not enough. I resolved to make the maximum effort to attend existing services in Russia, wherever possible. I asked Yossie Shuster, the JDC representative in Central Russia, the Volga, and the Urals, a Lithuanian-born Israeli with a warm Jewish heart, to arrange with the local rabbis a special minyan during my field visits so I could recite Kaddish.

And off I went.

In mid-February, Shabbat was over in Jerusalem at 6:00 p.m. A cab whisked me to the Ben Gurion Airport in time to catch an 8:15 p.m. flight to Moscow. I got to my hotel room at 2:00 a.m., slept three hours, returned to the airport to board the first flight to St. Petersburg at 7:30 a.m., landed at 8:35 a.m., and arrived in the Great Synagogue at 9:20 a.m., in time to say Kaddish!

There was a certain "Jewish bravado" to all of this rushing and running around, but the intention was real and honest. I was a son in mourning and wanted to do what was right. In addition, my situation had also created an unexpected opportunity to demonstrate to local Jews what it was like to live a traditional Jewish life.

A HIDDEN TREASURE IN ORENBURG

I had not visited Orenburg, located nine hundred miles southeast of Moscow, in many years and was amazed at the progress. The old synagogue, which had been expropriated by the Soviets and turned into the city archives, had been returned to the Jewish community and renovated. Chabad emissaries, Rabbi Goel and Kineret Meyers had come to town, restarted the shul, set up a kindergarten, day school, summer camp, and an active Hesed Community Welfare Center. They were typical of dozens of dedicated rabbinic families living in the periphery, maintaining and enriching Jewish life. Some of the rabbis even had acquired Russian citizenship and were planning on serving their communities for a lifetime.

Rabbi Meyers gathered a minyan of men at the shul so that I could say Kaddish. I used the brief break between the afternoon and evening prayers to speak to the group about their community, Jewish mourning, and my father.

I half-kibbitzed with them saying that I was not certain what the proper protocol was for this occasion: "Should *I* be thanking *you* for graciously gathering, particularly on a cold winter's afternoon, so I can say Kaddish, or, should *you* be thanking *me*, for the opportunity to come to shul and be part of a minyan?" Both were correct. I was, indeed, very grateful for all of their efforts, and honored that they allowed me to respect my father's memory.

I recalled my first visit to Orenburg, almost a dozen years previously, when things were slowly getting organized. The synagogue building was in disrepair, having only recently been restored to the community. The religious congregation consisted of a handful of older men. There were a few younger businessmen interested, but not a lot was happening.

Yaakov, who was the head of the community at the time, was eager to show me something from Orenburg's Jewish past. As we pulled up in front of a typical older-style wooden house, a woman opened the door and showed us in. I didn't quite know why we were there, but I was soon to find out. She led us to a wooden cabinet on the floor, inside of which was what appeared to be a rolled-up bolt of colorful cloth. With great care, she picked it up, set it on the table, and unwrapped the coverings.

Lying in front of us on the table was a Torah scroll. It had been removed from the once-functioning local synagogue before it was shuttered and was hidden away, in this woman's safekeeping. It was very important for them to show it to me, as a representative of the Joint and of the entire Jewish people.

And now, a dozen years later, sitting in the recently refurbished shul in Orenburg in 2008, I warmly acknowledged that they had proven worthy of the precious *sefer Torah* that was entrusted to their care, and had restored it to its rightful location. That was an extraordinary act of hope and faith in the Jewish future.

Everywhere I traveled in those days, Samara, Perm, Ufa, Chelyabinsk, and others, local Jews would gather so I could say Kaddish. I will be forever grateful.

A TIME FOR GOODBYES

Upon my return to Jerusalem from a field visit to the Urals in June 2008, Asher asked to meet with me, to convey some unexpected news. The JDC had decided to do some major restructuring, and my position, together with that of many other Russian department country directors and senior staff, was ending. Even though I had heard talk of major changes, nonetheless it still came as a shock.

In my remaining few weeks, there were many goodbyes and thank-yous I wanted to make.

I decided to take our youngest son, Shlomo Reuven, then twenty-two, along with me on a trip to Russia, while I still had the opportunity. I had taken one of his sisters, Batsheva Miriam, previously. We stopped in Moscow, saw Red Square, visited the Kremlin, ate at the Chabad center, and then spent a few lovely days in St. Petersburg, seeing the sites. We went to the Hermitage and to Peterhoff, and we took a late Russian evening canal ride. I was very glad that I was able to preserve at least some connection with my years at the Joint as part of our family's collective memory.

COMMUNITY FAREWELLS

Transitions are very important in life. I had been working for the JDC in Russia for fifteen years, since August 1993, and it was now July 2008. So much had changed and developed over that critical period. I wanted to mark what the JDC and the local communities had achieved together during that time, and how much those relationships meant to me, personally.

YESOD was the most fitting location for the St. Petersburg event. In addition to the local JDC staff, Asher flew in to be with us, and his presence was very much appreciated. The leaders of many of the local organizations attended, including Rabbi Pewzner from the Great Synagogue, Rabbi Stas from the Progressive Congregation, Genia Lvova from Adain Lo, Lenoid Kolton from Hesed, as well as the head of the Hesed in Murmansk.

In his comments, Asher referred to me as "a real hero." That certainly applied to my wife and family for supporting and enabling me to travel so extensively to the field, on the average of once a month for fifteen years. I had been on the road for a long time and looked forward to being at home again.

On our last morning together in St. Petersburg, I wanted to share some personal thoughts with Asher. I said to him that, even though my position with the JDC was concluding, I would be remiss if I did not thank him personally, from the depths of my heart, for the extraordinary experience, privilege, and mitzvah of the past fifteen years. He had invited me to join the Russian Department and had supported me throughout. Working for the JDC and being able to help shape and influence the future of post-Soviet Jewry was the privilege of a lifetime and would forever remain an integral part of me.

From St. Petersburg, I traveled to Yekaterinburg, for a different kind of good-bye. In addition to the JDC office staff, we were joined by the local Chabad rabbi, the representative of the Jewish Agency, and community leaders from all over the Urals, including Izhevsk, Perm, Ufa, Nizhni-Tagil, Chelyabinsk, Yekaterinburg, and others. Each of our private conversations brought to mind projects we had worked on together over the years, whether organizing a Jewish wedding, founding a Hillel, constructing a new community building, or opening a Hesed. We had taken the first steps together in supporting and developing each of their communities, which would hopefully continue to grow in the future.

I was especially moved when Alla Borisovna, head of the Menorah JCC in Yekaterinburg, who had been born before World War II, called me "the first rabbi she had ever met." What a powerful designation, weighty both in history as well as responsibility.

As we parted, perhaps never to meet again in the future, I said goodbye with a heavy, yet full, heart. I felt a deep personal connection to many of them and recalled with great affection our time together. I look back with great fondness at my work in the Russian periphery as one of the hallmarks of my years with the JDC.

THE FINAL FAREWELL – IN JERUSALEM

The season of goodbyes concluded with a gathering of colleagues at the JDC Russian Department in Jerusalem. Even though it was held on a weekday, I came dressed in my Shabbat best. They honored me with a special menu, including bottles of Diet Coke, my "beverage of choice" over the years.

The Jerusalem staff were all present. Working in one office together for fifteen years on a shared mission creates the feeling of close family. I was very appreciative of their support and friendship and welcomed the opportunity to thank them in person. My senior representatives from the field, Menachem Lepkivker, from the St. Petersburg office, and Yossie Shuster from Yekaterinburg, were there with their wives, as were Ralph Goldman and Stanley Abramovitch.

I expressed my profoundly felt thanks to all, and Asher, in his usual very gracious way, spoke on behalf of the JDC. He noted the "purposeful enthusiasm" which I brought to all that I did, particularly to all things Jewish.

The fifteen years at the JDC had passed very quickly. In the years to come, I would often wonder how things in Russia had developed after I left. How much was short-term or ephemeral, and how much was longer-lasting. A decade later, in person, I was to find out.

CHAPTER 25

Revisiting Jewish Russia

RETURNING THE BURNT BIBLE

It was the summer of 2018. I had been invited by Steve Zerobnick, a neighbor and friend, and one of the directors of Keshet Educational Journeys, to participate in a great adventure, to serve as the Scholar-in-Residence for a "Russian Jewish Journey" to Moscow and St. Petersburg. My role was to organize and guide the Jewish portion of the tour, which turned out to be the leitmotif of the entire visit.

As I was packing for the trip, it suddenly came to mind. I rummaged through all of my papers and storage boxes before finally locating the partially burnt and water-stained copy of the biblical book of Exodus, in Russian and Hebrew, which I had been keeping for years. The damaged book had long ago belonged in a burial place for worn and desecrated holy objects, but apparently, it still had sentimental and symbolic value for me, far more than I realized, and I slipped it inside my bag.

I had been to Russia many, many times, but this would be different: I was going to introduce Jewish Russia to a group of thirty-four active and sophisticated adults from America and Israel, all of whom were involved in their local communities and synagogues. Religiously, the group spanned the spectrum from Orthodox Neo-Hassidic to a Reform woman rabbi. One of the participants was a former USYer whom I had taken to Russia as a teenager nearly fifty years earlier.

We would highlight the Soviet and Russian Jewish experiences over the past century and look into the future. Since I had been a witness to much of what had transpired over the past fifty plus years, I would be able to add my perspectives as well.

On our first evening together in Moscow, I laid out the primary challenge of our trip: *we had come to visit a country that no longer existed.* With that, I spread out one of my old-time oversized Russian maps bearing the heading: "Union of Soviet Socialist Republics." We would have to begin our trip from there. We would constantly need to compare the current reality with what had existed in the past and delve into how much that legacy continues to impact the present day.

On a personal level, our journey affected me in ways I had never expected.

Under the Soviets, only a few synagogues were permitted to function in Moscow: the Choral Synagogue on Arkhipova Street and two unmarked *shtieblach* (prayer rooms), in hidden-away corners of the city. I had visited all of them over the years.

Now, on the opening day of our visit, we were sitting in the main shul of the impressive Marina Roshcha Synagogue and Jewish Community Center, constructed by Chabad. It housed an expansive synagogue, three kosher restaurants, a gym and health club, classrooms, a library, a Jewish book store, a fully equipped auditorium, and the offices of the Chief Rabbinate of Russia. Certainly, for visitors, not to speak of Soviet Jews, it was something to behold.

Our host, Rabbi Moti Weissberg, was recounting the history of the current synagogue-JCC building. He mentioned in passing that in Soviet times, a very modest prayer house had once stood there. It had burnt down at the end of December 1993 in a fire "of unknown origin," though it was officially ascribed then to an "electrical failure." Subsequently, Chabad decided to build the current structure in its place, at the same location.

In a sudden flash of understanding, and with great emotion, I interrupted Rabbi Moti's presentation.

I told the group that I had been in Moscow the day of the fire some twenty-five years ago. Upon hearing the shocking news that December morning, I rushed to the site of the still-smoldering ruins. The roof and walls had collapsed, firemen were sloshing around in the water with their hoses, and the floor was strewn with damaged, destroyed, and defiled holy books.

Realizing that everything in front of me would soon be dumped in the garbage, I bent over and retrieved a water-logged and fire-damaged copy of Shemot (the book of Exodus), put it into my bag, and brought it home with me to Jerusalem, where it sat for the next quarter-century, until…

And with that, I went into my backpack, pulled out that very same volume, and said to Rabbi Moti: "I have come to fulfill the mitzvah of *hashavat aveidah* [returning a lost item]. Twenty-five years ago, this holy book was nearly discarded in this very place, and today I have brought it home."

Stunned and emotionally overcome, we embraced. Tears of shock, surprise, recognition, relief, and great thanksgiving flowed freely.[1] (See photos.)

Our group looked on in wonderment and awe. It was an unforgettable and dramatic start to our trip.

---

1. A version of the preceding text appeared as "Dispatches from My 175th Visit to Jewish Moscow," *Jewish Week*, February 7, 2019, https://jewishweek.timesofisrael.com /dispatches-from-my-175th-visit-to-jewish-moscow/.

Rabbi Moti wrote me the next day: "*Todah Todah*! Many, many, many thanks for the extraordinarily emotional visit. I was especially moved by your singular presentation. It is a gift for the ages! You are a true friend of our community."

That burnt and water-stained book, with such deep spiritual significance, symbolized the Jews of Russia. Against all odds and in face of all adversity, they would survive as well.

Soviet Jewish Torah in Red Square

We were standing in the middle of Moscow's Red Square.

We had already seen the statue of Soviet war hero Marshal Zhukov, visited Lenin's Tomb, pointed out Stalin's grave, as I began describing the epic Moscow Victory Parade of June 24, 1945, celebrating the defeat of the Germans. I had brought with me the stirring photograph of Zhukov leading the parade, astride his white horse Kumir, almost floating in the air as he rode by the very spot where we stood.

The photo was taken by Yevgeny Khaldei, a Ukrainian Jew, who was one of the most well-known Soviet World War II photographers. He had shot the *second-most* famous picture of the entire war. He had seen Joe Rosenthal's iconic photo *Raising the Flag on Iwo Jima* from February 1945 and was inspired to create something equally memorable. He asked his uncle in Moscow to make a large Soviet flag out of bedsheets, which he took with him to Berlin, where he photographed his celebrated picture *Raising the Flag over the Reichstag* on May 2, 1945.

Khaldei was one of the half a million Soviet Jews who fought in the Red Army during the war, about a third of whom were killed, 160,000 decorated, and 150 honored as Heroes of the Soviet Union.

I showed another wartime picture Khaldei had taken in January 1945 in Budapest, of two dazed and fearful Hungarian Jews, a husband and wife, who had just emerged from the rubble of the fighting, still wearing their "yellow stars" on their coats. Initially, they were terrified of him, and thought he was a German soldier or SS man until Khaldei said to them in Yiddish: "*Ich bin oykhet a yid. Shalom aleichem!*" (I also am a Jew. Shalom!). He tore off their yellow badges and told them they were now free.

He was a Soviet Jewish boy, loyally serving his country as well as his people. His father and four sisters had been murdered by the Nazis. Subsequently, he was "downsized" by the authorities and, in October 1948, was fired from his photo-journalist position, precisely at the time of Stalin's purges of Jews. Khaldei himself attributed the firing to antisemitism.

I posed the following question to the group: what would you do if your two identities, as a loyal citizen and as a Jew, were in tension or collided? That was a situation that confronted Jews over and over again; not only in the USSR but in other diasporas as well, throughout Jewish history.

I shared with the group a piece of "Soviet Jewish Torah," a story from the Talmud (*Shabbat* 33b). It tells of a two-thousand-year-old conversation in then Roman Palestine, Israel of today.

> Rabbi Yehuda spoke first: "The accomplishments of this nation, Rome, are so marvelous! They laid out the streets and marketplaces, built the bridges, maintain public baths."
>
> Rabbi Yossi kept silent.
>
> Rabbi Shimon Bar Yochai responded as follows: "Everything they made was only for their own purposes: market places to house prostitutes; public baths to indulge themselves; bridges to collect customs duties."
>
> Yehuda Ben Gerim went and repeated their words until they reached the authorities.
>
> The Romans decreed: "Yehuda, who praised, should be elevated; Yossi, who remained silent, should be exiled; Shimon, who condemned, should be executed.

It was a timeless test of ultimate Jewish loyalty.

I had always imagined transposing this ancient exchange to Red Square, in Stalin's time. Imagine, say in 1950 or so, four Soviet Jews standing in Moscow exactly where we are now, looking over this magnificent plaza and the walls of the Kremlin.

Rabbi Yehuda, perhaps Yevgeny in Russian, launches into resounding praise of the Soviets, and by implication, The Leader: Look at their amazing accomplishments; look what they have built in only a few short years since the Revolution. Soviet Power is immutable. That is our future as loyal Soviet citizens and as Jews.

The next in line, Yossie, maybe Ilya, says nothing. He knows full well that he is expected to echo and elaborate upon what he had just heard, yet he doesn't utter a word. His silence is deafening and noticed.

Rabbi Shimon Bar Yochai, Semyon, speaks treason. He talks without fear or hesitation and calls a spade a spade. Everything the regime did is corrupt and immoral. All we see is a sham and a lie.

Yehuda ben Gerim, Misha, chatters too much, and the conversation reaches the KGB. Was he an informer? We are not told.

Yevgeny is rewarded, Ilya is sent to the Gulag, and Semyon is marked for death.

Suddenly, the two-thousand-year-old Talmudic tale no longer sounded so remote or distant. It had striking parallels in a society that demanded absolute allegiance. The story was set in Roman Palestine and repeated itself generation after generation. Soviet Jews were forced to struggle under the suspicion and accusation of having "dual loyalties" or of being "cosmopolitans," and were often required or expected to "prove" their faithfulness to the regime, often with dire consequences.

EXPRESSIONS OF JEWISH PRIDE

As we toured Moscow, we were struck repeatedly by public displays of Jewish self-respect, dignity, and success, in addition to the previously mentioned Marina Roshcha Synagogue-JCC.

The Jewish Museum and Tolerance Center, opened in 2012, featured a state-of-the-art interactive exhibition that took you from the shtetl, through Tsarist and Soviet times, to the present day. You could visit a Ukrainian shul, see an actual T-34 tank from World War II (the State Commissar for Tank Production was a Jew), admire an original of Khaldei's photograph *Raising the Flag over the Reichstag*, stand with Golda Meir in front of the Arkhipova Street synagogue in 1948, meet refuseniks in a Moscow forest, and view video interviews describing the rebuilding of Russian Jewish life today.

A coffee shop and Jewish bookstore greeted you on your way out. This place of immense local Jewish pride also reached out to non-Jewish schools and other visitors, demonstrating the positive role of Jews in Russian life. Contrasted with the past, when the Jews were either ignored, denigrated, or vilified, it was revolutionary.

The Kosher Gourmet food store-emporium supplied kosher products to Moscow, as well as all over the country, in as fancy a western-style as you could imagine, something previously inconceivable in Russia. It was long thought that religious Jewish life in Russia would be impossible to maintain, but apparently not. I knew that all the rabbis and their families observed kashrut and had established kosher kitchens in shuls, but still, I wondered how widespread it had become among local Russian Jews.

I recalled traveling in the Urals in the 1990s for a week when I had to bring all twenty-one meals with me. Kosher food, then unattainable, was now available to all who wished.

The Holocaust Memorial Synagogue at the Poklonnaya Gora Museum of the Great Patriotic War (World War II) has a permanent exhibition on the Holocaust in the Soviet Union, focusing on the role, valor, and sacrifice of Jewish fighters in the Red Army and partisans. Here, as an integral part of the official Russian

Victory Park Memorial Complex, the national site of memory, complementing a Russian Orthodox church and a mosque, there was a synagogue and Jewish museum. Funded by members of the Russian Jewish Congress and dedicated by President Boris Yeltsin in 1998, it was a powerful statement about the radically changed status of Jews in the post-Soviet era.

YESOD, the St. Petersburg Jewish Community Home, opened in 2006, which so impressed us during our visit, was a source of great Jewish community self-respect.

It was clear that local Jews were permitted and even encouraged to express feelings of Jewish national pride, something quite normal and acceptable in our home countries, but ground-breaking in a Russian context.

Each of these buildings, and others like them in other former Soviet cities, served as a new focus for current and future Jewish life. The message was clear: after decades of State-imposed suppression, concealment, and hiding, the Jews of Russia had returned to the public sphere with their heads held high.

Welcoming Shabbat in St. Petersburg

Nowhere was that renewed local Jewish spirit better expressed then when we joined the Shaarei Shalom Progressive Congregation in St. Petersburg, for Kabbalat Shabbat services. (See photos.)

Steve Zerobnick, our Keshet group leader, described it beautifully as follows:

> I looked around at the faces in the room at the Kabbalat Shabbat services at the Shaarei Shalom Progressive Synagogue in St. Petersburg. These were Russian Jews who had chosen to come to synagogue after seven decades of forced atheism, official antisemitism, and aggressive state-sponsored attempts to sever their connection with Judaism and other Jews. They finally had the opportunity to rejoin Judaism and the Jewish world, and they voted with their feet.
>
> They chose to be an active part of the Jewish people against all odds.
>
> As we sang the Friday evening prayers with them, replete with familiar tunes, the feeling of Jewish unity was palpable.
>
> Sitting together in the synagogue, we felt like family; through the language of Jewish text and prayer, we felt a sense of solidarity.[2]

---

2. Steve Zerobnick, from his blog entry "Welcoming Shabbat with the Jews of St. Petersburg," July 2018. Quoted with permission.

It was particularly heartwarming to join them that early Shabbat evening. It was apparent that the very "user friendly" setting, with congregational singing, family seating, and words of explanation and welcome, spoke to their hearts. One of our group members, Rabbi Dina Finegold from Kenosha, Wisconsin, delivered the sermon. In a country as large as Russia, there was plenty of room for different modes and expressions of being Jewish.

Moscow's Choral Synagogue

No visit to Jewish Moscow would be complete without stopping by the Choral Synagogue on Spasoglinishchevskiy Street, known in Jewish circles around the world by its former name, Arkhipova Street. It was sometimes difficult to locate in Soviet times, but now there were municipal street signs in Russian and English with little Stars of David on them, so you couldn't miss it! What the Soviets had sought to hide was now displayed for all to see.

As we stood in front of the shul, I reflected on its place and significance for local Jews. In its time, this was the central "Soviet Jewish address." In years past, Soviet Jews would gather there en masse on special occasions. On Rosh Hashanah 1942, it was completely packed. About a quarter of the worshippers were in uniform, reciting prayers for the victory of the Red Army and the survival of the Jewish people.

When Golda Meir arrived in Moscow in 1948 as the newly appointed Israeli ambassador to the USSR and attended High Holiday services, throngs of Jews came to see her. When she appeared, she was greeted with enthusiastic cheers of "*Am Yisrael chai*," to which she responded in Yiddish: "I thank you for having remained Jews." Golda's visit was so memorable and iconic, that a photograph of the event, with her face clearly visible, was printed on the old Israeli ten-shekel banknote, together with the words "*Shalach et ami*" (Let my people go).

Over time, the weekday minyan had shrunk to a few dozen of the elderly faithful, though a larger congregation would gather on Shabbat morning and holidays.

Elie Wiesel's account of Simchat Torah on Arkhipova Street in his 1966 book *The Jews of Silence* was a turning point in raising American and world Jewish consciousness to the plight of Soviet Jews. It drew me here for Simchat Torah in 1968 and changed the direction of my life.

I imagined that my warm recollections and memories were not shared by the large swath of Soviet Jews, for whom this synagogue and all others were foreign and often hostile places; but certainly, over the years, as Jewish life contracted and memories aged, it remained the Jewish venue for locals as well as visitors. It even successfully reinvented itself as the central meeting place for refuseniks with foreign tourists from the 1970s onward.

Moscow's Choral Synagogue and Arkhipova Street had played critical roles in maintaining a Jewish presence and awareness during the Soviet years. In the post-Soviet era, they had been supplemented by newly constructed and rebuilt synagogue buildings all over the former Soviet Union, but it had all started there. Some would say that without this central address, nothing would have survived.

HIDDEN SECRETS IN THE MALL OF RUSSIA

Moscow's upscale Afimall, the Mall of Russia, is a shopper's paradise: more than four hundred shops, fifty restaurants, an IMAX theater, and five shopping levels, all under a glass ceiling with an imposing view of skyscrapers towering overhead. It also boasts the Yaffo Restaurant, a very "cool" and trendy kosher eatery.

But that was not what was special about the shopping center. Following dinner and looking for a private place to meet with our evening speakers, we asked the Yaffo's manager if there was somewhere else in the building where we could gather. As if on cue, one of the staff said "come with me," and we followed him rather blindly through the maze of the shops and escalators, into the bowels of the building, opened an unmarked door, and in front of us was…a hidden synagogue, fully furnished with a holy ark, Torah scrolls, a reader's table, and prayer books!

I was immediately flooded by memories of my visits to Russia years ago, when I would open a door, and discover a room with elderly Jews, gathered to pray; only we were not in the late 1960s, we were fifty years later, in the heart of an upscale popular Moscow mall.

Our guide explained that "Afimall," was the brand name for "Africa-Israel Investments," a project of Lev Leviev, the billionaire Israeli-Russian businessman, originally from Bukhara, in Soviet Central Asia. Leviev was an observant Jew and a major supporter of Chabad projects throughout the former Soviet Union. He included mini-shuls in many of his buildings, even though there were no regular services, "Just in case." Perhaps he was anticipating our group! Indeed, three of Leviev's staff were overjoyed at our coming, since now they had a minyan to say Kaddish.

It was a most appropriate setting, in a hidden shul in the heart of a modern mall, to hear about the past, present, and future of post-Soviet Jewish life.

We had invited Russian Hillel activists from across the generations to share their stories. (See photos.)

Ilya, whose story we related earlier (see chapter 18), was a true pioneer. Born in 1970 in Tyumen, Siberia, he grew up in a typical Soviet environment with barely any mention of being a Jew, participated in a March of the Living visit to Poland in the early nineties, and organized one of the earliest Jewish festivals "Chanukah in Siberia." He was the first local to serve as a JDC Representative in Russia.

Anna, a decade younger, had attended Project Judaica, an intensive Jewish studies program at one of Moscow's premier universities, studied Yiddish language and literature at Columbia University and the Jewish Theological Seminary in New York, and was presently the director of education for Hillel in Russia.

Violetta discovered Judaism on her own as a teenager, with no apparent Jewish connections. She decided to study Hebrew at age sixteen, and a few years later stopped eating pork, as well as milk and meat products together. "Funny," one of her relatives remarked, much to her surprise, "your grandfather also ate like that." Without knowing it, she had originated from a Jewish family. She had already been to Israel six times, was studying for conversion, and planned on making aliyah.

As they recounted their journeys, our group was mesmerized. I wrote to our guests the following day:

> You can't imagine the deep emotional Jewish responses your heartfelt words of last evening evoked. In simple words: They loved it!
>
> Especially striking was the interconnectedness of the three of you, from Ilya to Anna to Violetta; the passing on the torch of Russian Jewish life and tradition, in the most powerful of ways.
>
> You gave us hope and faith for the Jewish people, as well as for our own local communities.

It was beyond encouraging and hopeful to hear such heartfelt Jewish stories in the depths of the Mall of Russia.

PARTING QUESTIONS AND FUTURE TASKS

Our Keshet Russian Jewish Journey participants were amazed and very moved by what we had seen. The experience had deeply impressed and affected them. So much had been achieved in little more than a generation since the fall of the Soviet Union. I was very proud to have done my part, together with my colleagues and our local partners, in reaching this point.

Even with all of this growth and success, it would not be an easy task to fully rebuild and reconstitute Jewish life in the former Soviet Union. Much remained to be done.

Many critical questions regarding the future of post-Soviet Jewry came to mind, including:

- Would this progress continue and take root? Did the local Jews have the financial commitment and staying-power required to support themselves, as well as to continue building? Would younger leaders emerge with the vision and wisdom necessary to lead the community in the years to come? Would the established leaders make room for the newcomers?
- What would the future Jewish community look like culturally, nationally, and demographically? Would the periphery empty, leaving major Jewish populations only in a few key urban centers? Who would take care of those remaining in remote locations, especially the elderly and needy?
- What would be the nature of Jewish religious and spiritual life? How would Jewish knowledge and tradition be passed on? How would the local rabbinate, which was overwhelmingly Orthodox, be able to address the expectations and needs of post-Soviet Jews, who were overwhelmingly secular? Would there be a way for those with Jewish roots to formally "rejoin" the Jewish people as full members?
- With more and more Russian-speaking Jews spread out around the world, including Israel, the US, Canada and Germany, would the remaining local Jews stay or relocate to their relatives' home countries? Might Russian Jews who had emigrated, contemplate returning? No Jewish community is more closely connected to Israel than post-Soviet Jewry. Would that continue and develop?
- How would the local and international political situations affect the future of Jewish life? In the post-Soviet period, Jewish life in Russia and Ukraine have flourished and expanded. Would future governments be as supportive of Jewish life as the present ones? Would antisemitism rear its ugly head once again?

These questions, of finances, leadership, demographics, religious life, conversion, relocation, Israel, local politics, and others are common to *all* Jewish communities throughout the world, not only in Russia. Perhaps that was the ultimate message of our visit: *Russian Jewry, despite its difficult and troubled past, was rejoining the ranks of world Jewry.*

Our Russian Jewish Journey group had come from the US and Israel to encourage the local Jews and to give them strength; instead, wherever we went, to synagogues, Jewish museums and memorials, kosher restaurants, JCC's, Hillels, and all the rest, we came away enriched, encouraged, and inspired by their

renewed Jewish spirit. Ultimately, the visit helped us to understand and appreciate our own Jewish lives.

Truly, in the words of the Jewish schoolchildren in Kiev thirty years ago:
"Here, we are all Jews," just like the rest of the Jewish communities around the
world.

CHAPTER 26

Closing Reflections on the Journeys

THEIR WORDS

My journeys to the Jews of the Soviet Union and Russia over the past half-century were deeply emotional and heartfelt; they became an intimate part of my life. As Ruchel, one of our former USYers, expressed it nearly fifty years later: "I still carry these people with me in my soul..."

Anyone privileged to meet and connect with Russian Jews during those times will never forget the experience. What can we learn from these encounters that speak to us today? What can we take with us for our own Jewish futures?

We should listen, once again, to their words and hear their voices. They capture the essence of their messages and wisdom, of their teachings and their Torah.

Words of Jewish courage: "Absolutely! [We will never give up hope!]" – Chacham Yitzchak from Tbilisi, 1968.

Words of Jewish longing: "I haven't spoken Hebrew for thirty years – and I am going to the Land of Israel" – A new *oleh* from Vilna in transit to Israel in the Vienna train station, 1969.

Words of anguish and challenge: "You aren't doing enough for us!" – Noach from Leningrad, 1970.

Words of incalculable loss: "Our shul, our home, was destroyed!" – Reb Yonah from Moscow, 1972.

Words of faith: "God knows that you and I are one." – Maria, the Pioneer Camp nurse in Kiev, 1972.

Words of Jewish memory and faithfulness: "You are just like our long-lost brother Joseph. You haven't forgotten us." – Reb Nechemyah from Leningrad, 1973.

Words of encouragement: "We are not poor, second-class Jews!" – Me, addressing Urals seminar, 1997.

Words of Jewish peoplehood: "You are a Diaspora rabbi – you understand us" – Participants in Urals Shabbat seminar, 1997.

Words of thanks: "Thank you for never forgetting that you were Jews." – Me, speaking to Russian Jews, 2000s.

Words of Jewish pride: "I never felt as proud to be a Jew as I did today." – An attendee at Professor Aumann's St. Petersburg YESOD presentation, 2007.

Unexpected and astonishing words: "My father was a major general in the Red Army; my son served in Tzahal, the army of Israel." – Elena from St. Petersburg, 2018.

And perhaps most evocative and compelling of all, words of inclusiveness: "Here we are all Jews." – Jewish schoolchildren in Kiev, 1992.

That phrase from the fifth graders spoke to my heart and to those of others as well. Whenever I would recount the story of that classroom visit to audiences in the post-Soviet Union, as I did on many occasions over the years, the invariable response was a spontaneous outpouring of emotion. People nodded and smiled; their faces brightened; they broke out into applause and even cheers. The youngsters' precious and profound words of welcome and acceptance reopened the doors for them, the listeners, to rejoin the Jewish people once again.

Those expressions, and many others, still resonate within me today.

SOME LESSONS

From all of my journeys, whether under the Soviets, in the post-Soviet era, or with *olim* in Israel, the following lessons stand out.

I experienced firsthand the power of Jewish faithfulness. It was inspiring and exhilarating to see their suppressed feelings of Jewish pride and identification unexpectedly revive and reawaken. The most heartfelt moments were seeing Jews, often distant from Jewish life for generations, choosing to return and identify with the Jewish people. *I learned from them never to give up hope or assume that someone is lost forever to Am Yisrael.*

In my eyes, they were genuine Jewish heroes.

As visitors from the West and Israel, we came with the assumption that we would bring them gifts and provide support; we soon realized that whatever we had thought to give them, we received even more in return. What we were carrying in our thoughts and suitcases, they were carrying in their hearts.

I was privileged to be a teacher of Torah in ways and circumstances I had never imagined. I was moved and humbled when they told me that I was the first rabbi they had ever met. In their eyes, I represented Jewish life, tradition, and the entire Jewish people. That was a weighty responsibility.

My early interest in the Russian language, which I had studied in college, was an invaluable and even a sacred tool in allowing me to communicate directly with local Jews in my own voice.

You couldn't leave Russia without sharing what you had just experienced with others. Often, that became life-defining and life-changing. In earlier times, many who visited aspired to be worthy of the message and calling that Elie Wiesel had entrusted to us; I was not alone; his words moved a generation.

There are broader communal lessons as well.

Imagine a Jewish world where it does not matter to which synagogue you belong or don't belong; if you affiliate or don't affiliate; if you identify as Orthodox, Conservative, Reform, Reconstructionist, Jewish Renewal, or "none of the above." Institutional connections and memberships do not matter; not even who your parents are. You choose to include yourself as a part of the Jewish people.

In the words of Dr. Eugene Weiner, the Israeli sociologist who worked as a JDC special representative in Moscow in the late 1990s, the Jews of the former Soviet Union were "post-assimilationist Jews," who wanted to reclaim their Jewish identity *as they understood it*. They consciously expanded the categories of being Jewish, based on their own experience.

To my mind, no Jewish community in the world is as connected to Israel as the Jews of the former Soviet Union. They are uncompromising and outspoken supporters of the Jewish state. They don't care about being "politically correct" and aren't afraid to speak their minds. That should not come as a surprise; after all, virtually all Russian-speaking Jews have family in Israel. From their Soviet upbringing, they learned the necessity for Jews to defend themselves without relying on the outside world.

Nearly fifty years ago in my article "The Challenge of Soviet Jewry" (*United Synagogue Review*, Spring 1974), I suggested that even more important than what we do for Soviet Jewry is what Soviet Jewry does for us. Ultimately, even though the events in this book are cast mainly in the lands of the Tsars and Soviets, the lessons are not limited exclusively to the Russian Jewish experience; this story is not solely about them. It is about us as well.

Their examples of Jewish pride, courage, and determination to remain Jews should inspire us today to support our brothers and sisters around the world, to defend the legitimacy of the Jewish State of Israel, to respond to antisemitism, and to create and build Jewish families for the future.

PARTING MEMORIES

It is impossible to visit Russia on so many occasions and not to be captivated by the memories. The following scenes are inextricably embedded in my deepest imagination.

Of Russian beauty and the Russian spirit: Visiting the remote and nearly inaccessible southern shore of untrammeled, pristine, and majestic Lake Baikal in the heart of Siberia, I spontaneously recited a blessing for the privilege of witnessing what God had originally formed at the time of the creation of the world, eons ago.

I was moved to recall that the lands of the former Soviet Union are among the richest and most blessed on earth, not only in physical resources but in the human spirit as well. I had met many such people during my travels and would carry their memories with me forever.

Of fighting common enemies: Overlooking Magnitogorsk in the heart of the Ural Mountains, the Soviet Union's largest iron and steel plant – whose factories had produced nearly half of all the steel used by the Soviets to make the tanks and shells that, together with the Allies, had defeated Nazi Germany – evoked the memories of the half a million Soviet Jews who fought in the Red Army, about a third of whom perished.

I was proud to stand in a place that helped to defeat the enemy of our peoples. There were select but decisive times, such as the war against the Nazis and support for a Jewish state in Palestine at the UN in 1947, when the Soviet Union was critical to the future survival of the Jewish people, and should not be forgotten.

Of Jewish solidarity, even to the end: Participating in a Jewish funeral in the heart of the Russian winter at the Leningrad Municipal Crematorium for a young man, Vitaly, a member of our local JDC St. Petersburg staff, who had died suddenly in a tragic accident. His parents desperately wanted to bring him to a Jewish burial. Unfortunately, the local Jewish cemetery was out of town and was inaccessible during the winter months. The only way he could receive a Jewish resting place was to cremate the body and bury the ashes in his grandmother's grave, in the nearby, but already full, Jewish cemetery in town.

I had never been to a cremation before but said we must go. We must not allow our friend and fellow Jew to leave this world by himself.

We gathered at the city crematorium, with "Ave Maria" playing in the background, as the local crematory official, dressed in her dark suit, conducted the ceremony, in the presence of the casket and a few family members and friends. When she asked if anyone would like to say something, I stepped forward and said: "In our tradition, at times like these, we say the following: *Yitkadal ve'yitkadash shemei rabbah.*" As I closed my eyes and began intoning the words, I was aware of a murmur rising from the crowd; nearly everyone in attendance was repeating the Mourner's Kaddish after me.

Our friend Vitaly did not leave this world alone. We accompanied him on his final journey.

RUSSIAN JEWRY AS A TALE OF JEWISH HOPE

After decades of governmental suppression and state antisemitism, the story of Russian Jewry is ultimately one of hope and renewal. Within the borders of the former Soviet Union or around the world, including Israel, North America, Germany, and other places, their story is still being written.

For us outsiders, who were privileged to take part in this incredible and moving saga, this was undoubtedly one of the great journeys of our lives. We entered Soviet and post-Soviet space with open eyes and open hearts and met long-lost brothers and sisters who affected us to our core.

We traveled there to affirm and demonstrate once and for all that the declaration "*Am Yisrael chai*" is not only a rousing and beloved song, but expresses the essence of the Jewish people around the world today, and we came away invigorated and inspired.

In Professor Gil Troy's stirring words in the foreword, the Russian Jewish story is a "salute to the magical power of Jewish memory, identity, solidarity, chutzpah, and hope."

Permissions

The author is grateful for permission to quote from the following.

Altshuler, Mordechai. *Religion and Jewish Identity in the Soviet Union, 1941–1964*. Translated by Saadya Sternberg. Waltham, MA: Brandeis University Press, 2012. Excerpts reprinted with permission.

Gitelman, Zvi. *A Century of Ambivalence: The Jews of Russia and the Soviet Union, 1881 to the Present*. 2nd, expanded edition. Bloomington, IN: Indiana University Press, 2001.

Goldes, Svetlana, translator, "The Rabbi's Son," by Isaac Babel.

Goldman, Rabbi Yossie. *Let My People Grow: Hillel and the Jewish Renaissance in the Former Soviet Union*. Jerusalem: Gefen Publishing House, 2020. Excerpts quoted with permission.

Kosharovsky, Yuli. *"We Are Jews Again": Jewish Activism in the Soviet Union*. Syracuse: Syracuse University Press, 2017. Quoted with permission.

Porath, Jonathan. "25 'Must' Places to Visit for the Jewish Tourist." In *The Jewish Almanac* , compiled and edited by Richard Siegel and Carl Rheins, 151–52. New York: Bantam Books, 1980. Used by permission of Penguin Random House.

———. "The Challenge of Soviet Jewry." *United Synagogue Review*, Spring 1974. Reprinted with permission of the United Synagogue of Conservative Judaism.

———. "Dispatches from My 175th Visit to Jewish Moscow." *Jewish Week*, February 7, 2019. https://jewishweek.timesofisrael.com /dispatches-from-my-175th-visit-to-jewish-moscow/.

———. "The Fallen Sukkot of Jewish Poland." *Jerusalem Post*, October 15, 2019, https://www.jpost.com/diaspora/dateline-warsaw-1968-604450. Used by permission of the *Jerusalem Post*.

———. *Jews in Russia: The Last Four Centuries; A Documentary History*. New York: United Synagogue Commission on Jewish Education, 1973. Used with permission of the United Synagogue of Conservative Judaism.

———. "A Moscow Simhat Torah Diary." *Jerusalem Post*, September 30, 2018, https://www.jpost.com/israel-news/a-moscow-simhat-torah-diary-568028. Used by permission of the *Jerusalem Post*.

———. "Pieces of Matza Wrapped in Copies of Pravda." *Jerusalem Post*, April 16, 2017, https://www.jpost.com/diaspora/pieces-of-matza-wrapped-in-copies -of-pravda-488088. Used by permission of the *Jerusalem Post*.

———. "Remembering My Teacher and Friend Elie Wiesel." *Jerusalem Post*, June 26, 2019, https://www.jpost.com/diaspora/remembering-my-teacher -and-friend-elie-wiesel-593764.

———. "Saving Soviet Jewry." In *The Third Jewish Catalog: Creating Community*, compiled and edited by Sharon Strassfeld and Michael Strassfeld, 51–61. Philadelphia; Jewish Publication Society, 1980. Used by permission.

———. "Visit to Russia." *Our Age*, October 5, 1969, 3. Reprinted with permission of the United Synagogue of Conservative Judaism.

Richter, Glenn. "Wiesel Inspired Free Soviet Jewry Movement." **JTA** July 3, 2016. Used by permission of JTA. This story may not be reproduced without JTA's permission; more information about JTA is available on its website at https://www.jta.org/.

Shachtman, Tom. *I Seek My Brethren: Ralph Goldman and "The Joint."* New York: Newmarket Press, 2001. Quoted with permission.

Schneiderman, S. L. "Soviet Jews Are Silent No Longer." *World Over* (a publication of the Jewish Education Committee of New York), February 27, 1970, 6–7.

Times of London. "Professor Rashid Kaplanov." January 7, 2008. https:// www.thetimes.co.uk/article/professor-rashid-kaplanov-6wgrfpd5k53. Quoted with permission.

Wiesel, Elie. *The Jews of Silence: A Personal Report on Soviet Jewry*. New York: Schocken, 2011. Copyright © 1966, 2011 by Elie Wiesel. Reprinted by permission of Georges Borchardt, Inc., on behalf of the author's Estate.

———. *Hadassah Magazine*, October 1968. Quoted with permission.

———. "We Can Be Proud of Jewish Youth" [in Yiddish]. *Der Algemeiner Journal*, December 6, 1974. Quoted with permission.

Yevtushenko, Yevgeny. "Babii Yar." In *The Poetry of Yevgeny Yevtushenko*, translated by George Reaves. London: Calder and Boyars, 1966. Now available as *Early Poems* by Yevgeny Yevtushenko. London: Marion Boyars, 1989. Quoted with permission.

Zerobnick, Steve. Blog entry "Welcoming Shabbat with the Jews of St. Petersburg." July 2018.

Meeting President Zalman Shazar (*right*) at the
Twenty-Sixth Zionist Congress in Jerusalem, 1964

USY group meeting in Moscow, 1970; *left to right:* myself, Chief Rabbi Levin, Rabbi Arnie Turetsky

In the courtyard of the Georgian synagogue in Tbilisi with Chacham Yitzchak (*center*),
the local shochet, 1972

Jewish schoolchildren in the courtyard of the Georgian synagogue in Tbilisi, 1972

USY group about to depart from JFK airport in New York City for Europe, 1970

USYers in Red Square, Moscow, 1973

Jewish mothers and children at Pioneer Camp in Vilna, Soviet
Lithuania, 1971

USY girls dancing in the small shul in Leningrad, 1973

With Shimon from Odessa (*left*) in the Kiev railroad station, 1973

Luba, our Jewish Intourist guide, 1973

With Elie Wiesel in the offices of the Elie Wiesel Foundation for
Humanity in New York City, 2013

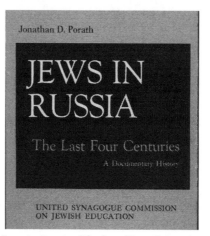

Jonathan D. Porath

JEWS IN RUSSIA

The Last Four Centuries

A Documentary History

UNITED SYNAGOGUE COMMISSION
ON JEWISH EDUCATION

Jews in Russia: The Last Four Centuries,
published in 1973, the first textbook on
Russian and Soviet Jewry for Hebrew
high schools and adult education

Soviet Jews on their way to Israel, at the Vienna
railroad station, 1969

Olim at Moscow's Sheremetyevo Airport, soon
to be departing for Tel Aviv, 1992

Chanukah program for new *olim* in Jerusalem,
organized by Keren Klitat Aliyah-Neve Orot, 1990

Neighborhood clothing warehouse for new *olim*, 1991; *left to right:* cochair of the
Keren Klitat Aliya Avraham Shafir, myself, Nancy Berlin, project coordinator Bertha
Khayat (a new *olah* formerly from Minsk), Louis Berlin. Nancy and Louis had just
delivered suitcases of new clothing from America for the new *olim*.

Natan Sharansky speaking to olim in Jerusalem's Ramot
neighborhood on Chanukah, 1991. In background, Moshe Khayat
and Avraham Shafir from Keren Klitat Aliyah-Neve Orot.

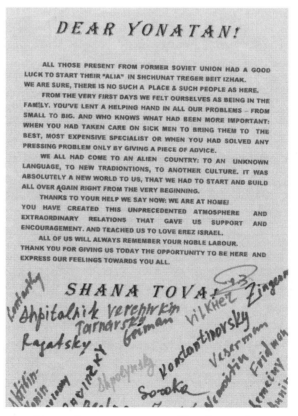

Letter of appreciation signed by *olim* on the
tenth anniversary of their arrival in Israel to the Jerusalem
neighborhood of Ramot, 2000

With prospective *olim* at the Israeli embassy in Moscow,
proudly waving Israeli flags in public, 1992

With Colonel Uri Sokol and his wife Leiba, director of the Moscow
Jewish Cultural Educational Society and library, 1992

In Tyumen, Siberia, for the Chanukah in Siberia festival, December 1995

Under the chuppah in Ufa, Russia, at the wedding of Inessa and Boris, 1996

Demonstrating the Havdalah ceremony at a "Shabbat in the Jewish Home"
presentation in Orsk, Russia, 1996

Visiting US, Canadian, and Israeli academics with the Israeli ambassador to the Russian Federation,
Madam Professor Aliza Shenhar (*center, in white*), for the annual SEFER conference in Moscow,
1996; *to her immediate right:* Professor Rashid Kaplanov, founding academic chair of SEFER

Participants in SEFER student academic summer school in Moscow during the COVID pandemic (note the masks), 2021 (courtesy of Dr. Victoria Mochalova and SEFER)

With Professors Mikhail Chlenov, current SEFER academic chair,
and Victoria Mochalova, SEFER director,
meeting visitors in Moscow, 2018

FSU Hillel staff in Kishinev shul, 1998; *third from right:* Rabbi Yossie
Goldman, director (courtesy of Rabbi Yossie Goldman)

The Hillel in Izhevsk, Russia, 2001; *from left:* Mark Goldin, community leader; Rabbi Nahum Amsel, Hillel FSU educational director; Ilya Goldin, student leader (courtesy of Rabbi Nahum Amsel)

Keshet Tour group meeting in the shul in the Mall of Russia with current and former Russian Jewish student activists, 2018; *speaking, second from left:* Ilya Pestrikov, cofounder of Chanukah in Siberia

With Rabbi Yossie Goldman (*left*) at the twenty-fifth anniversary celebration of the founding of Moscow Hillel, 2019

Rabbi Moti Weissberg from Moscow's Marina Roshcha Synagogue/JCC displaying the burnt and desecrated copy of a book of the Torah I had just presented to him, 2018

Friday evening Shabbat services at the Shaarei Shalom Progressive Congregation in St. Petersburg, 2018 (courtesy of Steve Zerobnick)

YESOD/St. Petersburg Jewish Community Home, 2017 (courtesy of Masha Aryeva and YESOD)

Purim celebrations at YESOD, 2017 (courtesy of Masha Aryeva and YESOD)

Keshet Educational Tours visit to YESOD, 2018; *kneeling, left:* Steve Zerobnick, group leader; *kneeling, right:* myself, scholar in residence (courtesy of Steve Zerobnick)

Index

Numbers preceded by *p-* denote photo gallery pages.

Made in the USA
Middletown, DE
21 April 2023

29259727R00152